Laughter in the Courts of Love

LAUGHTER *in the* COURTS *of* LOVE

COMEDY *in* ALLEGORY, *from* CHAUCER *to* SPENSER

By FRANCES McNEELY LEONARD

PILGRIM BOOKS, INC.
NORMAN, OKLAHOMA

Library of Congress Cataloging in Publication Data

Leonard, Frances McNeely, 1936–
     Laughter in the courts of love.

     Bibliography.
     Includes index.
     1. English poetry – Middle English, 1100–1500 –
History and criticism. 2. English poetry – Early modern,
1500–1700 – History and criticism. 3. Scottish poetry –
To–1700 – History and criticism. 4. Comic, The.
5. Allegory. 6. Courtly love.
I. Title.
PR317.C65L4   821.'009'17   81-10676
ISBN 0-937664-54-5   AACR2

Copyright©1981 by Pilgrim Books, Inc., Norman, Oklahoma,
Manufactured in the U.S.A. First edition.

To Bob, Suzanne, and Christopher,

who endure and triumph, both comically
and allegorically. Blessed are they.

Contents

		Page
Preface		ix
Chapter 1	Allegory and Comedy	3
2	Chaucer's Comic Visions	27
3	Laughter in the Courts of Love	57
4	The Pilgrimage of Love	105
5	The Comedy of *The Faerie Queene*	133
6	Comedy and Allegory	169
Selected Bibliography		173
Index		181

Preface

OST STUDIES OF COMEDY originate, I am convinced, in a season of despair. A class sits mirthless and stone-faced through "the funniest story written in America since *Huckleberry Finn.*" A critic ignores or even maligns humor while fitting a poem into a particular theoretical bed. Or worst of all, one laughs – and laughs alone. Then the light of wisdom shines. If they can't see what is obvious, give them what is obviously needed: a plain-spoken definition of comedy that will teach everyone when and where to laugh. So with a high heart, the scholar rides into battle; and a fearsome battle it is, for defining comedy, as Bergson has suggested, is like trying to capture the foam of the sea. As quickly as a thesis is built up, it vanishes, exploded by the intransigence of comedy itself. Above all, comedy is irregular, irrelevant, and cheerfully defiant of common sense.

Now if comedy defies common sense, the prolonged contemplation of medieval comedy in allegory must surely be a flirtation with lunacy. In the moonscape of allegory, nothing seems to be what it is, which may be either more or less than the poem leads us to expect. Allegory is a tease, and the sensitive reader may be excused for suspecting that when the allegorical point is comical, the laugh is actually on himself. All this can lead to sitting alone at midnight amidst the tattered shreds of sanity while one ponders how to proceed seriously and soberly, as one must when writing about comedy.

I have been fortunate in this undertaking to be sustained and encouraged by friends and mentors whose sagacity and patience have outlasted more than one round with doubt and timidity. Professors Michael Cherniss and Richard Hardin at the University of Kansas not only consented

Laughter in the Courts of Love

to the union of Chaucer and Spenser in comedy but vigilantly demanded precision of utterance, while Professor George Wedge did his best to curb excesses of style. To Professor Paul Ruggiers at the University of Oklahoma, I am indebted for an abiding faith and friendship which surpasses reason. Finally, I must thank Stephen Hawes for an unexpected but doubtless necessary lesson in critical humility. To my knowledge, *The Pastime of Pleasure* is no one's favorite poem. Long, often limp-metered, and occasionally tedious, it sprawls between Chaucer and Spenser, almost inviting the slings and arrows of critical scorn. But it is a genuinely encyclopedic poem which not only ranges from heaven to hell but also summarizes the philosophy of the age. It embodies a scope of vision and manifests an unassuming ambition denied to modern man. It is, in short, a poem which no *critic* can write. I hope always to remember this fact.

Frances McNeely Leonard

Laughter in the Courts of Love

1.

Allegory and Comedy

HE SUBJECT OF THIS book, to paraphrase Dante, is not simple, for it is concerned with the structures and meanings of comedy as they coalesce or sometimes collide with the structures and meanings of allegory. It is also concerned, though less directly, with the question of how our direct response to comedy impinges upon our understanding of an allegory. The question is perhaps unanswerable, since a reader's response is instantaneous, personal, surely idiosyncratic; but it is not idle. If an interpretation is based upon only one set of emotive devices in a poem to the exclusion of others, then we are reading only part of the poem. Because our critical strategies for analyzing allegory lead us to focus upon the serious and philosophical, we tend to dismiss the comedy as momentarily pleasurable but thematically frivolous and irrelevant. When we respond to comedy, we worry that the sound of laughter will banish the allegorical sense.

This book originated a dozen years ago at a moment when comedy and allegory seemed to collide. It began, literally, with a sudden halt, a slow and methodical rereading of the text, a burst of laughter, and an immediate concern that the laughter might be inappropriate, since it was provoked by a passage in the sage and serious *Faerie Queene*. In Book 2, Spenser narrates the adventures of Sir Guyon, whose mission is to find and destroy the Bower of Bliss. Because his horse has been stolen, Guyon is proceeding on foot through a sequence of less than honorific encounters when fierce Pyrochles, the embodiment of unprovoked wrath, charges down upon him (Canto 5). Guyon moves to defend himself – and by accident beheads a horse.

Now the implications of this scene invite contradictory responses. If we interpret the passage from the customary perspectives of allegorical criticism, then we are predisposed to see it as thoroughly serious, and we shall probably agree with the gloss in a widely used text that the scene conveys frustration, "mounting shame, injustice, and anger."[1] But the encounter is narrated in a comic style and is set, moreover, in a comic context, which invites laughter, and the effect of laughter is to dispel frustration, to deny the reality of anger, injustice, and shame. Either the laughter is inappropriate, or the meaning of this passage is far more complicated than that which is suggested by allegorical criticism alone. What did comedy, that "temporal" and "realistic" point of view, have to do with a mode that points upward toward immaterial ideals? It was in answer to this question that the following work was begun.

This book focuses upon the union of comedy and allegory as manifested in a representative selection of English and Scottish poems written between 1369 and 1599. All the poems may be termed *Chaucerian,* that is, written by Chaucer and his contemporaries or by later poets, including Spenser, who frankly acknowledged indebtedness to the "flour imperiall" of their tongue. They are further related in that all the narratives are concerned in some manner with the doctrine of Courtly Love: either the central figure is a lover, or his adventures bring him into contact with a society whose primary concern is *fin amour.* All the poems are critically designated as allegories, and all are informed, either totally or in central, defining passages, by a comic vision. They invite two sets of responses; they tease the reader out of complacency. They make us confront two fundamental questions: Did the poet know how to write allegory? Do we know how to read it?

Allegorical Expectations and Comic Realities

Allegorical poetry, particularly that produced by the courtly poets of the late Middle Ages and the early Renaissance, has long been the victim of literary prejudice, although its value has risen slightly in the critical stock market within recent years. For more than a century scholars have viewed courtly allegory as the peculiar aberration of a remote society, a deliberate turning away from the true stream of robust and realistic modernity that flows from *Troilus and Criseyde* and *The Canterbury*

[1]Robert Kellogg and Oliver Steele, eds., *Books I and II of* The Faerie Queene, p. 278n.

Allegory and Comedy

Tales to the present age. Courtly allegory was the stylized articulation of an elaborate system of analogies that composed the medieval poet's picture of the world. Modern readers, who have the advantage of historical perspective, know that this world was already collapsing, and they suspect that any poem that tries to re-create it is timidly refusing to face reality.

Since comedy is the child of reality, we do not readily think of comedy when we think of these poems. Comedy, moreover, is supposed to give pleasure, but these courtly allegories often seem devoid of that power. Readers whose literary tastes have been formed largely by Wordsworth's Romantic doctrine that poetry is "the spontaneous overflow of powerful emotions recollected in tranquillity" find that courtly allegory seems perversely directed away from both spontaneity and pleasure. Its language is difficult to understand; its systematized structure often lands both poem and reader in the dismal swamp of dullness; and its final effect is that of a tease, promising literary delights that it will not deliver. In practice as well as theory courtly allegory is shaped to serve a function more didactic than pleasure-giving, and yet, by intellectual and philosophical standards, the allegory is concerned with the commonplace, the conventional, the jejune, having virtually no traffic with the powerful or the original. It proceeds by consciously planned parallels and indirections, and it finds artistic expression only in terms other than those pertaining directly to itself. In short, the modern student finds that courtly allegory is not immediately sincere or original; it is an art form that bears in its face the visible signs of duplicity.

That much of the formal allegory produced in the so-called Age of Transition in England (1400–1550) is flat and barren, both aesthetically and intellectually, there is no refuting. Many critics have argued that allegory was in moribund condition even earlier, pointing out that while Chaucer took his poetic training in the school of courtly allegory, in his mature works he discarded much of the elaborate system of artifice for a more direct representational style that has at least as much kinship to our conventional realism as it has to formal allegory. Chaucer's contemporary, the moral John Gower, remained a very competent allegorist throughout his career, but the warmest praise accorded him suggests that at his best he is only slightly better than Chaucer at his worst.[2] My

[2]Derek Pearsall, "Gower's Narrative Art," *PMLA* 81 (1966):483.

point is this: In its aspect as the dominant mode of the times, allegory, like realism in the twentieth century, attracted virtually all writers, but particularly the secondary talents, for its very commonness implied that it was a mode anyone could manage successfully. Unfortunately, the engagement of a mediocre talent with a potentially intractable mode does not result in an entertaining or lively body of poetry. It does, as the critics have said, result in dullness, conventionality, artificiality — something of a literary desert.

For the most part the presence of comedy in this desert has been overlooked, or dismissed as a mirage, or accepted only as an incidental lapse that offers a momentary diversion from the real issues at hand. From a critical perspective comedy and allegory are seldom companions, much less conspirators at presenting a poetic vision. Usually they are cast as competitors, with one — alas, too often allegory — necessarily overcoming and banishing the other. Allegory, we are told, is Serious Business; like business often dull, dreary, mechanical, and sometimes even mindless, but even in its last and dullest phases, still a serious attempt to communicate high truths to low wits. Comedy is, if one need say it, not serious, and to attempt to defend it on the grounds that "comedy is serious" is to risk denying the primary effect of comedy, which is to dispel seriousness. Allegory, in the popular concept, tends toward elevation; its function is to imply that there are higher values than mere humanity, that these values are the proper study of mankind. Comedy teaches — if it teaches at all — that we should embrace life, rejoice in mere humanity.[3] Comedy and allegory, then, must be inimical, even when they appear together.

To judge by the testimony of critical studies, the reader's characteristic response to comedy in allegory is to treat it as a sign that the poet has momentarily lost faith in the allegorical mode, or else to assume that yet another third-rate Homer has nodded. Often the critic seems not even to

[3]This concept has descended to modern theorists from antiquity. Thus Evanthius says, "In tragedy the kind of life is shown that is to be shunned; while in comedy the kind is shown that is to be sought after." Evanthius, *De Comoedia et Tragoedia*, in *Commentum Terenti*, ed. Paul Wessner, vol. 1 in *Classical and Medieval Literary Criticism: Translations and Interpretations*, trans. O. B. Hardison, Jr., ed. Alex Preminger, O. B. Hardison, Jr., and Kevin Karrane, p. 305. A markedly different translation of the same passage is offered by J. V. Cunningham, who atttributes it to Donatus: "The moral of tragedy is that life should be rejected; of comedy, that it should be embraced." J. V. Cunningham, *Tradition and Poetic Structure: Essays in Literary History and Criticism*, p. 164.

Allegory and Comedy

notice the comedy, particularly if he is intent upon expounding the systematized implications of the letter. Some of the most devout explicators of allegorical poetry – D. W. Robertson, Jr., Bernard F. Huppé, and B. G. Koonce, for example – may declare that they see comedy in a poem, and they may even fetch up a laugh at what they see, but their laughter is like that of Troilus in the eighth sphere, the product of a genuine contempt for mere humanity and mere comedy. At bottom the patristic critic has the same attitude toward comedy as that of the general reader indoctrinated in the Arnoldian school of high seriousness: it is a form of moral and poetical frivolity properly reserved for holidays. Both kinds of readers are distressingly tone-deaf to modulations or outright changes of key in a work they have assumed to be monotonic.

As regards comedy in allegorical poems, a reader's assumption of allegorical seriousness stands between him and the poem, for the prime requisite for appreciating comedy is a predisposition toward recognizing it, coupled with the belief that comedy must establish its values in its own way and not according to any prior (or thematic) notion of what the poem really ought to be doing.[4] To notice the comedy, a reader must relinquish his presuppositions about how one reads allegory; to account for comedy, the reader may have to find new ways of interpreting allegory. In particular, he may have to give up some of his prejudices about what allegory ought to do, and he may discover that these prejudices are founded on a limited perspective of what allegory is, for even today allegory remains a largely unmapped tract, and most "definitive studies" of it lead to a dissatisfaction with the definitions.

Allegorical Structures

Allegory, to put the case bluntly, can be a vexatious bitch. It is variously a mode of writing, a process of reading, and an individual poem or passage of poetry that has been critically designated as "allegorical." As a mode of writing, it presumably originated with the Holy Spirit dictating the Scripture to earthly scribes. As a process of reading, it evolved from

---

[4]Jonathan Culler argues that to locate any work within a genre is to create a set of expectations that the reader will look for in the work. "Comedy," he says, "exists by virtue of the fact that to read something as comedy involves different expectations from reading something as a tragedy or as an epic." Jonathan Culler, *Structuralist Poetics: Structuralism, Linguistics, and the Study of Literature*, p. 137.

the early Christian conviction that although the Bible contained all history and all wisdom—and all pointing to the life of Christ—the specifically Christian quality of the truth was often veiled by an obscure or equivocal expression; hence the reader had to interpret the literal text to find the proper spiritual significance.[5] This practice was eventually codified as the "fourfold method" of reading; that is, the interpreter looked not only at the letter (or first level) but through it to the figural levels of meaning: the specifically Christian (also called allegorical), the moral (or tropological), and the anagogical, which is concerned with the ultimate, unchanging state of the soul.[6]

One difficulty that we have in reading medieval allegories is an often-repeated but erroneous assumption that since the process of reading was fully articulated in the Middle Ages it ought to be applicable to all medieval allegories, when in fact it is not. John Burrow has pointed out that most of the so-called allegories written during the last quarter of the fourteenth century rely upon exemplification rather than implication.[7] Moreover, not all allegories have a specifically Christian level of reference. While we may assume that most of the poets believed, at least generally, in the tenets of Holy Mother Church, their faith was not so all-possessing that it occupied center stage in all their poems. Far more likely, these poets were concerned with social relationships and ethical questions or, as poets and rhetoricians, with the conscious elaboration of their style. If, therefore, we look for four levels or even a specifically Christ-centered level of meaning in these poems, we usually look in vain.

Definitions of allegory, like definitions of comedy, try almost without exception to establish a singular set of characteristics that explain *all* allegories, but these resemble territorial maps made by imperialistic aggressors and their foes: they include either so much or so little territory as to be virtually useless. C. S. Lewis, for example, restricts allegory to

[5]For an invaluable survey of the theories of allegorical composition and interpretation, see Morton Bloomfield, "Allegory as Interpretation," *NLH* 3 (1972):301–17. Other useful commentaries on the nature of allegory include Gay Clifford, *The Transformations of Allegory*; Pamela Gradon, *Form and Style in Early English Poetry*, especially pp. 32–92 and 332–81; and Joseph Anthony Mazzeo, *Varieties of Interpretation*, pp. 47–69.

[6]The explanation of this method of reading, which has been ascribed to many sources, is most readily available to modern readers and nonspecialists in the "Letter to Can Grande della Scala," generally attributed to Dante and reprinted in virtually all translations of the *Divine Comedy*.

[7]John Burrow, *Ricardian Poetry: Chaucer, Gower, Langland, and the Gawain-Poet*, pp. 79–83.

mean only personification: ". . . you can start with an immaterial fact, such as the passions which you actually experience, and can then invent *visibilia* to express them."[8] Judson B. Allen has pointed out, however, that the medieval allegorizers did not connect personification with allegory but treated it separately as an element of style.[9] Lewis resolutely excludes from allegory that vast body of works which follow a counter movement from the visible to the immaterial. This countermotion, which Lewis terms "sacramentalism," or symbolism, belongs as much to allegory as personification does, and, in fact, it is not at all uncommon to find the two types appearing together in one poem. For instance, the goddess Fame in Chaucer's *The House of Fame* is a personification of an abstract concept; but the Eagle, who takes Geffrey to the House, is a symbol—moreover, a symbol that cannot be fully defined. Allegory, then, is not merely composition by means of personification, though personification is one characteristic device of allegorical style.

At the opposite pole from Lewis are those critics who either imply or state that any work that presents the conflict of dual forces is ipso facto allegory. Thus, when the good guys in white hats combat the bad guys in black hats, the television western, in its puerile fashion, is presenting an allegory. So broad a definition of allegory rests finally upon the reduction of any poem, novel, or play to its barest thematic outlines, its most abstract and least poetical form. All critics seem to agree that allegory requires a "marked dualism" of good and evil as absolute forces,[10] but it is neither logical nor critical to assume that such dualism is automatically allegory.

Still another difficulty in knowing what allegory is results from the original definition provided by Isidore of Seville that allegory is *aleniloquium:* "It says one thing, and another is understood," and that "the force of allegory is double; under some things it figuratively points to another."[11] Accepting this definition, we expect allegory to present a continuous set of implications so that we can read two, three, or four stories or messages at the same time. Both Angus Fletcher and Judson Allen support this expectation when they stress the isomorphic quality

[8]C. S. Lewis, *The Allegory of Love*, pp. 44–45.

[9]Judson B. Allen, *The Friar as Critic: Literary Attitudes in the Later Middle Ages*, p. 8.

[10]Angus Fletcher, *Allegory: The Theory of a Symbolic Mode*, pp. 222–23.

[11]Isidore of Seville, *Etymologiarum*, 1.37.22, 26, trans. by Allen in *The Friar as Critic*, p. 7.

of allegorical structures, suggesting that a poem can be properly termed allegorical only when it has a fully developed figurative form that parallels point by point the narrative form of the poem.[12]

In actuality allegory (in an important parallel to comedy) is *generally* polysemous; but, to adapt an aphorism from Poe, not everything in a long allegory can be or need be allegorical, just as not everything in a comedy can be comic. Great comedies have essential passages that are not funny, that sometimes may be downright pathetic. Some allegories likewise have passages in which even the most diligent reader may be hard-pressed to find as many as two levels of meaning. Particularly the courtly allegories modeled upon the *Roman de la Rose*, including Chaucer's early poems and those of the later Chaucerians, tend for long stretches to fulfill themselves on one level of meaning only, that being the quasiliteral realm in which "Ira" and "Anger" become so totally wedded that there is no *need* to translate from one level to another. In other words, allegory can become such a self-contained artifice that it lives in neither the material nor the immaterial world but in some hermetically sealed sphere between the two. The poet's emphasis is not upon creating a second meaning but upon stating one meaning with as much elaboration as possible.[13]

Although we talk about allegory in terms of its meaning, we need to remember that it is a fundamentally dramatic "way of thinking about man and the universe" that reveals and examines the vital influences that man and his world have over each other.[14] As a poetic mode allegory is the imitation of an action revealing "that moving of the will toward good or evil which is an integral part of the didactic theory."[15] In allegory man is an actor, and his world is an actor also, for both participate in a ceaseless struggle against anarchy and chaos. In her study of allegorical imagery Rosemond Tuve stresses the centrality of action when she points out that a poet of the 1580s could not depict a vice without depicting escape

[12]See Fletcher, *Allegory*, chap. 4, where he discusses the symmetry of structure and substructures; see also Allen, *The Friar as Critic*, p. 118.

[13]Rosemond Tuve, *Allegorical Imagery: Some Medieval Books and Their Posterity*, pp. 233–84. See also Allen, *The Friar as Critic*, pp. 18–20.

[14]Edwin Honig, *Dark Conceit: The Making of Allegory*, p. 7. For a more recent study that stresses the dramatic quality of Renaissance allegory, see Mark L. Caldwell, "Allegory: The Renaissance Mode," *ELH* 44 (1977):580–600.

[15]Rosemond Tuve, *Elizabethan and Metaphysical Imagery: Renaissance Poetic and Twentieth-Century Critics*, p. 400.

from it, capture by it, or its conquest by (or victory over) the opposing virtue.[16]

In its imitation of an action allegory usually moves on two planes of reference, which may be termed the literal and the figurative, or the "real" and "more real" worlds of human experience. There is in each allegory a literal world described by the words of the poem as "real," no matter how fantastic the inhabitants or incidents, and there is also an implied world, which may be the physical world of ordinary existence or the completely immaterial world of idealized, perfected humanity. Allegory achieves its dual reference by relying upon either personification or symbolism or the two modes of presentation in combination. Particularly in the courtly allegories the poet relies chiefly upon personification, and he selects for his setting a fantasy world that may refer both to the physical world and to the ideal world. The courtly allegorist is most directly concerned with patterns of conduct and the system of moral values that are implied by these patterns. He is seldom overtly – sometimes not even covertly – engaged by questions of Christian theology, except insofar as morality has been subsumed by Christian doctrine.

With the single exception of book 1 of *The Faerie Queene*, all the poems to be dealt with in this book are more secular than theological in their bias. They therefore share in a characteristic tendency of secular allegory toward a reduced number of potential meanings. But however few levels it has, each allegory has its distinctive tone, either comic or serious, which is determined by the *letter*, in which the tone is first manifested. To keep in touch with the tone of an allegory, the reader has to believe in the importance of the letter. He has to forgo his intellectual preference (and a compelling one it is) for what Charles Donahue describes as the Greek method of interpretation, whereby "the original meaning is destroyed once the allegorical meaning is discovered."[17] To appreciate comedy in allegory, the reader must begin by understanding that comedy is not an evasion of morality and doctrine, nor an attack upon them, but a component of both the literal and the figural levels that

---

[16]Tuve, *Allegorical Imagery*, p. 118. Morton W. Bloomfield, in "A Grammatical Approach to Personification Allegory," *MP* 60 (1963):161–71, says that in personification allegory the grammatical stress is on action, that is, on the "verbs and predicates" (p. 165).

[17]Charles Donahue, "Patristic Exegesis in the Criticism of Medieval Literature: Summation," in Dorothy Bethurum, ed., *Critical Approaches to Medieval Literature*, p. 66.

stresses that the letter too is a form of reality and that total reality on all possible levels is really quite complex.

Comic Strategies

As an art form comedy is the result of a way of viewing human experience that, despite the risk of a pedantic circularity, must be called the comic vision. Comedy is the expression of an attitude toward man and his place in the universal scheme that dictates how one shall behave, what he shall do, and how one ought to respond to that which is being done. Comedy, says L. J. Potts, is "a way of writing; or . . . a way of drawing, or dancing, and so forth."[18] As regards poetry, comedy implies not only a way of writing but also a way of reading, for if the reader is not attuned to the ways in which comedy functions, then he is unlikely to notice its presence and is almost certain to miss its implications.

To state the existence of a comic vision that governs form is, of course, easy enough, and to believe in it is not difficult either; to prove it, however, can finally be done only by analogy, for the comic vision is the soul of the comic poem or incident, and like the soul of any created organism it is discernible not in itself but in its becoming. "It is not perceived save in operation, nor manifested except by its effects, as life [is manifested] in a plant by the green leaves."[19] The comic vision, then, can be discerned only by the perception of its product, that is, by comedy itself. And yet the comic vision is not *what* is seen but *how* the subject is seen; it is, in effect, the artist's astigmatism that confers peculiarities of size and shape, the knobs, bumps, and unexpected curvatures that signify a departure from the norm.

[18]L. J. Potts, *Comedy*, p. 9. Other significant theoretical and critical studies that can aid in the understanding of medieval and Renaissance comedy include Lane Cooper, *An Aristotelian Theory of Comedy, with an Adaptation of the* Poetics *and a Translation of the* Tractatus Coislinianus; George E. Duckworth, *The Nature of Roman Comedy: A Study in Popular Entertainment*; Northrop Frye, "Old and New Comedy," *ShS* 22 (1969):1–5; Nevill Coghill, "The Basis of Shakespearian Comedy: A Study in Medieval Affinities," *Essays and Studies*, n.s. 3 (1950):1–28; C. L. Barber, *Shakespeare's Festive Comedy: A Study of Dramatic Form and Its Relation to Social Custom*; and Paul G. Ruggiers, ed., *Versions of Medieval Comedy*.

[19]Dante, *Purgatorio*, 18.52–54, trans. Francis Fergusson, in Fergusson, *The Idea of a Theatre: A Study of Ten Plays; The Art of Drama in Changing Perspective*, p. 11. Although I shall seldom have occasion to quote from Fergusson's book, I should like to acknowledge a general indebtedness to his theory of poetic structure and dramatic action as it has influenced my understanding of the structure of comedy.

Allegory and Comedy

At heart the comic vision is a celebration of human existence. It is the bone-deep awareness that human life is all we have, whether on earth or in heaven or hell (for there we shall still have been human, though confounded or redeemed), and this awareness teaches us that life in all its forms is to be embraced and endured. Endurance is not, however, the focal point of the comic vision, for monkeys can endure. What the comic vision really sees—and this can make hard work for patristic critics—is man's capacity to *triumph*, "by wit, luck, personal power, or even humorous, or ironical, or philosophical acceptance of mischance."[20] The ultimate meaning of this triumph is man's gratification of his desire for immortality. Comedy is an acting out of the ways in which man tries to achieve immortality: in everyday life by maintaining his physical and emotional balance, in history by reduplicating himself—begetting children, and in the Christian universe by attaining to the state of paradise through having been human.

A second characteristic of the comic vision is more frequently noted than is its focus on Man Triumphant: the fact that it is not a single but a double vision. Wylie Sypher describes the comic character as being marked by a "deep ambiguity"; he is not only the enemy of God but the very image of God, and as such he is endowed with a double nature and is driven at last to a double fate of both body and soul.[21] The two sides of the comic character or situation or action or speech are by natural tendency contradictory; also by nature, both are palpably present. As Charles Muscatine says, "If it is true that Chauntecleer and Pertelote are rounded characters, it is also true that they are chickens."[22]

The double vision of comedy bestows a special irony upon the ways in which man triumphs over adversity. For instance, he may keep his emotional balance only by losing it; so Chaucer establishes the down-to-earth center of his character Geffrey in *The House of Fame* by stressing the abject terror that Geffrey suffers in flight with the Eagle. Geffrey's unwillingness to be "stellyfyed" points up the norms of human existence, for while man seeks immortality, he seeks it in his own being: he is a man and not a star.[23] The usual way in which man seeks immortality, through

[20]Susanne K. Langer, *Feeling and Form: A Theory of Art*, p. 331.

[21]Wylie Sypher, "The Meaning of Comedy," in Wylie Sypher, *Comedy*, pp. 230–31.

[22]Charles Muscatine, *Chaucer and the French Tradition*, p. 238.

[23]The special appeal of Dante's Purgatory and Paradise is the luminous quality of humanity, both

begetting children, is especially amenable to comic treatment, for sex itself is of a double nature. While man may spiritualize sex by establishing religious and moral codes to govern it, it is a drive that he shares in common with beasts but not angels. It is a union of the sublime and the ridiculous, and the comic vision never totally blots out either extreme.

A third aspect of the comic vision is that it is inconstant, yet patterned. It is not a steady and unblinking point of view but a rapid movement of the mental eye, focusing, blurring, focusing anew. Its changeability is not random, however, but rhythmic. The comic view returns again and again to its original focus, repeating a pattern until the pattern becomes as visible as the object seen. The prominence of a pattern repeated without significant variation is a defining characteristic of comedy, and it accompanies, perhaps paradoxically, an awareness that life is basically a discontinuous experience. Comedy does not depend upon a long process of development; rather, it is the result of a series of movements that are quick, short, almost random. Comic life is determined not by any sober fate but by Fortune.[24] As conceived of comically, Fortune does not turn a gigantic wheel whose single cycle determines the full shape of man's life. Rather, Fortune is equated with rapidity, momentariness, quick and persistent change. Adventure is potentially, if not really, misadventure, and man as a comic being is a slave to some passion or else a free agent capable of manipulating those who are spiritual slaves. But freedom is not absolute in comedy, nor is slavery, for all men are heirs to folly. The comic vision sees that all men "dance the same measure," and the comic action is the recreation of this measure.[25]

The comic vision, then, dictates how we shall see the subject that is the comic poem, and, like a true autocrat, it decrees also how we shall respond and what the outward manifestation of these responses will be. A great deal has been said about the relationship of laughter to comedy, mostly to prove that the occurrence of one does not automatically ensure

---

erring and redeemed, and Dante's insistence that one's human identity endures from earthly existence throughout eternity. All the saints in Paradise are well aware that they achieved the state of grace through having been human, for salvation is God's gift to man and not to angels, nor to beasts.

[24]Langer, *Feeling And Form*, p. 331.

[25]Sir Philip Sidney, *The Defence of Poesie*, vol. 3 in *The Prose Works of Sir Philip Sidney*, ed. Albert Feuillerat, p. 23.

the presence of the other. True enough, and yet most critics still rely on their natural tendency to say that laughter really does prove the existence of comedy. Here instinct is probably more reliable than much learning, for the reasonable critic believes that the reasonable reader will laugh at what is funny. The effect of comedy varies naturally according to the technique and the topic, but the most common comic response is an impulse in the direction of laughter.[26]

There is a second and distinct comic response, however, which is characterized more by feeling good than by laughter. This is the final effect intended by Shakespeare in the romantic comedies that end with marriages, feasts, dances. In its intense forms this response is one of sheer jubilation, the most heightened instance being that moment in Dante's *Purgatory* when Statius achieves purgation, the mountain quakes, and the souls sing "Alleluia." Dante reveals the proper—and comic—response through the narrative events, and the reader shares in the sense of triumph himself, unless he is a moral and emotional clod. This kind of comedy provides what Sir Philip Sidney calls *delight*, when he says that delight as well as laughter may be a proper response to comedy. Laughter, Sidney says, is indicative of the downward or baser motion of man's existence and attitudes, whereas delight moves upward, reflecting the instructive, morally uplifting effects of comedy.[27]

From these two movements with their two responses we must learn finally that there is no one basic term that defines comedy, for comedy comes in many forms and provokes many responses. It is protean and will not be wrestled to the ground, but it cannot be taken as the enemy, for it relies upon our sense of complicity to achieve its effect.

We discover comedy, however, not in theories of the comic vision but through our immediate response to the technique and style of a given poem. It is universally remarked, and truly, that there is no topic that is

[26]Elder Olson, in *The Theory of Comedy*, pp. 16–25, says that there exists what may be called a laughter emotion, the relaxation of engaged interest when we suddenly perceive that something assumed to be serious is really trivial. This relaxation of tension, which he calls *katastasis*, is a necessary prelude to laughter and to "feeling good." He weakens the general applicability of this theory, however, by insisting upon a very narrow definition of comedy that is modeled upon Aristophanic farce; thus *katastasis* is the relaxation of interest that accompanies the vitality of Aristophanic comedies but not the mental patterns of high comedy nor the romantic form of Shakespeare's most popular comedies. Olson has nothing to say about nondramatic comedy.

[27]Sidney, *The Defence of Poesie*, pp. 40–41.

always genuinely comic in itself, but there are methods of development that are comic, that inevitably lead toward comic responses, and that had better be avoided unless one is aiming for a comic response.

Most theories of comic technique and devices have been drawn from analyses of dramatic forms,[28] and there runs throughout most discus-sions of comedy a strong sense of the dramatic. This is perhaps accidental but not at all unfortunate, for the source of comic criticism highlights a basic quality of comedy, distinguishing it from its components of wit, irony, and humor. Comedy is fundamentally an action, the working out of a rhythmic pattern of events that stresses the random, the accidental, the incidental and ends in either a triumphant crescendo of responsive laughter or a leveling off onto a plateau of general good feeling. As its basic ingredients comedy requires a character in a situation attempting to gratify a desire, for an action can be expressed only through the medium of an actor.[29]

The character in a comedy is often conspicuously uneasy in his relation to dignity, or he lacks the capacity to inspire awe. Frequently he is a stock figure—a braggart, a hypocrite, or a pedant—rather than an indi-vidualized being acting in accordance with his type and not in response to the situation. However noble the goal he starts toward, he is easily deflected from his course and spends much of his time pursuing incidental events to their ignoble or trivial ends, arriving virtually by chance at his original destiny.

[28]J. W. H. Atkins explains how a critical theory of nondramatic comedy developed: Through Isidore's confused designation of Plautus and Terence as representing Old Comedy and of the satirists Horace, Persius, and Juvenal, as representing New Comedy, and through "the absence of any clear idea of ancient dramatic form," genres merged, "comoedia came to be regarded as a nar-rative in elegiac verse, written in familiar style and with a happy ending; and this conception resulted in the appearance of a new literary genre in the twelfth century, namely the medieval com-edy which was none other than a versified tale." English Literary Criticism: The Medieval Phase, p. 32.

[29]It has become customary in recent years for critics of Chaucer and Spenser, notably D. W. Robertson, Jr. (in A Preface to Chaucer: Studies in Medieval Perspectives), Roger Sale (in Reading Spenser: An Introduction to The Faerie Queene), and Paul J. Alpers (in The Poetry of The Faerie Queene), to stress that the poetry is "undramatic." Their definition of "dramatic" is, however, based upon the Romantic and Victorian concept of drama as the sincere expression of the emotional life of the character. Robertson, for example, bases his definition on Gustav Freytag's Die Technik des Dramas, an exposition of the pyramid structure of the well-made play, first published in 1863. Freytag's study can most kindly be called dated, and the definition of drama that he proposes and these critics embrace plays a very minor role in contemporary theories of drama.

Allegory and Comedy

His experiences en route to his destiny provide the shape – or plot – of the comic action. Generally there are conceded to be two or three basic shapes of comic action, which in actual execution become individual and distinct from all other shapes and, more important, from all other appear-ances of the same shape. These plot forms have been named the para-bolic, the processional, and the Thomistic or transformational.[30] The im-portance of these plot forms is not their name, however, but their power to establish a set of expectations that the poem must gratify. If the action is resolved by a series of discoveries or disclosures that help the charac-ter to discover who he is and permit him to achieve his goal, then the plot is essentially parabolic. It is the parabola shape to which Maynard Mack refers when he says that "the curve of comedy" is self-exposure.[31]

The parabolic plot is characteristic of New Comedy as written by Plautus and Terence and as written by Shakespeare in his romantic com-edies. The comic protagonist sets out along a straight line to accomplish a goal but finds himself blocked by a figure or force more powerful than he. He endures a series of small crises and petty catastrophes, which form the arch of the parabola, before the discoveries enable him to come to rest at the point of triumph – the end of the original straight line. The world he moves in is usually inverted; that is, the common authority figures do not function as they ought. Parents may behave like children, or masters like slaves, thereby forcing the children and slaves to assume the vacated roles. Although the world is inverted, there is yet a reasonable sort of motion that leads from one ludicrous incident to the next until all is set right. Cause and effect, though not serious as in tragedy, determine the sequence of events, which generally *have* to follow one after another in time.

The second basic plot form, the processional, has been derived by critics from the Aristophanic tradition of comedy. It is marked by a general absence of causality and a diminished significance of time order. Incidents here are sequential because literary and dramatic forms cannot create a true simultaneity of all events. The plot form is basically spatial; it is the pattern provided by

[30]Northrop Frye, "The Argument of Comedy," in *English Institute Essays, 1948*, p. 73. See also Northrop Frye, *A Natural Perspective: The Development of Shakespearean Comedy and Romance.*

[31]Maynard Mack, "Introduction to *Joseph Andrews*," in John Jacob Enck et al., eds., *The Comic in Theory and Practice*, p. 100

a grouping of characters rather than a march of events. . . . [The plot is] the contrast and balance of characters. . . . It does not matter whether the events have any particular connexion with each other; it does not even matter what order they come in; and they are all trivial and mostly fantastic.[32]

This plot form is episodic, in precisely the sense that Aristotle meant when he declared the episodic plot a weak form for tragedy.

The third comic plot form is the transformational – what Northrop Frye calls the Dantean or Thomistic – in which the outcome of the action involves a metamorphosis into a different, and usually higher, sphere of being.[33] This metamorphosis may be an actual physical transformation, like that of the loathly lady in The Wife of Bath's Tale, or an improvement in behavior, like that of the knight-husband. But there is a basic change in the character, or at least in his perception of values and his mode of behavior. The character learns through education and experience to give up his original goal, and for this sacrifice he is rewarded by grace from a higher power. This pattern of education, change, and reward – the basic transaction of the plot – marks a sharp distinction between the transformational and other comic plots, wherein the sequence of events "uncovers" the comic character, though he makes no discovery about himself and does not essentially change. In a transformational plot cause and effect are present, but only as a general and, in fact, vague law that something once begun must finally come to an end. More stress is laid on the logical divisions of the subject and on the thorough disquisition of each division. Once the disquisition is completed, then the metamorphosis occurs.

These are not exhaustive categories, obviously; they are the names of generalized patterns that events usually follow in working to a satisfactory conclusion. In regard to comedy there is a very real sense in which the Romantic doctrine applies that each work is its own genre, and there is the equally real fact that almost no comedy belongs to one category alone but has the characteristics of several.

The signal characteristics of all comic plots are brevity of incidents,

[32]Potts, Comedy, p. 130.

[33]For a further discussion of transformational comedy see my "The School for Transformation: A theory of Middle English Comedy," Genre 9 (1976):179–91.

sudden transitions, repetition, and a sense of discontinuity – the feeling that the poem is constantly contradicting itself. The separate incidents of comedy are marked by an implicit insistence upon energy as the source and manner of personal behavior. In comedies produced on the stage, energy is communicated through the speed at which incidents are played.[34] In narratives energy is implied by the snowballing of events, that is, making as many things as possible, involving as many people as possible, happen in as short a time as possible. Other comic devices commonly used are the inversion of a customary procedure (the slave giving orders, or the peacemaker causing trouble); the self-contradictory action (conducting serious business in an undignified position); or nonincremental repetition. Northrop Frye says flatly that had J. M. Synge's *Riders to the Sea* been a "full-length tragedy plodding glumly through the seven drownings one after another, the audience would have been helpless with unsympathetic laughter long before it was over."[35] Any event that recurs without significant variation or growth is destined to provoke laughter. Repetition, inversion, exaggeration, speed, and other common comic devices are patterns of development that lead inevitably to comic responses.

Style is, of course, the primary tool available to the poet who wishes to communicate his perception of the self-contradictory, or mechanically repetitious, or inverted situation. "It is in the style of a play or novel that we first recognize comedy; and that is probably a surer touchstone than any theory."[36] The comic style corresponds with the "comic in actions and in situations, and is nothing more . . . than their projection on to the plane of words."[37] It insists upon small, concrete details that are them-

---

[34]As theater historian George R. Kernodle has noted, "Played fast enough, any emotional scene will produce laughter." "Excruciatingly Funny *or, the 47 Keys to Comedy,*" *Theatre Arts* 30 (1946):720.

[35]Northrop Frye, *Anatomy of Criticism: Four Essays,* p. 168.

[36]Potts, *Comedy,* p. 64.

[37]Henri Bergson, "Laughter," in Sypher, *Comedy,* pp. 132–33, undeniably the best single discussion of comic techniques and style available to us. Bergson's theory of the comic is founded upon his philosophical concept of *élan vital* – that life is vitality. Bergson sees comedy as basically corrective in its function: it reveals to us what is not vital and provokes us to laugh at it. The content and manner of comedy either contradict our sense of vitality or else counterfeit vitality without being genuinely vital. Whether or not we accept Bergson's reduction of the comic to one principle (almost all critics practice reduction, by the way, and generally with less success than Bergson does), the fact remains that the techniques that he points out are universally accepted as comic and the metaphoric names

selves and not symbols; it highlights our involvement with trivia: woolen underwear, small change, the tendency to count anything that can be counted.

The language of comedy has been traditionally characterized as "low" or "humble," but such a description is not fully accurate, for the language may be very elaborate and eloquent, chosen for its inappropriateness to the topic. Usually the poet achieves a comic style by relying upon age-old verbal tricks that are, paradoxically, perennially fresh. The poet may put an unexpected item into a well-established formula, as Chaucer does when he interprets art as meaning love in the formula "Ars longa, vita brevis" at the beginning of *The Parliament of Fowls*. The poet may apply jargon to everyday life, or he may steadfastly refuse to use technical terms even when they are needed. He may insist upon following a logical concept to its furthest point, at which it is no longer logical; or he may eschew the clearly reasonable in favor of the remote and unreasonable. He utilizes traditional figures of speech that stress the potential ridiculousness of his topic: oxymoron, litotes, and hyperbole, in particular.

As important in comic style as individual words and figures of speech is the element of rhythm. Rhythm in comedy may be an accelerating beat that leads to a crescendo, like the cry "Water!" that climaxes and unites both plots of *The Miller's Tale*, or it may be a sustained and steady pattern that is conspicuously out of synchronization with the events, or yet it may be a basic pattern that is established to be broken by sudden, even violent, variations in its movement and direction. Chaucer uses this rhythmic scheme in the Invocation to book 1 of *The House of Fame*, when he turns a smooth and eloquent prayer for good dreams into a vehement curse calling down nightmares on disbelievers. The primary point is that the rhythm tends to be noticeable, calling attention to itself, like a distinct actor in the comic action. The rhythm and language of comedy are, in effect, self-conscious of their existence as rhythm and language, and they exist not only as a medium of communication but as a celebration of themselves. In other words, comedy, through all its structural and expressive elements, signals that it is comic, and it invites the reader or audience to share in its vision of reality, its celebration of the humble glories of being human.

---

that he gives to comic actions—the "snowball," the "dancing-jack," the "jack-in-the-box"—all illuminate the mechanical and nonvital materials of comedy.

Allegory and Comedy

Here it becomes important to make a necessary distinction between cnmedy and satire, for readers often confuse the two, and it is common to hear one speak of satire when actually he is referring to comedy. Alternately, when the patristic critics of the 1960s tried to illustrate comedy in their allegorical exegeses, they succeeded in making it sound like satire. The source of this confusion is a function shared by both comedy and satire: criticism. All readers know that satire criticizes its subject; too many forget that, while comedy criticizes also, its criticism comes from a different perspective and serves a different end. The comic poet sees his topic as a part of human life, which he embraces, even in its flawed entirety. The satirical poet rejects his topic and human life with it.[38] The satirist "[stands] off to one side . . . saying: Let us laugh at other people."[39] Despite these differences in perspective, satire is closely akin to comedy, for it uses many of the same devices, techniques, and tricks of style that comedy does, and it may be outrageously funny in its effect. Many comic poems contain passages or characters that are satiric, that require the reader to exclude them from the final comic world. Both Chaucer and Spenser shift from comedy to satire when it is required by the nature of a subject that cannot be incorporated into a celebration of human life.[40]

If the end of comedy is to produce lightheartedness and gaiety through a celebration of being human, then its relationship to allegory, particularly as conceived of by the general reader, is indeed suspect. The alliance looks unholy, and it cannot be defended honestly upon the grounds of how much the two have in common, for what they *seem* to have in common is often a point of least similarity. Both comedy and allegory are defined as being fundamentally dual in conception and execution; but whereas the dual aspects of allegory tend to move closer toward a philosophical or moral unity, the two aspects of comedy pull as far apart as possible, as if to emphasize the potential disunity of all existence. On its ethical level allegory tends to move upward, to suggest a mode of conduct by which man may improve himself. The morality of

[38]Potts, *Comedy*, pp. 153–54.

[39]Louis Kronenberger, *The Thread of Laughter: Chapters on English Stage Comedy from Jonson to Maugham*, p. 192.

[40]For an excellent analysis of the structure of satire, see Alvin Kernan, *The Cankered Muse: Satire of the English Renaissance*, Yale Studies in English, vol. 142, pp. 1–36.

comedy tends to be practical and down-to-earth.[41] It stresses the conservation of energy, the importance of being socially acceptable, the need for conformity. In interpretation the finite details of allegory tend to blur the edges of their first identity; the finite details of comedy tend to remain emphatically themselves to the end. By abstract definition comedy and allegory seem to have little in common, but abstract definition deals with ideals and not with the ordinary, imperfect executions that make up literature. Allegory can be comic and still be allegorical – allegory often is both; and in its union of two modes of presentation it offers a complex view of humanity.

Structures, Strategies, and Response

The difficulty of observing both comedy and allegory as they function simultaneously can be easily illustrated by *The Morall Fabillis of Esope the Phrygian*, by Robert Henryson, a so-called Scottish Chaucerian who wrote near the end of the fifteenth century. Henryson displays in several of the fables a very sophisticated comic sensibility, and he also provides a *Moralitas* at the end of each fable in which the several senses of the poem are explained. Henryson recognizes the presence of the comedy, saying in his "Prolog" that it accords well "with sad materis sum merines to ming," so that the mind will not be dulled by too much seriousness.[42] The real fruit of the fable is the moral lesson; the humor is but chaff. Thus Henryson himself indicates that there is no firm union between morality and comedy, and he makes matters harder for the reader who seeks a unity by frequently imposing a *Moralitas* that has only a tangential relation to the fable, that may be, indeed, utterly humorless. In some cases, for instance in "The Taill of the Cok and the Jasp," the effect of the *Moralitas* is diametrically opposed to that of the fable itself. While there is not so great a disparity between the moral and tale of "How this foir-said Tod maid his Confessioun to Freir Wolf Waitskaith," there is,

---

[41]Most recent studies of comedy have tended to stress the dubious morality and the pressures for social conformity that are revealed in comedy. See, for example, Robert B. Heilman, *The Ways of the World: Comedy and Society*; Allan Rodway, *English Comedy: Its Role and Nature from Chaucer to the Present Day*; Derek Brewer, "Afterword: Notes Towards a Theory of Medieval Comedy," in *Medieval Comic Tales*, trans. Peter Rickard et al., pp. 140–49; and Morton Gurewitch, *Comedy: The Irrational Vision*.

[42]Robert Henryson, *Poems*, ed. Charles Elliott, line 26. Further references are incorporated in the text.

nonetheless, a marked tendency to stamp out the comedy in order to allegorize.

The tale of the Fox's confession is a delightful comedy of human weakness whose humor arises from quick and ingenious moral compromise. The fox, Lawrence, looks at the skies, reads in the stars that death awaits him shortly, and determines to prepare for his destiny: "Thairfoir I will ga seik sum confessour, / And schryiff me clene off my sinnis to this hour" (654–55). This resolution he follows with a lament over the cursed life allotted to thieves. Then he discovers the "worthie Doctour in Divinitie," Freir Wolf Waitskaith, and makes confession to him. In being shriven, the Fox faces difficulties, for he cannot feel contrite over the delicious meals he has stolen, he cannot promise to abstain from further stealing, and he can take penance only if it is "licht, Schort and not gre-vand to my tendernes." He is, says the *Moralitas*, "throw consuetude and ryte, / Vincust with carnall sensualitie" (lines 782–83).

Although fully aware of his indefensible position, the Fox requests special consideration. When his penance is pronounced, "Thow sall...forbeir flesch untill Pasche," he bargains (lines 726–29):

> "I grant thairto, swa ye will giff me leif
> To eit puddingis, or laip ane lyttill blude,
> Or heid or feit or paynchis let me preif,
> In cace I fall no flesch unto my fude."

Yet he really intends to forbear flesh, to live on fish, until he arrives at the river and sees the water and wild waves. He is so dismayed that he is ready to die from the mere anticipation of hunger, until he sees a trip of goats. At the opportune moment he seizes a kid, carries him to the edge of the sea, and "dowkis" him twice or thrice, saying, "Ga doun Schir Kid, cum up Schir Salmond agane!" After feasting on "salmon," he goes to a hiding place in the woods and lies under a bush to bask in the sun (lines 758–60):

> And rekleslie he said quhair he did rest,
> Straikand his wame aganis the sonis heit:
> "Upon this wame set wer ane bolt full meit."

As if in response to a request, the goatherd sees him, draws his bow, and pricks the Fox fast to the earth. With his final breath the Fox criticizes the way of the world: "Me think na man may speik ane word in play, / Bot nowondayis in ernist it is tane" (lines 770–71).

The Fox's response to being slain illustrates the final form of human triumph suggested by Susanne Langer: the philosophical acceptance of mischance that diminishes its power over the victim–that, in fact, subordinates it to the victim. That is, the Fox, while dying, triumphs verbally over death by pointing out that it is in error–death has misin- terpreted a "word in play" as being "in ernist." Insofar as the Fox can con- vert everything to the level of words, he is the master of his little world; he takes the controlling power out of divine or astrological hands and grants it to himself as the creator of his own existence. The Fox controls his own destiny from beginning to end in a way that no serious or tragic figure could, and he achieves this control through a finely developed capacity for compromising moral and theological standards. He will suf- fer penance only if he does not have to suffer; he will abstain from the name of meat but not the form. His baptism of the Kid is a flash of seman- tic genius, the highest creative act in a world that is made of words only. His unwillingness to give up sin *ought* to be morally repugnant to us, but the ingenuity with which he tries to say yes and no simultaneously is far from repugnant. In fact, it engages not only our attention but also our moral complicity, for his cleverness seems so desirable a fault that to con- demn the Fox is to condemn our desire to be clever, and this we cannot fully or freely do.

The *Moralitas* tells us that the Fox is a lost soul, erring mankind who loves his sin too much to leave it. Henryson draws a practical moral for conduct from the experience of the Fox: the folk ought to amend and give up their pleasant sins, for fear of the suddenness of death's coming. They must cease to sin, be remorseful of conscience, and obey God, and they "sall wend" after death "to blis withouttin end." Allegorically the Fox is the sinner who brings himself to confusion through refusing to leave his sins. Comically he is the conquering hero, the clever man who somehow triumphs over adversity. His transformation of the Kid into salmon is a parody of the sacrament of baptism, an indictment of corruption in the Church, as represented in the fable by the Priest-Wolf; it is also the ad- mirable ploy of a human being struggling against a hostile environment. The Fox is, in a real sense, our agent enacting our victory.

Thus the poem stands: Allegorically it damns the Fox; comically it

Allegory and Comedy

elevates him. The *Moralitas*, while clearly and logically appropriate, has little to do with our basic response to the poem; in fact, it creates a totally dual aspect for the poem. It does not really contradict or fail to fit the story—it has a logical consistency and appropriateness that carry its own conviction. In other words, we are logically engaged by the *Moralitas* and emotionally engaged by the tale, and the two responses do not seem to come together, at least in any contemporary sense of unity.

We have here, then, a medieval "dissociation of sensibility," and we cannot be certain that Henryson ever intended what we would call an aesthetic unity, or that any medieval poet who included comic passages in an allegory intended a unity as we define it. Modern critics who seek for unity ordinarily find it at the expense of the comedy, but by granting the poet high seriousness of allegorical intention, they deprive the poem of a primary source of vitality. They leave unanswered the question of how jest and earnest can coexist and cooperate within a single work. It is this question that we shall try to answer in the following chapters as we look at the comic allegories of Chaucer and his successors.

2.

Chaucer's Comic Visions

EOFFREY CHAUCER BEGAN his poetic career by writing an allegory that contained comedy and ended by writing an extended comedy that contained allegory. As a result of his shift in emphasis he has become a man of two reputations. For the two centuries following his death he was honored as a rhetorician, the "well of English undefyled," and a maker of allegorical models for his successors to imitate. He became the revered master of a poetical tradition in English that influenced not only the late medieval Chaucerians — Lydgate, Henryson, Hawes, Dunbar, Douglas, and Skelton — but also poets of the English Renaissance, including Edmund Spenser. Beginning in the late seventeenth century, however, when Dryden and then Pope chose *The Canterbury Tales* for their "translations" and imitations, Chaucer's reputation came to be founded on his achivement as a maker of realistic comedies, and for these poems he is now honored as the greatest comic poet in English.[1]

The problem with these two reputations is that, while both are direct reflections of Chaucer's poetical practice and development, they tend to split his full achievement in halves that are then set in opposition to each other. They suggest, with a degree of accuracy, that Chaucer had difficulty in establishing a balance between comedy and allegory, that, rather than balancing the two, he selected narrative forms that subordinated one to the other. But instead of illustrating that comedy and allegory can be mutual components of one construction, Chaucer's two

[1]For a brief and engaging survey of Chaucer's reputations through the ages, see E. Talbot Donaldson, "Chaucer in the Twentieth Century," *Studies in the Age of Chaucer*, Publications of the New Chaucer Society, vol. 2, ed. Roy J. Pearcy, pp. 7–13.

reputations suggest that they are almost irreconcilable enemies, each fighting for mastery as though serious thought and laughter cannot coexist.

For the most part, criticism of Chaucer's poetry has borne out this impression, both intentionally and inadvertently. The older school of critics who focused their attention on comic realism tended to discount the seriousness of Chaucer's commitment to allegory. Trained in an era when the Coleridgean prejudice against allegory governed most theories of poetry, they believed that allegory – particularly the dream vision – was already dead when Chaucer began to write. Moreover, they defined allegory as the literary opposite of realism, and since comedy, however fantastic its material, is realistic in its implications, Chaucer's increasing emphasis upon comedy naturally indicated a corresponding disinterest in allegory. This belief is explicit in the introductory essays that F. N. Robinson provides for the standard edition of Chaucer's works[2] and in Wolfgang Clemen's *Chaucer's Early Poetry*, which purports to document Chaucer's farewell to allegory.[3] It is also implicit in as recent a work as James Winny's study of Chaucer's dream poetry.[4]

On the other hand, much of the recent criticism that emphasizes Chaucer's allegory offers an inadvertent testimony that comedy and allegory do not blend, at least for critical purposes. The exegetical critics tend to discuss irony and satire rather than comedy: irony because it is a tone rather than a form and is more open to theological interpretation, and satire because it is already designed to convey moral attitudes and statements. The structuralist critics, while trying to look squarely at Chaucer's poetry rather than at the world around it, nonetheless warp their interpretations by insisting that his true allegory is an evolving thesis about the nature and function of language and that his comedy is fundamentally a matter of puns and sometimes exquisite wordplay. If the exegetical critics project an image of Chaucer as a stern preaching friar who inexplicably disguised himself as an urbane courtier, the structuralists convey the impression that he is the very first of our twentieth-century semanticists.

[2]*The Works of Geoffrey Chaucer*, ed. F. N. Robinson, 2d ed. All quotations are taken from this edition.

[3]Trans. C. A. M. Sym.

[4]*Chaucer's Dream Poems.*

Chaucer's Comic Visions

All these attitudes toward Chaucer's allegory are grounded upon distinctive features of his poetry and his world, though we may justifiably
wonder whether the foundation is not ice rather than stone. We must
grant the point of the skeptical realists that *Troilus and Criseyde* and *The
Canterbury Tales* omit the dream-vision frame and make limited use of
personified abstractions; but our preference for the so-called realism of
these works may tell us more about our literary prejudices than about
Chaucer's aesthetic principles. We can join the exegetical critics in being
certain that Chaucer subscribed to the Christian doctrine, but, as recent
studies indicate, he may have worn his faith comfortably, even casually,
without the nagging insistence upon its centrality that patristic criticism
imputes to his poems.[5] Finally, Chaucer does stop poems in their narrative or declamatory tracks to comment upon diction, metrics, and matters of structure, and he cautions that words may be true or false; but
verbal self-consciousness is as much a device of comedy as it is a philosophical inquiry into the nature of language. In sum, all these approaches
to Chaucerian allegory can leave the reader dissatisfied.

The problem is that the allegory, especially in the dream-vision poems,
continually baffles our expectations of how allegory should work. To
begin with, it is not particularly evocative. There is a world of suggestive
difference between Chaucer's knight dressed in black and Spenser's Red
Cross knight, whose new suit of armor is dented and battered from many
a blow. Chaucer's image is self-defining and self-contained; Spenser's
teases us into discovering that this knight is wearing the whole armor of
God. Moreover, Chaucer's parallel narratives and inset tales, like his images, literalize rather than imply. They do not lead to a structure of implied meanings. For the most part, his meaning is stated and restated in
the very surface of these poems, obscured only by the fact that we do not
expect or want it to be so open and obvious. Finally, and most troublesome of all, the dream-vision poems are not remarkably Christian in their
concerns or implications. They do not suggest that the Christian vision
enables man to see the world whole. In fact, Chaucer frequently turns
the narrator's faith into a comic obtuseness that precludes his really see-

[5]For recent studies that have done much to redress the earlier overemphasis upon the religious
solidarity of the Middle Ages and to explore the fourteenth-century sense of "unknowing" that may
have contributed to Chaucer's ironic view, see Derek Brewer, *Chaucer and His World*, pp. 165–80;
and Sheila Delany, *Chaucer's* House of Fame: *The Poetics of Skeptical Fideism*. See also John Gardner,
The Poetry of Chaucer, pp. xv–xxv.

ing what he has seen. Although fully grounded in virtue, the allegory can seem as unstable and slippery as Criseyde's heart.

The point is now well taken by scholars that Chaucer did not abandon allegory, despite giving up some of its mechanical appurtenances, but continued to use it to the end of his career. We recognize that the older critics erred in believing that Chaucer had to choose between comedy and allegory. But a good many allegorical studies run into ditches of their own making by simplifying or altering the nature of his comedy to make it fit an interpretation of the allegory. At times we can find some truly hilarious passages being dismissed as merely farcical "chaff";[6] at other times we hear critics telling us how heartily Chaucer's audience laughed when our own judgment keeps us sober. In speaking of allegory, we are always challenged by Chaucer's comedy.

From *The Book of the Duchess* through *The Canterbury Tales*, Chaucer is intent upon evoking both serious reflection and laughter, and to this end he frequently relies upon the pull and tug of constructions that seem on the surface to be incongruously juxtaposed within a single frame. His is a complex art, in which the mixture of comedy and allegory may be meant not to coalesce into a single statement about human existence and aspirations but—quite the reverse—to suggest how various and contradictory human experience can be.

A Model for Chaucer

Although Chaucer has been called the reverend master of a poetical tradition in English that still bears his name, he was not the first poet, even in England, to try uniting comedy and allegory. Rather, he was working in the tradition of that most influential of medieval poems, the *Roman de la Rose*, and under the more direct influence of the French poet Guillaume de Machaut.[7] Apparently Chaucer began his career as poet by making a translation of the *Roman* into English.[8] It is certain that the poem exercised a pervasive, lifelong influence on him that may never be fully documented.

[6]See Bernard F. Huppé and D. W. Robertson, Jr., *Fruyt and Chaf: Studies in Chaucer's Allegories.*

[7]For a full-length study of the French influence, see James Wimsatt, *Chaucer and the French Love Poets: The Literary Background of* The Book of the Duchess.

[8]See Dean S. Fansler, *Chaucer and the* Roman de la Rose.

Chaucer's Comic Visions

In the *Roman* he found character types whose qualities he expanded or contracted and shaped into some of his own most memorable personages. The most famous of these is the Wife of Bath, whose original is La Vieille; but perhaps the most broadly influential figure in the *Roman* is Faus-Semblant, who bears a strong family resemblance to several of the Canterbury churchmen: the Friar with his easy enjoyment of lust and luxury, the Summoner with his new doctrine that "Purs is the ercedekenes helle," and the Pardoner with his devotion to corrupting the incorruptible. A second lesson Chaucer may have learned from the *Roman* was how to turn anticlerical sentiment into the form and content of poetry, a conversion he achieves so deftly that the false churchman is presented intact in his self-delusion, while all readers see him instantly as the expansive figure of a balloon, filled with air only. A third influence of the poem upon Chaucer may be traced in his steady development of the technique of unconscious self-revelation (the transformation of confession into a comic device), which figures prominently in the action of all his comic poems. Closely related to this is the device of the obtuse narrator who cannot or will not learn from his own experiences, even when he sees clearly that they are instructive and miraculous. A final influence upon Chaucer's early poems is the use of the dream-vision as a framework to structure the contents of the poem. The authors of the *Roman* did not create the dream frame, for it goes back in Latin poetry to the *Somnium Scipionis* and in the Christian tradition to the prophetic books of the Old Testament and the Book of Revelation in the New Testament, but the *Roman's* immense popularity certainly helped maintain the dream vision's dominance over all other allegorical forms in Europe for three centuries.

In other words, we may trace directly or indirectly to the *Roman de la Rose* the roots of several distinct characteristics of Chaucer's poetry, particularly the combination of comedy and allegory into one vision and statement. John V. Fleming has argued very persuasively that Guillaume de Lorris set in motion a deeply ironic narrative, told by an ignorant, self-deluded Dreamer, about one man's pursuit of a love that is really narcissistic infatuation with the self. Jean de Meun completed the story by having the Dreamer reject Raison on the stupidly prudish grounds that she speaks indelicately of sexual organs. Then he allies himself with false "virtues" and creates a sweeping movement toward sin that deludes even Nature into assuming authority over matters beyond her realm, before he achieves his original desire – raping a rosebush.[9]

The *Roman* is an extravagant comedy about man triumphing in his belief that he can disturb the universe to gratify his own desires, a triumph he achieves by casting out his own reason and impiously conferring a spiritual significance upon his lust. Especially in Jean de Meun's continuation, there is a combination of parody, satire, and farce that defines the world of Amis, Amours, La Vieille, Nature, and Genius. There is a parodic strain to the analogy of the Lover and the spiritual pilgrim, particularly in the equation of his sexual organs with the scrip and staff carried by the seeker after holy shrines. The literal overthrow of the old society of Jalosie and Peor and the establishment of a new order, figured by the mating of the Lover with his Rose, suggest that the movement of the poem is typical of Roman New Comedy, wherein attention is directed toward marriage and the procreation of a new generation. The society overthrown, however, is that headed by Raison, while the new world is founded upon violence, lust, and rape. The poem narrows to a pun at the end to reflect the destructiveness of the hero's triumph, which grows out of his persuasion that the natural man is true master over the rational. Our laughter at the end is not in admiration of his victory but in surprise at his self-delusion, a delusion that the allegory has pointed out repeatedly.

On his way to the brave new world created out of the wreckage of the old, Jean emphasizes the Lover's ludicrous view of life by creating broadly farcical scenes. The climax of the first battle outside the castle of Jalosie descends from heroic warfare to slapstick when Suerté defends herself from Peor:

> To give example to the rest, she seized
> Her enemy by both the ears; and Fear
> To her did likewise. Others intervened
> And, grabbing one another similarly,
> Struggled in pairs. Never was battle seen
> So joined before![10]

[9]*The* Roman de la Rose: *A Study in Allegory and Iconography*, p. 53. For a kindlier, more romantic reading of the poem, see Alan M. F. Gunn, *The Mirror of Love: A Reinterpretation of* The Romance of the Rose.

[10]Guillaume de Lorris and Jean de Meun, *The Romance of the Rose*, trans. Harry W. Robbins, ed.

Chaucer's Comic Visions

The sudden stress upon the physical body, the exchange of sword and shield for hands and ears, and the reduplication of the first encounter by all the other warriors—these are typically farcical. By making the warriors enact the adage "All's fair in love and war," Jean reduces both the adage and the conflict to their least glorious denominator and so illustrates the debased nature of any love that provokes war. The comedy of the battle makes a philosophical point in the allegory by ridiculing the speed with which man resorts to unmanly conduct when he relies only upon natural inclination to guide him through life. Allegorically, comically too, man is a union of rational and natural impulses, and he cannot come to a proper physical or spiritual destiny if he denies the importance of reason.

A Comic Elegy

Jean's achievement in the *Roman* set a very high level for Chaucer and his descendants to aim at: the subtle and skillful blending of comedy and allegory into one mode of knowing that evokes simultaneous and cooperative responses from emotion and intellect. Chaucer's early dream visions are products of his attempts to arrive at a complex unity provoking comparable responses, but they are not, properly speaking, exact imitations of the *Roman*. Chaucer's comic vision is his own, generally more benevolent and less condemnatory than Jean's, and his allegorical implications reflect the quality of his own intellect working upon the contents of his mind and heart. Although the comic devices that Chaucer relies upon to express his vision are traditional, even standardized, materials of comedy, they become uniquely "Chaucerian" as they are modified by his style and are shaped into his own creations. In comparison with Jean's satiric intent, Chaucer's comedy serves functions that are infinitely more complex, even in the earliest dream visions. It is generally meant to elicit a variety of simultaneous responses rather than a single attitude like scornful laughter, and these responses may either complement or contradict one another, depending upon the context they spring from.

It is only fair to admit that such complexity borders on confusion, for it requires great artistry to control the materials so that intended order

---

Charles W. Dunn, p. 331.

Laughter in the Courts of Love

does not dwindle into chaos. Much of the criticism of Chaucer's second dream vision, *The House of Fame*, has been devoted to evaluating the degree of order or chaos in the poem, for there is general disagreement about whether Chaucer actually kept control of all his materials in this ambitious undertaking. But even regarding *The Book of the Duchess*, a poem that is relatively clear and direct, the question of unity has been raised by those who find comedy inappropriate in an allegory about the "Deeth of Blaunche."[11]

I have said that *The Book of the Duchess* is a relatively clear and direct poem, and so it is, in comparison with *The House of Fame*; but it is, in its own right, a complex poem, an allegory about human feeling and understanding that is narrated by a comic figure whose participation in the action invites laughter. The narrator introduces his poem by announcing his amazement that he is alive, since he has been unable to sleep for eight years as the result of a sickness that he will neither name nor analyze. He is incapable of feeling: joy and sorrow to him are alike. Moreover, he has no hope of being cured, for there is but one (unidentified) physician who can heal him. On a recent evening, however, after debating whether to play at chess or backgammon or to read a book, he took up a romance and read the tale of Seys and Alcyone, in which he was introduced to the figure of Morpheus, the god of sleep. Inspired by desperation, he prayed to Morpheus, whereupon he fell immediately to sleep and dreamed the adventure that constitutes the remainder of the poem.

In his dream he awakens to a beautiful May morning, rises to join a hunt, in which the trail is ultimately lost, follows a fawning whelp into a grove, and there discovers a solitary Knight dressed in black, who laments the loss of his "faire White." The dialogue between the Dreamer and the Knight is made up of eloquent praise for the lady, heartfelt lamentations by the Knight, and comic fumblings by the Dreamer, who seems compassionate and yet incapable of understanding what the Knight

[11]In recent years *The Book of the Duchess* has become a very popular subject of critical studies by those who view the poem as an allegory of linguistic and poetical concerns. See, for instance, Phillip C. Boardman, "Courtly Language and the Strategy of Consolation in the *Book of the Duchess*," *ELH* 44 (1977):567–79; and Judith Ferster, "Intention and Interpretation in the 'Book of the Duchess,'" *Criticism* 22 (1980):1–24. For an older historical view explaining that the mixture of tones and styles is traditional, see E. R. Curtius, *European Literature and the Latin Middle Ages*, trans. Willard R. Trask, pp. 417–35.

means. Thus the dialogue seems to go in two directions, one pointed by the sorrowful Knight and the other by his obtuse listener; but the two come together at last in the statement of the Dreamer, who finally understands the Knight's grief: "Be God, hyt ys routhe!"

As allegory, the poem is a classic illustration of Isidore's definition of allegory as *alieniloquium*: "One thing is said, and another is meant." What is meant by the poem is the one word never uttered: Blanche. She is identified as a "fers," the "faire White," and a lady who inspired true courtliness in a callow youth, but never as herself. Otherwise, the point of the poem is stated outright: Blanche is dead, and it is a pity. Her death is a loss that even the obtuse, insensate Dreamer must understand and *feel*. Once that fact is accomplished, the poem is completed. There remain only the closing details, the end of the hunt and the end of the dream, which are summarized in short order. Chaucer offers no consolation, neither Christian nor philosophical, as P. M. Kean has pointed out, because that was not his purpose in writing the poem.[12] What he said, both literally and allegorically, was what he meant to say: It is appropriate to grieve deeply at the death of so noble a lady as Blanche.

Chaucer approaches this depth of feeling, however, through indirection and through comedy. The poem is filled with images and expressions of loss, mostly trivial, which lead finally to the Knight's loss. The Dreamer has lost his sleep, his sense of feeling, his hope of being cured. He reads a tale of a queen who has lost her mate, but he misses the true point of the story and focuses instead on a subordinate detail. He joins a hunt in which the quarry is lost, and when he tries to catch the whelp, it flees from him and is gone. The Dreamer inhabits a world in which loss seems consistent, but not serious.

The comedy of the poem is centered in the figure of the Dreamer. From the beginning he sets himself up as willfully ignorant, refusing to analyze why he cannot sleep; furthermore, he reveals himself to be an awkward combination of skepticism and gullibility. After he discovers the figure of Morpheus in the tale of Seys and Alcyone, he prays to him, even though he never knew but one God, offering him "in game"—providing that he actually exists and has the power to make men sleep—"'of down of pure

12P. M. Kean, *Chaucer and the Making of English Poetry*, vol. 1, *Love Vision and Debate*, p. 66. For another very sensible view of the "nature of consolation" and the relation of the Dreamer to the Knight, see A. C. Spearing, *Medieval Dream-Poetry*, pp. 71–73.

dowve's white . . . a fether-bed"' (lines 250–51), which he would deliver *if* he knew the location of the god's cave. The pledge is a delightful composition, made up basically of the comic devices of accumulation and contradiction and concluded with an unconscious revelation of true motive. Throughout his speech the Dreamer is a self-conscious embodiment of cautious impulsiveness, offering Morpheus "'moo feës thus / Than ever he wan" but canceling the earnestness of his offer by his prefatory rejection of the deity as the one true God. In describing his bribe for sleep, the Dreamer accumulates little concrete details: the feather bed will be striped with gold and covered with imported fine black satin, and every pillowcase will be made of cloth of Rennes. He dwells fondly on the material details of his imagined gift and lingers over the thought of luxurious sleep on the featherbed: "Hym thar not nede to turnen ofte" (line 256). Such devotion to detail for the love of detail itself is comic, particularly when accompanied by the Dreamer's implicit desire to enjoy the bed and the sleep himself.

The pledge to Morpheus helps characterize the Dreamer as a literalist of the imagination, and it is his literalism—his inability to recognize figurative speech—that counterpoints the pathos of the Black Knight's lament. When he hears the Knight say that he wishes to die because he has lost his "fers" in a game of chess with Fortune, the Dreamer hastily interjects that even the loss of a dozen "ferses" is no proper cause for suicide, which will surely lead to damnation. With firm common sense he concludes, ". . . ther is no man alyve her / Wolde for a fers make this woo!" (lines 740–41). His failure to identify the "fers" with the Lady leads the conversation onward through the Knight's narration of his courtship and happiness, until at last the Knight is forced to state his loss directly, without any figure of speech. The Dreamer now is faced with a real cause for grief that he cannot misunderstand, that he must respond to directly; he has undergone an education in feeling and knowing as a result of his comic blunders throughout the encounter. His capacity for fearful empathy, which he expressed upon reading about Alcyone's grief and also upon first seeing the Knight, is now joined with a knowledge that transcends his former literalism and his refusal to investigate the causes of conditions and situations. He, like Alcyone and the Knight, has come to know grief.

The Book of the Duchess, then, is both a literal statement and an allegory of grief offered to John of Gaunt as a tribute to Blanche. In its structure the poem traces a spiral, beginning with a laughable statement of loss and grief so trivial, so remote, that it seems quite irrelevant to the death of Blanche, yet moving steadily inward as it continues to circle figuratively about the literalized center. The narrated legend of Seys and Alcyone, taken from Ovid's *Metamorphoses*, mirrors the story of the Knight and his Lady (appropriately reversing their roles), but because the Dreamer emphasizes Morpheus as his significant discovery, the parallel seems more decorative than emotive. The dream itself begins with a statement of felt pleasure, the Dreamer's delight in the sunshine, the decorated windows of his chamber, the singing of birds, and the anticipation of enjoyment in the hunt. Although the spiral is moving closer to its center, the narrative is still focused on a peripheral concern. Once the dreamer rides out to join the hunt, however, he is on his way to a discovery that cannot be denied.

The dialogue between the Dreamer and the Knight continues this pattern of moving around the subject and looking at its reflection. Although the Knight's first speech states explicitly that his Lady is dead and gone, the Dreamer interprets it as "a lay, a maner song, / Withoute noote, withoute song" (lines 471–72). Next the Knight states his loss figuratively, saying that he has lost his queen to Fortune in a game of chess. The Dreamer interprets this literally, finding it incredible that any man would be so forlorn over the loss of a single chesspiece. The Knight now tells his story a third time, casting it in the terms of Courtly Love, which the Dreamer can dimly understand, though he suspects that the Lady has proved either unresponsive or false. To correct this error, the Knight must speak bluntly: "She ys ded!" and the Dreamer *must* respond: "Is that youre los? Be God, hyt ys routhe!"

The spiral structure of the poem, with its movement from figurative speech to literalness, from comedy to acquaintance with grief, serves to honor Blanche. She is the center of the poem, the virtuous lady who inspired virtue in others. Her death is a loss that must be felt, that cannot, must not, be minimized by a rush to consolation. The structural function of comedy in the allegory is twofold. First, it heightens our sense of the Lady's goodness, by contrasting her excellence with the Dreamer's shortcomings. It is a form of comic relief that intensifies the ideal of virtue. Second, it tells its own moral story about the importance of knowledge that leads to appropriate responses to human experience. The loss of Blanche is a great loss, which must lead to profound grief; any other response is to misunderstand the value of the Lady. The comedy of Chaucer's elegy makes the poem a complex and moving allegory of the human heart and mind.

Toward the Meaning of Fame

The Book of the Duchess is essentially an allegory that is modified by comedy, while *The House of Fame* may properly be called a comedy that is allegorical. That is, Chaucer subordinates comedy to allegory in the first dream vision, but in the second he seems to be working out new relationships in which comedy and allegory are balanced together. Each book of the poem illustrates a different relation: In book 1, as in *The Book of the Duchess*, comedy is clearly subordinate; in book 2, comedy is dominant—in fact, Chaucer uses it to provide statements that are customarily made through allegory; and in book 3 comedy and allegory are united as satire. Technically, *The House of Fame* is an extremely ambitious poem, and it is perhaps natural that so many critics have questioned Chaucer's success. A. C. Baugh, for example, terms it "a badly proportioned, incomplete, and utterly delightful poem."[13]

The reader's introduction to the poem is provided by the same figure who introduced *The Book of the Duchess*—the greatest of Chaucer's comic inventions, the Chaucerian *persona*. This figure moves, often unwillingly and sometimes only because he is shoved, through the dream visions and on to Canterbury. Obtuse, sententious, timid, and tenderhearted, he is distinguished by a fondness for details (he seems to have total recall and a near-total inability to evaluate the quality of his recollections) that has its overwhelmingly logical conclusion in the "murye tale" of Melibee, an interminable analysis of moral and theological probability. Simultaneously gullible and suspicious, the persona veers from one attitude to the other, never suspecting that he contradicts himself. Though others scorn and ridicule him, he is stubbornly true to his own perceptions, defending them at times with obstinate silence. The Chaucer persona is a unique creation in English poetry: the only comic presentation of self that is accomplished without any self-preserving gestures. He is not Chaucer,

[13]A. C. Baugh, ed., *A Literary History of England*, p. 253.

even when named "Geffrey," but rather is Chaucer's comic treatment of himself, his spokesman, who must be brought clearly into focus if we are to understand the stories he tells us, adventures which he himself is trying to bring into focus.

It is the persona's struggle to express a marvelous dream that provides at least a mechanical unity to *The House of Fame*: the Narrator insists that this is all one dream that makes intelligible points about human existence. In the proems and invocations, which provide a comic frame around the dream frame, "Geffrey" mediates between the dream and the audience, directing them toward an appreciation of its significance, while at the same time he establishes a comic perspective on the allegory. As he pronounces the formal prefaces to his narrative, Geffrey reveals himself to be a contradictory union of knowledge and willful ignorance, charity and venom, modesty and pride, with each quality triumphing in its own turn and fully replacing that which preceded it, sequential attitudes that are never balanced under the yoke of temperance.

The effect of Geffrey's self-disclosure is oxymoronic, and the acting-out of his disunified personality gives much comic momentum to the poem. He recognizes that his dream of December 10 is significant: ". . . no man elles me beforn / Mette, I trowe stedfastly, / So wonderful a drem. . ." (lines 61–63); neither "Isaye, ne Scipion, / Ne kyng Nabugodonosor, / Pharoo, Turnus, ne Elcanor" (lines 514–16). But he relies upon assertion rather than analysis to prove the importance of his vision. In fact, he stubbornly refuses to classify his dream or to analyze it, declaring not only his ignorance of the kinds of dreams and their causes (though he names them) but also his determination to know nothing of kind or cause.

Besides struggling with the significance of his dream, the Narrator also engages in a losing battle with uncontrollable aspects of his personality and his craft. He announces that he will begin by making a proper invocation to the god of sleep, Morpheus, but almost immediately he redirects the invocation to Christ, asking His blessing upon all listeners – unless they do not believe him, in which case he asks Christ to curse them with bad dreams, whether they dream barefoot or shod. In the Invocation to book 3 he begins a sonorous address to Apollo, "O God of science and of lyght," but soon dwindles to asking that his rhymes may please the audience, even if his metrics fail in a syllable or two. The distance between his epical intention and troublesome metrics is a comic measure of his headlong tumble from dignity to awkward confusion, the same distance that he falls between the meritorious blessing and vehement curse in the Invocation to book 1. Figuratively speaking, he slips on the banana peel of his own nature and unintentionally illustrates that he cannot come to terms with his own impulses, much less with his dream.

The dream itself comprises Chaucer's most ambitious efforts in the visionary genre, an attempt to unite poetry, science, moral philosophy, and cultural history in a single structure. In combination with the proems and invocations, the three books of the dream make up a remarkably changeable poem whose tones and values can seem different upon each reading. Most critical reaction to the poem is troubled by the notion of unity, for each book seems a discrete segment, scarcely related to the other two in tone or structure, and the absence of an ending leaves the narrative unresolved, hence "disunified."[14] But apart from the puzzle over the "man of gret auctorite," who never appears, the lack of unity is more apparent than real. There is an intelligible pattern to the abstract argument of the poem, expressed through the thoughts and emotions of Geffrey the Dreamer, who undergoes a relatively complete and meaningful experience. He learns the true nature of Fame and concludes that he will lead his own life in stoical indifference to the desire for or fear of Fame. Moreover, as Kean has noted, by tracing a movement from a completed poem back to the wealth of ideas which the poet has to select from, he has discovered how makers of poetry contribute either truthfully or falsely to the world's notion of characters and events.[15] This pattern of experience, however, is set in contrast to the confusion and lack of control expressed by Geffrey the Narrator in the proems and invocations, where he seems completely overwhelmed by the significance of his

[14]For studies of unity and suggestions about the ending of the poem, see Paul G. Ruggiers, "The Unity of Chaucer's *House of Fame*," *SP* 50 (1953):16–29; B. G. Koonce, *Chaucer and the Tradition of Fame: Symbolism in* The House of Fame; Bertrand H. Bronson, *Chaucer's* Hous of Fame: *Another Hypothesis*, University of California Publications in English, vol. 3, no. 4; John M. Manly, "What Is Chaucer's *Hous of Fame?*" in *Anniversary Papers by Colleagues and Pupils of George Lyman Kittredge*, pp. 73–81; J. A. W. Bennett, *Chaucer's Book of Fame: An Exposition of* "The House of Fame"; John Leyerle, "Chaucer's Windy Eagle," *UTQ* 40 (1971):247–65; Sheila Delany, *Chaucer's* House of Fame: *The Poetics of Skeptical Fideism*; Kay Stevenson, "The Endings of Chaucer's *House of Fame*," *ES* 59 (1978):10–26; and John M. Fyler, *Chaucer and Ovid*, especially pp. 24–25, 58.

[15]Kean, *Chaucer and the Making of English Poetry*, 1:85–111.

dream and so clings stubbornly to his pretensions to ignorance. While the dream-vision moves forward to enlightenment, the frame around it moves backward into a comic chaos that, paradoxically, clarifies the meaning of the poem.

Besides the complex juxtaposition of the poetical frame and the dream, there is a further complexity of structure in both the allegory and the comedy of the poem. To begin with, the poem seems to be an experiment in allegorical styles, for there is a shift midway from symbolic allegory to personification. Moreover, although books 1 and 2 have symbolic structures, the central symbols and their allegorical implications differ markedly. An additional complexity in the poem is its comic structure. As I shall explain shortly, the action is presented as processional comedy, which is made up largely of absurdities, *non sequiturs*, and patent contradictions of itself.

As allegory the poem relies upon both symbol and personification to create its statement and to relate this statement to human experience. After setting the scene, Chaucer devotes most of book 1 to a narration of the story of Aeneas, with special emphasis on Dido, a pathetic victim of Fame and Love. The defining symbol of book 1, she introduces the two major terms of the allegory, Fame and Love, providing an initial definition and demonstrating the consequences of their interaction. She arouses both pity and confusion in the Dreamer by her lament (which he dreams rather than reading in the brass tablets). Having given up all the world for love, she finds herself given up; then, from fear of Fame, she kills herself. Filled with symphathy, Geffrey begins an impassioned denunciation of all faithless lovers but stops when he must admit that according to the book (Virgil's *Aeneid*), Aeneas left Dido because he was ordered by Mercury to sail for Italy. Hoping to learn more about the temple where he found the narration, Geffrey goes outside and discovers himself alone in a sandy waste. Now he prays to Christ for salvation from "fantome and illusion," and his prayer is answered by the coming of the Eagle, surely the greatest phantom and illusion of his life.

While book 1 places emphasis on Dido's desolation and death, book 2 is a comic celebration of life, manifested through the glorious golden Eagle. The flight through space literalizes the interior journey toward knowledge that Geffrey began in the Temple of Glass, with the loquacious Eagle replacing the brass tablets as teacher. But insofar as book 2 extends

Laughter in the Courts of Love

and modifies the definitions of Fame and Love offered in book 1, it does so in surprising ways. In his lecture the Eagle converts the terms to scientific elements, defining Love as speech, which is broken air, and Fame as a telephonic receiver of all those waves of broken air. Thus Love and Fame come together physically, but in space high above the earth. When he relates the terms to actual human experience, the Eagle offers only disinterested or negative evaluations, assuring Geffrey that he has not been granted the fame of stellification but is being given instruction because he is so unsuccessful as a lover. Cheerfully contemptuous of Geffrey's human limitations, the Eagle has no real concern with Love or Fame as emotional or social issues.

In book 3 Chaucer returns his focus to Love and Fame as vital forces shaping the life of man, and to clarify his meaning he shifts from symbolic allegory to personification. Rather than centering upon man, who must love and live with his fame (he has already done that in book 1), he presents these aspects of human existence as being human in themselves. The abstractions define themselves by acting out their own attributes. Fame is the embodiment of change and instability, capable of stretching up to the heavens or shrinking to less than a cubit in height. Covered with more ears than a beast has hairs, she listens to petitions for her favor, but responds to her own impulses (lines 1820–22):

> "Al be ther in me no justice,
> Me lyste not to doo hyt now,
> Ne this nyl I not graunte yow."

The lovers who come before her reflect the varieties of the emotion – they are proud, humble, generous, selfish, true, and false – and they ask for favors that reflect the nature of their love.

By watching the behavior of the petitioners and the responses of the goddess, Geffrey learns that it is futile to base one's actions upon the importance of reputation, for one can never predict the reputation he will be granted. This lesson provides a final oblique criticism of Dido, who tries to escape her reputation through suicide. For himself, Geffrey concludes that self-knowledge is best (lines 1876–78):

> "Sufficeth me, as I were ded,
> That no wight have my name in honde.
> I wot myself best how y stonde. . . ."

Chaucer's Comic Visions

Learning to disregard Fame does not satisfy Geffrey, however, for he says that he knew this already, and, besides, he has been promised *new* tidings of Love. Therefore, he goes to the whirling house of twigs, where human murmurs are given palpable form. Here he sees lies and truths blending until they are indistinguishable, but, most important, he hears of the imminent appearance of a man of great authority and joins the throng of listeners waiting for an important pronouncement. Perhaps he is to see the embodiment of proper human love or to hear a definition that will resolve the conflict between Love and Fame apparent from book 1. However, his final lesson in Love is left unlearned forever.

Through the three books of the poem Chaucer works out the definition of his key terms Love and Fame. In book 1 he presents them through human experience, inadequately defined. The Eagle separates the terms from human experience and relocates them in abstract knowledge. The pageantry in the House of Fame dramatizes the true nature of Fame and satirizes man's tendency to make reputation a judge of Love. At various points in the poem Chaucer uses comedy to support and repeat the allegory, especially in book 3, where the narrative is constructed as satire. But for the most part the comedy of the poem assumes its own structure, separate from that of the allegory, and makes its own state-ment, which may be correlated to, although not identified with, the statement of the allegory.

As comedy *The House of Fame* follows the form of processional Old Comedy. The comedy begins by establishing the identity of a stock figure, the *eiron* (Geffrey), who dons the mask of ignorance that will make folly and error reveal themselves. When the *eiron* is juxtaposed against another classic type, the braggart or *alazon* (the Eagle), then the action turns into a verbal equivalent of slapstick and farce. Following this is the defining scene, the procession itself, disorderly, illogical, and delightful. Sitting as judge is the goddess Fame, unreliable, impulsive, distinctly injudicious. In all, nine companies of petitioners come before her, good lovers and bad, but in no definable order, save that the last group provides an anticlimax to the proceedings. Fame grants their wishes or denies them or serves petitioners the opposite of their request, according to whim. Insofar as she acts by principle, it is to contradict herself as frequently and emphatically as she can. The procession con-cludes when the ninth "route" comes "lepynge in . . . / And gunne choppen al aboute / Every man upon the crowne" (lines 1823–25). Their proud clamor for "shrewed fame" earns them a loud and malodorous blast from the black trumpet of Eolus, a fanfare that comments significantly upon the entire procession.

Processional comedy is to be defined, however, not only in terms of the procession but chiefly through the personality of the characters and the sequence of events that make up the total action of the poem. What the procession in book 3 does is to present in vivid physical terms the lapses of logic and the virtual absence of proportion between desire and gratification that plague Geffrey throughout his adventure. The brass tablets in book 1 give him so much information that his intellect is set at odds with his emotions; the Eagle is an overwhelming answer to prayer; but the lesson that Geffrey learns in the House of Fame is something, he says, that he knew already, and it cannot gratify him. Geffrey's comic education is structured by such departures from logic as discontinuity, sudden contrast, anticlimax, and irresolution; and the events of his dream unfold in sequences that follow each other temporally but with minimal reference to cause and effect.

The comedy of the dream begins on a very low key of irony expressed through Geffrey's confused response to the *Aeneid*. Although he is filled with sympathy for Dido, he has to admit that Aeneas, according to the author, acted properly; and caught between his feelings and his knowl-edge, Geffrey proceeds by contradiction and confusion. He says that he will not report her lament, but he does; then he begins an impassioned catalogue of faithless lovers comparable to Aeneas, but stops short when he must admit that Aeneas does not fit the category. It is his identifica-tion of himself as a confused man of feeling–thoroughly human–that leads into the comic action of book 2.

The events of book 2, which come about as a direct and incredible answer to prayer, get under way with Geffrey fainting, thereby forcing the heavenly messenger to assume the role of nursemaid. Upon recover-ing his wits, Geffrey comes logically enough to the conclusion that he is to be "stellyfyed," and he makes a totally human protest against his fate. Whether in space or on the mountain of ice, he clings obstinately to his identity as "mere" man and in so doing reaffirms the principle that com-edy teaches us to be human. The point is made ironically, however, through the understated conclusion to the argument that the Eagle wages against Geffrey's books.

The center of attention in book 2 is not Geffrey, however, but the glorious Eagle, who outshines him both physically and intellectually. Filled with sincere admiration of himself, the Eagle dismisses Geffrey as an unfortunately dull and heavy fellow, one who sits at his books until he is "domb as any stoon," while *real* life goes on all around him. The embodiment of knowledge (not to be confused with wisdom), the Eagle has learned everything through experience: after all, he dwells with Jove, and the territory of the heavens is his native ground. He promises Geffrey that instead of having to be content with knowledge from books, he too can learn by experience. When Geffrey looks about and concludes that his authorities, Martin Capella and Alan of Insulis, have described the heavens accurately, the Eagle cries sharply, "Lat be thy fantasye!" Then he offers to point out all the stars so that Geffrey will understand his books.

The Eagle is fundamentally comic, for he is audibly and intellectually a man, visibly and instinctually a bird; and no matter how human he seems, his avian nature is always present, waiting to assert itself. Because he is undertaking an ordinary flight through space, he has little sympathy with Geffrey's fears and astonishment. Because he knows things naturally, he belittles Geffrey's dependence on books. Because he is not human, however, he is finally defeated by Geffrey's insistence that his human habits serve him well enough. In response to the Eagle's offer of firsthand knowledge, Geffrey says that books tell him all he wants to know. Geffrey's triumph is small and ironic but a triumph, nonetheless, that lets him retain his human identity.

The comic conflict between Geffrey and the bird is, in essence, a dramatization of the medieval debate over authority and experience.[16] It is not articulated as pointedly here, however, as it is by the Wife of Bath in her Prologue, perhaps because Geffrey is so nearly mute in holding up his end of the argument. Yet it extends beyond Geffrey's ironic humility and the Eagle's arrogance to provide a unifying theme for the entire dream. The Dreamer's experience in the Temple of Glass is governed by the authority of books, especially Virgil's *Aeneid*; moreover, he expresses his emotions through allusions to books. In book 3, Geffrey

[16]Dorothy Bethurum, "Chaucer's Point of View as Narrator in the Love Poems," *PMLA* 74 (1959):514.

observes actual experience, the raw materials from which books are made. The brass tablets in the temple confuse him, while life in the palace disturbs and repels him without teaching him anything new. Between the temple and the palace occurs the defining argument over experience and authority. With characteristic irony Chaucer refrains from establishing either as preferable but uses each to correct the errors of the other. Geffrey must learn in the House of Fame how to recognize fallacies in books and to avoid the excesses that books can produce, while simul-taneously his acquaintance with books helps him evaluate what he sees and hears.

Geffrey's decision that it is worthwhile to be human is central to the tone of book 3. Here the comedy is quieter and more diffuse; also it is more sardonic, for it is directed at revealing the ways in which man fails to live a worthy life on earth. Geffrey moves from initial wonder at the marvelous place to a final rejection of human folly that manifests itself as ceaseless, misdirected energy.

The narrative of book 3 falls into three divisions: the description of the mountain and the palace, the ceremonial processions, and the house of Rumor, and each section is filled with feverish activity. The House of Fame is crowded with musicians, jugglers, and rushing courtiers; even the statues on the eight pillars are jostling verbally for place. The peti-tioners run in seeking their reward. In the house of Rumor, the people are so eager to hear tidings that they climb upon each other until they are "alle on an hepe." The central embodiment of this pointless activity is the goddess herself, indescribable, indefinable, infinitely changeable. Against all this commotion Geoffrey stands in stoic immobility, amazed at their conduct and their aspirations. But this response is not a rejection of his essential humanity; quite the contrary, it stands as an affirmation that man can live, indeed must live, in this world both wisely and well.

In book 3 comedy and allegory coalesce in a satiric presentation of man as misdirected pilgrim. The instructional force of the poem is clear: since man cannot predict or control the relationship of Fame and merit, he must forget about Fame if he wishes to be properly human, properly directed toward supreme good. The comedy persuades us to see error clearly and to laugh at it. In book 2, however, the comedy is not satiric but joyous, a celebration of the modes of experience and knowledge available to man. The comic conflict of man and bird provides a transition from the emotional confusion of book 1 to the satiric and corrective vision of book 3 by honoring man, who undergoes confusion and correction. Thus the significance of the allegory is founded on the comedy of being merely—and triumphantly—man.

An Allegory of Love

From the ambitious complexity of *The House of Fame*, Chaucer turned in his next dream-vision poem to a simpler use of comedy and allegory, and here he achieved a harmonious balance securely grounded on a well-defined structure. Of all the dream visions *The Parliament of Fowls* is the most skillfully wrought and aesthetically gratifying. From the delightful opening stanza, in which Chaucer subverts the reference of Hippocrates' formula "Ars longa, vita brevis" from art to Love, to the joyous closing hymn of the mating birds, there are a sureness of direction and a delicacy of implication that surpass his achievement in the earlier dream-visions.

As in book 3 of *The House of Fame*, the allegorical significance of the poem is literally present: the successive incidents are presentations of different aspects of human love. The kind of love that receives most attention is sexual love, but sexuality is not the only means of expressing love, nor is it necessarily the highest form of love accessible to mankind. Within the context of the poem Chaucer establishes two governing principles, "commune profyt" and "kynde," which must be incorporated into a proper definition of love. In the parliament that ends the vision, Nature, who is God's Vicar, indicates that that love is best which ennobles both the individual and the community, which, in following her dictates, fulfills the divine commandment to multiply and replenish the earth.[17]

The Parliament of Fowls is at heart a comic allegory, a celebration of the natural impulse to love and a criticism of those definitions of love that deny the lover his essential human nature. As comedy the poem follows the pattern of New Comedy, in which incomplete and repressive patterns of conduct are overruled so that the law of Nature can prevail.

[17]See Charles O. McDonald, "An Interpretation of Chaucer's *Parlement of Foules*," *Speculum* 30 (1955):444–57. For studies concerned with the question of unity in *The Parliament of Fowls*, see especially Kathleen E. Dubs and Stoddard Malarkey, "The Frame of Chaucer's *Parlement*," *ChauR* 13 (1978):16–24; and M. R. Kelly, "Antithesis as the Principle of Design in the *Parlement of Foules*," *ChauR* 14 (1979):61–73.

Laughter in the Courts of Love

Despite the elaborate machinery of the poem, the stern classical guide, the ornate temple, and the formal proceedings of the parliament, there is a domesticity of tone suggested by the Narrator's account of his quiet day and manifested in the birds' motive for gathering around Nature. The insistence upon mating (marriage) as the expression of love sanctioned by Nature is the standard resolution of New Comedy.

In *The Parliament of Fowls*, as in *The Book of the Duchess* and *The House of Fame*, Chaucer moves obliquely and slowly into his topic, beginning at a remote point and constructing separate segments that finally accumulate into a general conclusion. The structure of his allegory is dialectical, setting up a thesis (Love is a concern for common profit) and an antithesis (Love is a personal response to sexual instincts) and then drawing a conclusion that mediates between the two by modifying their exaggerations and correcting their exclusion of the other from a definition of love. Africanus is introduced as the spokesman for common profit, which, according to Scipio's *Somnium*, is best achieved by an ascetic self-denial. Africanus's definition of love, however, is only the first premise and not the concluding perspective from which we are to judge the nature of love. In fact, Africanus as a character is omitted from the narrative shortly after he shoves the Dreamer through the gates into the Garden of Love; but his summoning the Dreamer to go on a journey suggests the need to illustrate how his definition of love can function in relation to the ordinary human need for sexual fulfillment. He helps to define the concept of community as a natural union in which human impulses are valuable in their folly, a comic community in which man is unabashedly human, loving himself, his neighbor, and his God. This concept of common profit is at heart the basic value of Christianized New Comedy, the orderly continuation of human society achieved by removing obstacles and correcting errors so that young lovers can choose their mates and replenish the earth.

In creating his comic allegory, Chaucer moves indirectly toward the presentation of the central issue. He introduces the art of Love immediately in the first two stanzas, along with the confession that he personally knows nothing about it. In truth, he confesses, when thinking about Love, "Nat wot I wel wher that I flete or synke." Then, making an apparent shift in subject, he begins talking about a love that he does understand, the love of reading. Recently, he says, he happened across an old book, and, in hopes of learning "a certayn thing," he spent the day reading. Now he synopsizes what he read, the *Somnium Scipionis*, interpreting it as a treatise on ideal values that advises man to shun the world's delights so that he may come into the serenity of true virtue. He responds to the lesson by falling into a heaviness of spirit; in effect, he has advice for scorning his human nature but no advice for *being* human. Africanus comes to him in a dream, however, to reward him for his labor by leading him to a reinterpretation of the lesson taught in the *Somnium*.

Africanus takes the Dreamer to a gate, over which are two contradictory inscriptions, one in gold, promising bliss, grace, and good fortune, and the other in black, promising fruitlessness, sorrow, and imprisonment. Since these inscriptions are over the same entryway to the same garden, they suggest that love is a complex, even contradictory, emotion. Faced with this implication, the Dreamer hesitates until at last Africanus seizes and shoves him through the gate. After so inglorious an entry, the Dreamer has his stature further reduced by Africanus's assurance that he has nothing to fear, since the inscriptions do not refer to one who has so clearly lost his taste for Love.

The garden itself is a version of Paradise, a realization of harmonious and fruitful nature filled with growing plants and trees, sweet odors, melodious song, and peaceable animals. As he progresses through the park, the Dreamer begins to observe the personified forces of self-centered Love so situated that as he draws closer to each he is ineluctably led onward to a temple of brass, the court of Venus, which resounds with endless sighs of hot desire. The scene through which the Dreamer passes suggests the attractive power of sexual love with its promise of pleasure, but the temple itself reveals emptiness of spirit and a general paralysis of the will to deny oneself on behalf of someone else's good. Within the temple, in a "privie corner," is Venus herself in disport with the porter Richesse, oblivious of a young couple kneeling before her, vainly pleading for favor. The temple is filled with broken bows, symbols of despite to Diana, the goddess of chastity. The kind of love that Venus personifies distresses the Dreamer as greatly as did his interpretation of the *Somnium*, and he leaves the temple to "solace" himself. Venery, insolent and indifferent to the welfare of others, is the polar opposite of the love that the book taught, and undeniably inferior, but both are thus far given such extreme interpretations that neither seems to apply to the common behavior of common man, unless to suggest that all who yield to natural impulses are automatically given over to meaningless sensuality and spiritual desolation.

The first two premises of Chaucer's poem have posed an apparent dilemma: as his ideal of love one must choose either common profit or human sexuality; he cannot have them both, despite the fact that man is created both flesh and spirit. Chaucer's next logical step is to synthesize the two premises; this he does through the delightful comedy of the parliament of birds. The Love debate that finally upsets the parliament provides the resolution to both the allegory and the comedy.[18]

Up to this point Chaucer has depended primarily upon the comic presentation of his persona as a timid bookworm to emphasize that the definitions of love are either limited or misdirected. In laughing at the persona, we also laugh at the distortions that he looks upon as truth. But in the parliament, where wrong love threatens to become a way of life, Chaucer marshals a steady flow of comic devices designed not only to ridicule old error but also to establish a viable definition of love that radiates the energy of common life. His primary device is the creation of characters with an irreconcilable double nature. The birds are, of course, human beings, but they are incontrovertibly birds, so that when they blush the action is funny because they are birds. When pushed beyond the limits of their patience, they forget their human voices and respond, "Kek kek! kokkow! quek quek!" Chaucer heightens his comedy by presenting the birds in an artificial action that ends in anticlimax. By ordinary standards the parliament *ought* to work; it breaks down, however, because all the speakers offer pointless arguments, each purported to be the one solution to a problem that does not really exist. The three tercels wish not to be advised but to be selected by the formel eagle, and yet she has no chance to speak until everyone else present has had his say. Then, by refusing to select a mate, she reveals that much of the day and all of the argument have been wasted.

The parliament takes place on a hill where the birds, who have gathered on Saint Valentine's Day to choose their mates, sit in ordered groups about the goddess Nature, who rules there. The selection of mates is meant to follow a logical and social order, beginning with the

[18]Dorothy Bethurum, "The Center of the *Parlement of Foules*," in Richmond C. Beatty et al., eds. *Essays in Honor of Walter Clyde Curry*, pp. 39–50.

noblest bird and descending through the lowest ranks. The first choice made, however, sets off a debate that lasts until the sun hangs low in the west. The royal tercel, speaking in gracious courtly tones, claims Nature's favorite, the formel, as his sovereign Lady—he would never be so presumptuous as to make her his "fere"—promising that if she finds him untrue then all the other fowls may tear him asunder. Instantly he is challenged by a tercel of lower degree who claims to have loved the Lady longer and who will consent to die like a common criminal should she find him false. A third eagle then claims to have loved her not long but most intensely, without any question of being untrue. The differences among the three protestations are genuinely minimal in content and even in hyperbolic style. What does mark the second and third speeches is their animosity, poorly concealed in the claim to superior merit and then frankly revealed in the eagerness with which they accept a misinter-preted call to fight for the Lady. Fighting for one's Lady, as Gardiner Stillwell has noted, ordinarily meant attacking her foes, not her sup-porters.[19]

To end the debate and the ensuing uproar among the fowls, Nature lets each group select a spokesman who will offer its common advice to the royal birds. But just as courtesy turned to hostility, now counsel as readily becomes contest. The tercelet falcon nearly precipitates a battle while advising the formel to select the suitor of highest state and longest service in knighthood. The goose then offers the advice of the water-fowl, that the tercels find new loves. The turtledove blushes with shame at such a notion, insisting that they must serve the Lady all their lives, even though she may die and leave them desolate. The cuckoo asks only to gratify himself, without bothering to resolve the debate. With counsel, argument, attack, and counterattack the parliament threatens to prove as endless as the original pleading, until Nature intervenes to restore the peace. "I have herd al youre opynyoun," she says, "And in ef-fect yit be we nevere the neer" (lines 618–19). Then she instructs the formel to make her choice—which proves to be no choice at all but a re-quest that she postpone her choice for a year.

After all the argument and anger the debate is ended, and the other fowls are at last free to choose their own mates and to wend their ways nestward, as soon as they have sung their joyous roundel to the coming

[19]Gardiner Stillwell, "Unity and Comedy in *The Parlement of Foules*," *JEGP* 49 (1950):490.

summer. The song is the fitting conclusion to Chaucer's love comedy, Nature's harmony that symbolizes the music of the spheres. The kind of love so celebrated is dedicated to replenishing the earth and to serving the common good of both partners and of all society. While idealistic and sexual, it is neither the stern asceticism of the *Somnium* nor the voluptuous dalliance of Venus, but a happy balance between the two. The roundel is the culmination of both the comedy and the allegory, the balanced conclusion in which the future spreads before the mated lovers, and the summer world waits to be used for the common profit of God's people.

The Poet in the Court of Love

Chaucer's final dream vision, the Prologue to *The Legend of Good Women*, is at once the most curious and the least-studied of all Chaucer's allegories.[20] In many ways it resembles the allegories produced by fifteenth-century poets more than it does Chaucer's earlier poems. Gone are the distinctive devices of the early poems, the bumbling Dreamer, the marvelous birds, the ornate temples, and the rambling conversations. Here Chaucer brings the mythological beings of the Court of Love to the center of his stage, where they enact a Love judgment against the poet himself. In this poem Chaucer creates an inverted world in which mythology seems to engulf Christian doctrine. The high god is Cupid; the revered saint, Venus; and the queen of heaven, Alceste. All authorities, even the Church fathers, are interpreted as being true servants of Love. Only the poet is seen as being too old and unworthy for love.

Because it exists in two distinct versions, the Prologue to *The Legend of Good Women* offers very useful insights into Chaucer's mature efforts to make comedy and allegory serve the same end. The allegorical significance of both prologues is essentially the same: that the concept of love represented by Cupid and Alceste is founded upon exclusion, ignorance, and falsehood and is supported by suppression of the truth; it is, therefore, unworthy of the name of love. The point is made through inversion, by having the poet brought to trial and convicted of being a bad

[20]For a full-length study see Robert Worth Frank, Jr., *Chaucer and* The Legend of Good Women. See also Gardner, *The Poetry of Chaucer*, pp. 191–215.

poet. His plea that he has sought to honor love by distinguishing between true and false forms (by revealing the false as false) is rejected imperiously, and he is instructed that if he cannot say only good things then he ought to say nothing at all. For penance he is to leave off translating such poems as the *Roman de la Rose*, which makes wise folk hate love, and he is not to make his own poems about women like Criseyde, which suggest that a woman may be faithless. Instead he is to write a legendary of such martyrs as Cleopatra, Medea, and Dido, who are heavenly examples of true love.

Between the two prologues, however, there is a distinct difference in the structure and tone of the comedy, which is achieved in part through altering and balancing the characters of the little drama and also through relocating or omitting points of emphasis. In the F, or earlier, Prologue, the confrontation between the poet and the gods begins with a figurative sense of apotheosis. The poet, kneeling over the daisy, slowly raises his eyes to see a goddess-daisy walking toward him. By directing the eyes of the Dreamer (and the reader) upward from the flower to the Queen, Chaucer heightens the potential wonder and joy of the scene, implying that all things are made possible through the power of love. In the G Prologue the focus is different. The poet speaks of "roaming" the meadow rather than lying in admiration before the flower; instead of lifting his eyes, he looks straight across the meadow and sees the royal procession enter. Queen Alceste is still the daisy incarnate, but whereas the flower honored her, now she seems to honor the flower. The scene in revision has lost part of its luminous sense of awe; it is more curious than alluring and more appropriate to the poet's moral and aesthetic reservations about the doctrine of Love implicit in it.

A second change of emphasis in the G text occurs in the increased number of lines devoted to books, particularly in Cupid's discussion of worthy texts about women. While the F text presents the comic criticism of a poet, the G text is a comic essay in literary criticism, especially bad criticism. Alceste and Cupid reveal no understanding of literature in their speeches, yet both undertake to judge poetry and poets without the slightest doubt about their capacity to do so. One of Chaucer's master strokes in the G Prologue is having Cupid continue the argument for "auctoritee" that the poet introduced in the opening passage but invert its meaning by misreading the authorities he refers to.

Laughter in the Courts of Love

Some differences between the comic qualities of the two prologues come, then, from the change of focus and emphasis in details and incidents. The primary distinction lies, however, in the presentation of the characters. The major change is in the Narrator, the Chaucer persona. In the F Prologue, the persona is still something of a bumbler, an enthusiastic lover of books and daisies. He begins his poem sententiously with a proverb that leads to his argument about the value of books; next he moves from his love of books to his love of the daisy; then, seeming to recall his "true" topic, he returns to the value of books to promise that he will say more when it is time. He seems to give up books for flowers altogether in his excuse, "I may not al at-ones speke in ryme" (line 102). In the later version he presents himself as more competent and self-assured, though humble, moving obliquely yet firmly through his prefatory comments on authority, experience, books, and flowers before narrating his dream. By redefining himself as a knowledgeable poet, he adds credence to his plea that he meant to honor love when he wrote his *Troilus*; moreover, he highlights the ignorance of Cupid's speech on books and intensifies the irony in Alceste's defense of his motives.

The other major change in characterization is in Cupid. In the F Prologue he is presented as an arrogant and ignorant buffoon, innocent of logic and devoid of charity, yet presiding as the final judge of reason and love. When he sees the poet, he condemns him, saying he would rather see a worm near his flower, for the poet has both translated and created poems dishonoring Love. Moreover, he condemns the poet for failing to honor Alceste, in omitting her name from a balade composed in her honor. What he seems to demand here is an impossible construction, both logically and grammatically, for the balade is a catalogue of famous beauties and lovers all of whom are inferior to "My Lady." In the G Prologue, Cupid's ignorance is revealed more explicitly and at greater length. After condemning the Dreamer's poetry, he recommends that he learn how to write about women and love by reading model texts by Valerius, Titus, and Claudian and by Saint Jerome, especially his anti-feminist treatise *Against Jovinian*. All these books, he says, describe true love, but Jerome provides an excellent model for the poet to follow in honoring women and Love. The humor comes not so much from his unfounded arrogance now as from the irony of giving advice that contradicts his intention. As a logician Cupid is blind, and as a literary critic he is incompetent, however well-meaning he tries to be.

Set against the imperious ignorance of Cupid is the gentle figure of Alceste, whose role is essentially the same in both versions. She is the embodiment of kindness and mercy, and she comes to the Dreamer's defense with an argument that, despite her good intention, exonerates by damning. When Cupid criticizes the poet, she asks for mercy through an analogy that reduces the Dreamer to the least significant of insects: the noble lion (Cupid) does not attack the fly (the poet) when it offends or bites him but brushes it off with his tail "al esely." Even more derogatory are the excuses that she offers for the poet's sins. If the charges are not false, then perhaps he is still innocent because he is "nyce" (ignorant of what he says) or because he has misread his sources and "rekketh noght of what matere he taketh" or because he is someone's poetical lackey, ordered to write the offending poems and "durste yt nat withseye." At any rate, she concludes, even though he cannot write well, he has made ignorant folk delight in serving Cupid. The comedy of Alceste's defense derives from her insensitivity to what she is saying; moreover, the excuses that she offers actually provide a description of Cupid's theory of poetry.

The Prologue ends with the maker unmade, judged a bad poet because he has not subordinated poetry to Cupid's doctrine. He is then ordered to become Alceste's poetical lackey, writing a legendary of all women who have been true servants of Love, as a penance for his sins. He may define love in Cupid's terms only, always speaking affirmatively. By negating logic, by negating poetry, the poet may thus gratify the god's doctrine of Love. In both versions of the Prologue, but especially in G, Chaucer presents an ironic defense of the poet's freedom to use both pretense and logic as he sees fit. Through the parodic court trial he has argued that the subject of love is not divorced from logic, that it can "counterpleted be," especially when it is in error. What he has created in the two prologues is an incisive comedy that deftly severs the poetical head from the critical body and pronounces the body, the misdirected criticism of poetry, dead, while the head lives on.

In the Prologue to *The Legend of Good Women*, Chaucer unites comedy and allegory to animate and criticize error, to illumine false concepts of poetry and love. This is essentially a negative function of comedy, however, that directs the reader to reject what the poem seems to praise. It is unlike the all-embracing farce of *The House of Fame*, book 2. There the comedy leads to an affirmation that it is worthwhile to be human and limited. In the face of this comedy many readers have questioned whether *The House of Fame* — or any of Chaucer's other dream visions — has ascertainable validity as allegory, despite all the machinery present. Wolfgang Clemen speaks for an entire school of critics when he states that the allegory is incidental, an accident attributable to the poetic style of the times, whereas the comedy is Chaucer's real creative concern.

Clemen's argument obscures the point that both comedy and allegory are Chaucer's real creative concerns and that he is always trying to link them in a complex manner of seeing and knowing. At times he may subordinate the comedy, as in *The Book of the Duchess*; or he may give it primary emphasis, as in *The House of Fame*, book 2; or he may strike a felicitous, almost delicate balance of comedy and allegory, as in *The Parliament of Fowls*, or a satiric balance, as in *The House of Fame*, book 3. The success of these poems suggests that Chaucer is at his best when he works with allegory and comedy in a structure firmly enough delineated to restrain his digressive impulses. When he finds his structure in an established ritual like a court procession, a meeting of the Parliament, or a trial, then comedy and allegory interact freely and easily. These are very special creations, however, and they seem to be forms that Chaucer did not wish to repeat. In his great poems he does not try to balance comedy and allegory but rather selects forms where one, usually comedy, contains the other. It is these early poems, however, with their ambitious complexities and tenuous balances, that influenced allegorists of the next two centuries so profoundly.

3.
Laughter
in the Courts of Love

OR MOST POETS OF the fifteenth and early sixteenth centuries, Chaucer stood as the great exemplar, a maker who not only proved that "barbaric" English could be made to yield up brilliant poetry but also provided models that they could follow in their own practice. As a matter of sometimes sorry fact, in their practice they tended to follow the models of Chaucer's disciple John Lydgate more often than they did Chaucer's, but all at least voiced the opinion that Chaucer had set a standard of excellence that they could not really hope to achieve.

What they praised and did not hope to equal was his style; what they borrowed and turned to their own use was his content. Occasionally the borrowing was of a complete work, as when the Scottish poet Robert Henryson "finished" the history of Criseyde. More often the borrowing was of episodes, situations, characters, and images. Thus in William Dunbar's *The Golden Targe*, as in the Prologue to *The Legend of Good Women*, a courtly company comes upon and challenges the Dreamer. The image of Alceste and "her faithful nineteen" appears in both the Prologue to the *Legend* and the anonymous *The Court of Love*, and the dissolute Ryote of John Skelton's *The Bowge of Court* largely derives from the Pardoner of *The Canterbury Tales*. What proved most useful to these poets, then, was Chaucer's power for clearly defined, self-sustaining constructions that were sufficiently suggestive of moral values to seem useful in other settings.

Chaucer's gift to later poets was not of style and content only. Of greater importance was his provision of models in English that united comedy with allegory so that the poem illustrates a way of perceiving meanings that in itself establishes their value. That is to say, Chaucer's comic vision is in itself a moral vision, and in his poems the comedy makes much the same point as the allegorical implications. For the most part Chaucer escapes the pitfalls that usually await the moralist-comedian. His laughter is not often scornful or derisive; he is not armed with whips to lash men to better conduct. On the other hand, his morality is not so easy that it proves mere pragmatism. Instead, he balances laughter with joy, rebuke with elation, so that truth becomes pleasant and good conduct desirable. In the final analysis Chaucer's comedy and allegory lead to the same goal. He is writing poetry that is *utile et dulce* for himself and his audience.

Like their master, the so-called Chaucerian poets of the fifteenth century continued working out allegory in comic terms and comedy in allegorical terms. To transmit their understanding of human existence, they relied upon allegorical images that embodied a moral judgment of man's aspirations and delights, and they connected these images in a narrative structure made up of comic devices and expressed in a comic tone. The seriousness of sin, salvation, and eternal destiny is balanced against the levity provoked by man's propensity for being fallibly human.

The same allegorical images dominate all four poems to be studied in this chapter: John Gower's *Confessio Amantis*, William Dunbar's *The Golden Targe*, John Skelton's *The Bowge of Court*, and the anonymous poet's *The Court of Love*. The human figure, the Dreamer, is presented as a lover or a seeker who tries to gain access to his vision of worldly delights, the Court (usually of Love). He is either assisted or opposed by representatives from the court, who are personified aspects of his own nature, and he usually suffers a sequence of events that make him alter or abandon his old aspirations. In brief, all four poems tell essentially the same moral tale.

What distinguishes these poems is not the allegory, then, but the comic style and structure. Each poet has his own sense of the comic, which dictates the particular tone, and therefore the meaning, of each allegorical image. Thus each Dreamer has his own foibles and illusions, his own human personality; and each Court, symbol of the Dreamer's worldly desires, differs from all other Courts, not so much in its composition as in the style of comic presentation. In this chapter the focus is on the *process* of the poet in creating his work: what allegorical images he uses, what levels of meaning he makes operative, what comic devices he relies upon, what effects he aims at, and how well he unites comedy and allegory into one total form.

The Court of Love

One significant legacy that Chaucer, along with his contemporary, John Gower, left to later poets was the poetical presentation of a moral attitude to be taken toward the Court of Love. There appears in *The House of Fame*, *The Parliament of Fowls*, and the Prologue to *The Legend of Good Women* and in Gower's *Confessio Amantis* a construction that draws its impulse from the pagan goddess Venus and has a direct relationship to affairs of the human heart. It is presented variously as a temple or court, in the sense of a building; or a court, in the sense of a congregation of persons under the banner of a "royal leader," usually Cupid. Chaucer also presents it as a court of law. Those present in the Court – figures usually taken from poetry and pagan mythology, but sometimes from popular history and even the Bible – are there because they have loved, often disastrously and nearly always unhappily; still they are renowned for the fervor of their love. The Court, which commonly appears to the narrator of the poem in a dream, projects itself as a desirable destiny for man, equivalent to the popular image of Heaven as a place of singing and dancing in golden slippers along golden streets. From it emanates the attitude that any right-thinking man would want to enter it, for membership in the Court is the highest good that the Court knows. Entering the Court poses one small problem, however, for, while those in the Court are dead, the man who ought to desire entry is alive. To gain admission, he must live like those in the Court; he must become a Lover.

Thus, when the Court and the man come into conjunction, the discourse centers on that "Love" honored by the Court, sexual love. Implicit in the discourse is the notion that only select initiates know how to love properly, for love is an art that must be learned through arduous training. The man who wishes to enter the Court must practice certain principles of conduct in his daily life at the same time that he carefully shuns any hint of impropriety. Once he has established a reputation for probity of character, he may then approach a Lady in hopes of becoming her lover, or, more nearly, her slave. If she gives him some faint hope of success, he is then ready to begin anew the hourly process of proving his worthiness. He has become a "Lover." Unfortunately this Lover is still not admissible to the Court of Love, for he yet has more to give and gain. He must win the Lady and give up himself entirely; he literally must lay down his life to enter the Court.

D. W. Robertson, Jr., explains the "secular doctrine of love" that governs human preparation for entering the Court of Love as consisting of two parts: an inner heart, or generative force, and an outer body, a series of rules that the lover is to follow to nourish the heart. The heart of Courtly Love is a prolonged sensation of passionate fervor, the heyday in the blood, as Hamlet says. It is a state of obsession in which everything is subordinated to *feeling*, and this feeling has to be fed, lest it burn itself out. The obsessional phase of passion, Robertson notes, is common to all people, though it is usually a temporary state through which lovers pass on their way to a more stable and lasting relationship. In Courtly Love, however, the Lover's intention is to make the temporary permanent: he tries to lengthen a day into a year; he wants to convert a moment's ecstasy into a way of life. Accordingly he follows a pattern of conduct designed to enlarge his capacity for feeling fear and uncertainty, tremulous hope and restlessness. In effect he binds himself to a wheel of fire, for he has undertaken a hopeless task that yet requires him to be forever hopeful of success.[1]

Such is the composition and doctrine of the Court of Love as it is presented in Chaucer's and Gower's vision poems. A constant feature of Chaucer's comic technique is his a priori exclusion of the Dreamer from the Court. He is "unsuccessful" in Love, or, worse, "ignorant" of Love, no Lover at all. The standard conclusion of his allegory is a rejection of the Court as unsatisfactory and an affirmation that the Dreamer's welfare lies precisely in his exclusion. Gower, however, squarely confronts the dilemma of desirable damnation and makes it the central issue in *Confessio Amantis*. What Chaucer provides, and Gower, too, in his own fashion, is a method of presenting a poetical commonplace so that the correct moral attitude toward it is at all times manifest in the poem.

Whether or not the ritualized conduct of love affairs required by the Court of Love ever existed as an actual practice in medieval society is a topic of considerable debate, unresolved even by the sympathetic

[1]D. W. Robertson, Jr., *A Preface to Chaucer: Studies in Medieval Perspectives*, pp. 394–401.

Laughter in the Courts of Love

studies of Joan Ferrante and George Economou or the pontifical disquisitions of Robertson.[2] The fact remains, however, that the Court of Venus is a very popular image in visionary literature and that much other poetry is concerned with a formalized conduct of affairs of the heart. Debating the historical existence of Courtly Love seems off the point, particularly if we keep in mind Northrop Frye's dictum that literature is made up out of other literature, having its primary reference to verbal inventions rather than to external reality.[3] In those poems that deal with Courtly Love, the emphasis upon ritualized behavior, formalized rhetoric, and stylized emotion (expressed as sighs, tears, sleeplessness, and paleness of face) suggests that Courtly Love's primary existence was mental rather than social.

As a poetical image Courtly Love seems to have had a very broad appeal from the beginning because of its self-conscious pose as "art." The rendering of love as artifice made actual love less "real" and thus more useful as a vehicle for presenting the actuality of human experience. The universality of the love impulse would have made the topic directly relevant to virtually all readers, while the "rules" extended outward to suggest a relationship with all other areas of human knowledge that had also been systematized. Thus the "art of love" could be used as a device for ordering and expressing more recondite subjects; it provided a way of rendering them poetical. As C. S. Lewis points out, the very easy analogies between a code of love and a code of ethics enabled the poet to move freely from one to the other, as he would want to do when his concern was the decay of ethics and society that resulted from the corruption of the individual man's love instinct.[4]

But if the formalized analysis of love granted the poet a certain freedom of creative movement, at the same time it confronted him with an ethical dilemma as regards the content. Either he had to accept the doctrine of "Love" with its very obvious bias toward venality, or he had to reject it and make his rejection meaningful in terms of the poem he was writing. In allegorical poems Courtly Love is usually presented as a pattern of conduct that must be corrected by translation into a symbol of higher love or

---

[2]George D. Economou and Joan Ferrante, Introduction, *In Pursuit of Perfection: Courtly Love in Medieval Literature*, pp. 3–15. See also Robertson, *A Preface to Chaucer*, pp. 391–448.

[3]Northrop Frye, *Anatomy of Criticism: Four Essays*, p. 97.

[4]C. S. Lewis, *The Allegory of Love*, p. 213.

Laughter in the Courts of Love

refuted outright or else set aside in favor of more natural and construc-
tive behavior. As enunciated by Andreas Capellanus in the first book of
his treatise and as practiced by the Lover of the *Roman de la Rose*, the art
of love makes unnatural demands of lovers and ultimately obstructs the
progression of natural instincts toward physical union and procreation.
The service of Venus is made to oppose the service of Nature, though
Venus herself says that she works *with* Nature and will permit no one
who is unnatural to enter her court.[5]

Robertson may well be correct when he argues that Andreas meant to
mock human love in order to heighten his charge "Walter's" appreciation
of divine love; certainly this is the process that John Gower has completed at the end of his confession. The craft of love is presented in *Confessio Amantis* as a source of meaningless humiliation leading to spiritual
despair. Because the action of the poem centers on the admission of
human sinfulness and the determination to seek righteousness, Courtly
Love as manifested in conduct and feeling must be rejected, and the love
impulse itself refined through education and elevated into the pure
desire for the love of God.

The Vision of Love

Confessio Amantis is, in the words of the narrator, "A wonder hap which
me befell, / . . . / Touchende of love and his fortune (1.67, 69). On a
bright May morning the narrator goes into a garden, where, overcome
by the fruitlessness of his efforts as a lover, he prays to Venus for some
share in her grace. The king (Cupid) and queen (Venus) of love appear,
but Cupid merely glances at him with wrathful eyes and turns his
countenance away, but not before casting a fiery dart into the very root
of his heart. Venus, however, stays to ask who he is and why he has
called upon her. When the lover expresses concern that he may not live
long enough to tell of his sickness, she then calls upon her priest Genius,
for it is her desire that he be "shriven." The priest, she continues, is now
approaching to perform that very office. The remainder of the poem is, as
its title states, the lover's confession.

In making Courtly Love the primary topic of his lover's confession,

---

[5]John Gower, *Confessio Amantis*, vols. 2 and 3 of *The Complete Works of John Gower*, ed. G. C.
Macaulay 8.2322–49. All subsequent references are incorporated in the text.

Laughter in the Courts of Love

Gower seems to be following the pattern set by Guillaume de Lorris and Jean de Meun in the *Roman de la Rose*; but in his treatment of love he follows more the practice of Dante in the *Divine Comedy*. Gower, like Jean and Dante, sees Courtly Love as essentially the false flourishing of a natural seed, a hothouse growth carefully cultivated in the stead of true growth. The ordering of events in these poems is meant to make the lover recognize his false growth so that he will return of his own accord to a state of harmony with Nature. Then he may love correctly. But whereas Jean's Lover pushes aside elaborate rules of conduct to gratify his passions, Gower's and Dante's lovers transcend the passions.

The course of action in Gower's poem is loosely analogous to that in the *Divine Comedy*. It begins in a state of despair and ends in happiness, or at least peace and repose. At the outset Amans, the lover, is trapped in his venality, suffering a spiritual paralysis that prevents him from even knowing himself. In the end he is able to identify himself as "John Gower" and to recognize himself as an old man. Although Amans does not attain a joyous state of grace as Dante does, he is at least freed from his spiritual bondage, and he is able for the first time to smile. Russell Peck has noted that the lover's movement toward learning his own identity parallels the movement toward self-knowledge in Boethius's *The Consolation of Philosophy*.[6] More important, the establishment of identity defines the movement of the soul from a state in which its name can only be "miserable sinner" to a state of grace in which the redeemed soul regains forever its unique human identity.[7] If, as it may be argued, the lover is not saved at the end of his confession, he is nonetheless capable of being saved; certainly he has been converted. Paradoxically, now that he is an "Old Man," the future opens before him, whereas he was doomed as long as he played the young courtier.

In its cure for love, then, *Confessio Amantis* more nearly resembles the *Divine Comedy* than the *Roman de la Rose*; so also in the tone of its overtly moralistic and didactic passages and in the pointing of its allegorical implications.[8] Both Dante and Gower emphasize that the im-

[6]Russell A. Peck, Introduction, John Gower, *Confessio Amantis*, ed. Russell A. Peck, p. xi. Peck has amplified this thesis and extended his analysis of the poem in *Kingship and Common Profit in Gower's* Confessio Amantis.

[7]Paul G. Ruggiers, notes for a lecture on Dante's *Paradiso*, University of Oklahoma, December 13, 1959.

[8]The question of Dante's possible influence on medieval English poets has usually been answered

pulse to love underlies not only personal conduct but also the establish-ment of governments and religions. Both diagnose the corruption of church, state, and common man as a direct result of distorted love, and both intend their poems to be didactic illustrations of how love may be corrected. There is a strong strain of moral indignation in both poems, though Gower confines his largely to the Prologue and expresses it without the passionate intensity that makes Dante's anger memorable. Finally, both poems focus not upon human existence alone but upon the interaction of divine and mundane as it occurs in the act of redemption.

If a comparison of the two poems helps clarify certain of Gower's allegorical intentions, then also it may help explain why modern readers so often have difficulty in coping with Gower's poem. Both poems have as their basic action the progress of the soul through self-discovery and purgation to a state of grace or readiness for grace. Dante, however, presents this progress as a physical movement across a tangible terrain, whereas Gower's soul remains static in its sylvan confessional. There is at all times in the *Comedy* a sense of purposeful forward motion. In *Con-fessio Amantis* the focus is upon a system of interrelated definitions that remain largely abstract because Amans stubbornly refuses to give up his sin and move off dead center. As a result the *Confessio* seems to exist in a topographical as well as moral void until the very end, when a virtual miracle opens the future to Amans. While the allegory of the ending is genuinely beautiful and moving, the immobility of the hero weakens the structure of the narrative level of the poem.

Despite being a virtually unmanageable poem for modern readers, the *Confessio* has had a number of remarkable achievements claimed for it by critics.[9] C.S. Lewis says that Gower is "surprisingly good at architech-tonics," that he "almost succeeds" at weaving his numerous threads into

negatively; some Chaucer scholars even question whether Chaucer "really knew" Dante's poems. Certainly, however, both Chaucer and Gower were acquainted with a Dante legend in which the Florentine was represented as a great moral "maker." Several of the extant manuscripts of *Confessio Amantis* contain an *exemplum* in which Dante is the central figure, though this passage appears to have been edited out of the standard text. Macaulay reprints this as a variant reading in 8.2328–43 (Gower, *Confessio Amantis*, ed. G. C. Macauley). I do not claim that any direct line of influence ex-isted; my point, rather, is that both Dante and Gower were working in the same mode with the same materials and that many of the same attitudes obtain in their poems.

[9]For recent studies highlighting Gower's skill with irony and wry humor, see Samuel T. Cowling, "Gower's Ironic Self-Portrait in the *Confessio Amantis*," *AnM* 16 (1975):63–70; and Patrick J. Gallacher, *Love, the Word, and Mercury: A Reading of John Gower's* Confessio Amantis.

one complete fabric.[10] Russell Peck believes that Gower actually does succeed in uniting the nonfictional social criticism of the Prologue with the love fiction; the digressions, he says, "have dramatic relevance" to the narrative.[11] Derek Pearsall sees as "one of the achievements" of the poem Gower's development of a "dry and rueful comedy."[12] Implicit in all these judgments is a recognition of perhaps the most remarkable aspect of the poem: its extensive variety of topics.

Like the *Roman de la Rose* and Dante's *Comedy, Confessio Amantis* is an encyclopedic poem. Its topics of discourse are legion, ranging from a spirited protest against war to a history of the development of alchemy. Moreover, it is a long poem, its text running to 33,444 lines in the Macaulay edition. Gower begins in his Prologue at the broadest possible point, with an analysis of the decay of the world as it is manifested in the conduct of the three estates, the Nobles, the Clerics, and the Commons. The cause of this decay, he maintains, is division; that is, the placing of singular interest above common profit, which occurs when will triumphs over reason. Decay is further intensified by the "way of the world" as it is expressed through the statue that Nebuchadnezzar reputedly saw in a dream, the "Man of the Mountain." The descending value of the statue's composite metals, from its golden head to its feet of steel and clay, represents the progressive decay of society that is caused by passing time. Not only is man sinful; he is born into a world that has been corrupted by successive centuries of sinfulness. Gower hastens to add, however, that man is not trapped in this time-wrought decay; he can escape by learning how to love properly, and his model to imitate is the act of God, who so loved the world that he gave his Son for it. If man could learn to place common profit above singular interest, then perhaps Arion would return to play the music that draws all creatures together in harmony.

The Prologue expresses a tension that arises from the contest between hope and despair. Despair prevails in the anatomy of the world; hope, in the memory of God's gift and the final image of Arion's harmony. The poet expresses a great sense of loss – he has lost the golden age, the best state of the Church, the sense of direction that the Commons once had.

---

[10]Lewis, *The Allegory of Love*, pp. 198–99.

[11]Peck, Introduction, *Confessio Amantis*, p. xix.

[12]Derek Pearsall, *Gower and Lydgate*, Writers and Their Work, no. 211, p. 14.

Laughter in the Courts of Love

What he hopes for seems to be a backward motion, the return of an ancient Edenic peace before the Fall. This, however, is denied him, and as for the world he lives in, it has fallen into so dreary a state that "non bot only god may stiere."

The distance between this anatomy of the world and the confession of the self-centered lover seems so immeasurable that it is tempting to follow the lead of C. S. Lewis and omit the Prologue from a discussion of the poem. Gower brings the two together, however, by making a bridge out of Courtly Love. The lover is a little world, and, like the big world, he has gone astray through loving wrongly. The craft of Love that Amans practices is, in the end, a way of death, while the debased love of the world has reduced it from gold to steel and clay. Thus Courtly Love, which is the very real cause of the lover's corruption, stands as a symbol of all the wrong loves in the larger world. The world and the man have both driven so far off course that only supernatural aid can set them aright. For both, God must steer. God, however, does not force his direction upon man or the world, despite offering salvation freely to all who seek it. For Amans to be rescued, he has only to ask, but first he must learn what to ask for. Through confession he must discover his need to be released from a love that reaches but to dust. He has to restore Reason to its proper authority so that it can govern his cupidinous will. The office of confession exists to teach him how to replace the old art of Love with a new art of proper asking.

As allegory, Gower's analysis of individual and universal love ranges from the occasional flatness of images and fables that evoke nothing to richly suggestive passages that invite multiple interpretations. By casting his poem in the form of a confession, Gower imposed a general structure capable of being interpreted on varying levels of reference. That is, confession centers first on the human personality, revealing in this case the lover's futile struggle to gratify sexual desires that endanger his soul. But confession also investigates the ethical nature of man, especially as it is expressed in social relationships and legal and political establishments. Finally and supremely, confession analyzes and corrects the relationship of man with God.

When placed within this framework, most images and incidents of the literal love dialogue have the capacity to evoke meanings on other levels of the poem. For instance, Amans' confession of incapacitating fear in the presence of his lady implies on the tropological level the fact that in a corrupt society laws are made out of fear, not love,[13] and on the allegorical or theological level that an irrational fear of God's wrath can lead to a sense of despair over God's mercy. Because the poem is about a living man suffering earthly sorrows, the anagogical level is largely absent – or else present only in the negative implications of sin, eternal damnation, and Hell – until the ending when the confessor advises, "Take love where it mai noght fail." What up until now has been an anatomy of secular Love in a fallen world is suddenly transformed into an illustration of divine and lasting love in the heavenly Paradise.

The literal action of the poem, C. S. Lewis says, is Amans's accepting the death of love.[14] Literally, the poem is an analysis of the ways in which man has broken the commandment to love his neighbor as himself. Allegorically, the poem implies the birth of the new man rising Phoenix-like from the ashes of his old desire. At the beginning of his experience, Amans is revealed trapped in his desire, pierced by Cupid's fiery dart and stung by Venus' suspicion that he is a "faitour" who would enter her court to do her dishonor. When Venus's priest, Genius, arrives to hear his confession, Amans has to admit his total despair: he has looked on Medusa and turned to stone; he has heard the sirens and driven onto the rocks. Recognizing the gravity of Amans' condition, Genius abandons his original program of purifying the five senses and sets forth upon a confession proper, following the order of the seven deadly sins. Until the lover knows in his heart and mind what sin is, it is futile to discourse merely of the outward body.

Starting with the root sin of pride and concluding with lechery, Gower devotes each book of the *Confessio* – with the exception of book 7 – to the definition of a cardinal sin in its personal, social, historical, and religious implications. Amans has to confess his guilt to each primary sin and also the "ministers" or secondary forms (he is guilty of a staggering number, I might add). To make sure that the lover knows exactly what he is confessing to, Genius illustrates each sin with many *exempla* ranging in length from two or three-line allusions to full-fledged tales that extend nearly two thousand lines (over forty pages of text). The *exempla* are

[13]Cf. Prologue, lines 118–35.

[14]Lewis, *The Allegory of Love*, p. 217.

chosen because they impinge, sometimes tangentially, upon the sin being defined. The effect that some tales have upon the process of definition is occasionally curious or unsettling, for the tale quite often goes in a direction opposite to the moral point being made. The tale of "Canace and Machair" is introduced as an illustration of the disastrous consequences of wrath, whereas it is actually an emotionally charged narration of the disastrous effects of imprudent and incestuous love. The princess Canace and her brother, Machair, are reared together, apart from other company, until at last they fall in love and yield to their sexual impulses. When Canace grows great with child, Machair feigns a cause to go on a journey, leaving his sister behind to face the consequences. Discovering how his daughter has disgraced him (but not with whom), the king orders her to kill herself; then he has the baby abandoned in the wilds where it will be devoured by animals. The center of attention is the pathetic situation of Canace, who must suffer the consequences of blind passion; the "cruel" wrath of her dishonored father seems to be an almost incidental issue.[15] Despite the ambiguity about which sin is being exemplified, there is, however, no doubt that the confessor is illustrating immoral behavior.

As the confessor warms to his opportunity to discuss something other than Love's lore, he moves away from personal analysis into the more abstruse topics that constitute the "digressions" of the poem. In book 3, under the topic "Homicide," there is a discourse upon the evils of war, questioning in particular whether Crusades are justifiable.[16] In book 4 the confessor explains that all human inventions, from alphabets to alchemy, are the fruits of man's labor. The major digressions, however, are those that relate the history of religions (in book 5) and Aristotle's program of education devised for Alexander the Great (the subject of book 7). These digressions, according to Derek Pearsall, function "not as organic parts of a work of art with its own internal validity, but as the intellectual and informational basis of a programme which has external

---

[15]Cf. 3.143–336. It could be ingeniously argued that the *real* point of the tale is that cruel wrath makes even incest pitiable and defensible. It is not impossible that Gower had such an interpretation in mind, but neither is it probable.

[16]This may be a reference to attempts by Pope Boniface IX to promote "crusades" against his opponents. Cf. Russell A. Peck, *Kingship and Common Profit*, p. xiii.

validity...in its relation to the world of action."[17] In other words, the digressions are not really lessons that the lover must learn but are a definition of the world that the lover and the reader live in and an explanation of why patterns of conduct are established for all men.

Russell Peck, on the other hand, sees the digressions as repeating and exemplifying the analysis in the Prologue of the decay in the three estates.[18] Since these three estates are fused microcosmically within Amans, the digressions serve a "dramatic" function in teaching him how to regain his spiritual, social, and emotional balance. They restore him as governor over the kingdom of his heart.[19] While Peck's argument seems overly ingenious in its stress upon "dramatic appropriateness," it does relate the Prologue and the concluding prayer for England to the central issue of the lover's confession, and it points out a developmental sequence between the two. In the beginning the poet is able only to leave the state of the world in God's hands, but at the end he is able to pray for England. Confession has taught him that he may participate in God's steering of England and all the world.

The confessor who educates the lover is, both aptly and ironically, a priest to Venus, bearing the original charge to prepare Amans for entry into her court. From the outset, however, he is ambitious to be what he calls a "true priest" (lines 238–43):

> "I mot algate and nedes wile
> Noght only make my spekynges
> Of love, bot of othre thinges,
> That touchen to the cause of vice,
> For that belongeth to thoffice
> Of Prest, whos ordre that I bere."

Genius belongs to the train of allegorical instructors in medieval Latin and vernacular literature that includes the Lady Philosophy in *The Consolation of Philosophy*, Raison in the *Roman de la Rose*, Virgil in *The Divine Comedy*, and even the Eagle in Chaucer's *The House of Fame*. His name is taken from the confessor Genius in the *Roman de la Rose*, but C. S. Lewis errs, I believe, when he concludes that both simply represent

[17]Pearsall, *Gower and Lydgate*, p. 17.

[18]Peck, Introduction, *Confessio Amantis*, pp. xix–xxii.

[19]Ibid, p. xxix.

the generative force of propagation rather than the genius who is "the second self" or the "familiar of men."[20] Granted, Genius arrives trailing clouds of sexuality behind him, but given the opportunity, he argues so strongly for virginity that at last Amans timidly suggests that too much virginity will abolish propagation and the race of man. Genius in Gower's poem seems to view propagation as a purely metaphorical process: purity of spirit will beget purity of spirit—and the word *beget* has no physically creative force.

Genius is, in fact, the "second self" of Amans. Russell Peck approaches but does not really investigate this identification of Genius when he points out that the shift from dialogue to narration in the closing debate suddenly refocuses the scene, so that the debate seems to be going on within the lover-as-lover, while the lover-as-poet looks on from above.[21] The shift in focus reaches beyond the scene, in fact, to relocate the entire confession *within* the lover. Amans thus is the body trapped in its own desire, while Genius is the soul, trying to save itself and the body as well.

As the spiritual half of the lover, Genius at first seems to be as far from heaven as Amans is from love. In the beginning he grounds his principles of conduct on the code of behavior for lovers, but at the end he has a new foundation for his principles: truth. "Mi Sone, unto the trouthe wende / Now wol I for the love of thee" (8.2060–61). The truth enables him to love charitably, and charity frees him to speak truthfully. From venality Genius has come to virtue, and, by the grace of God functioning through Venus, he brings Amans to virtue too.

The fine irony of the conclusion, in which the pagan goddess becomes the agent of divine love, sheds a glow of Christian charity over the entire poem. After all, the purpose of confession is to bring the human will into proper conjunction with Christ, not Venus. Christ is discussed forthrightly only twice in the poem—in the Prologue, where he is presented as exemplifying the pattern of love that ought to prevail in the three estates, and in book 5, where Christianity is described as the true religion of the world—but there appear in various tales evocative

[20]Lewis, *The Allegory of Love*, p. 362. For two more recent studies that view Genius as a more complex and sophisticated figure, see George D. Economou, "The Character Genius in Alan de Lille, Jean de Meun, and John Gower," *ChauR* 4 (1970):203–10; and Denise N. Baker, "The Priesthood of Genius: A Study of the Medieval Tradition," *Speculum* 51 (1976):277–91.

[21]Peck, Introduction, *Confessio Amantis*, p. xxvii.

Laughter in the Courts of Love

passages that imply his presence in the life of man. C. S. Lewis has commented that "the heathen theogamies which form the pivot of *Mundus and Paulina* and *Nectanabus* are conceived in the light of the Christian sentiment that surrounds the story of the Annunciation."[22] The account in "Nectanabus" of the so-called miracles attending the birth of Alexander suggests the violent reaction of the earth to the death of Christ. Perhaps the image most evocative of Christ (one, by the way, that is repeated with heavily ironic undertones in "Nectanabus") appears in the tale of "Constance," who herself symbolizes both the steadfastness of human faith and the unchanging love of God. After all her perils and her reunion with her husband, King Allee, Constance sets out "Upon a Mule whyt amblaunt" to meet her father, the Emperor. Constance coming into Rome, like Christ into Jerusalem, is a child of the king coming into the king's city. Such an image functions like a lighthouse, gathering up all the implications of Christ and radiating them outward, shedding light over the surrounding darkness of human error.

The figurative and literal presence of Christ in the poem makes possible the anagogical implications of the conclusion. In his last speech Genius, who himself has been redeemed by the confession, reminds Amans of the finality of human choices: "Now ches if thou wolt live or deie" (8.2148). Amans must not enter into a false paradise at the cost of losing the true. Even Venus serves the divine plan of salvation when she forces Amans to look into the mirror and see that he is an old man. Paradoxically, it is through this realization that Amans is given new life: in recognizing the old man, or sinner, he finally admits his sin in Christian terms and so brings himself to the gateway of salvation.[23] With a smile he goes his "softe pas" home.

But though Christ is immanent in the poem, and though the lover has been transformed from "caitif" to "John Gower," there is, nonetheless, a sense of melancholy attending his redemption. C. S. Lewis refers to it when he says that the poem is about the death of love,[24] and Russell

[22]Lewis, *The Allegory of Love*, p. 212.

[23]D. W. Robertson, Jr., discusses the allegorical and scriptural significance of the "Old Man" in *A Preface to Chaucer*, p. 334. See also Robert P. Miller, "Chaucer's Pardoner, the Scriptural Eunuch, and the Pardoner's Tale," *Speculum* 30 (1955):180–99.

[24]Lewis, *The Allegory of Love*, p. 217.

Peck, when he classifies the poem as a consolation.[25] Allegorically, the conclusion illustrates God's grace coming in sufficient measure to save one who wishes to be saved. Literally, it dramatizes man coming sadly to terms with himself as a dotard. Because Amans has struggled so desperately against this judgment of himself, the victory of spirit over flesh is not made a cause for celebration. Rather than hosannas and danc-ing, it is attended only with a smile.

The pattern of consolation in the poem necessarily raises a problem in classification: can the *Confessio* properly be called a comedy? Consola-tion, after all, implies the protagonist's admission of loss or failure in his pursuit and his acceptance of a substitute for his original desire. This ob-viously is not the triumphant resolution familiar to most comedy. To make matters worse, the pattern of consolation insists that the new reward is not merely something in the place of another, but rather is far better than the original, which was faulty because it was merely human. Consolation is accomplished by distancing—moving from the first level of earthly reality onto a higher plane of symbolic values. From this new perspective the protagonist, Amans, for example, can see that divine love is superior to any merely human love on earth. To be consoled, Amans must give up his old human wishes; he has to make a repudiation that runs counter to ordinary comic rejoicing in common humanity. Moreover, there is, in the character of Amans, no joyous transformation to highlight the worth of his new persuasion. Amans is corrected, cured, and redirected, but he is not a transfigured man, only a man capable of be-ing transfigured. In fact, there is at the core of Amans's experience a passiveness not easily correlated with comic energy and vitality. If we focus on Amans alone at the end of the poem, then we must conclude that whatever comedy obtains is dry and rueful in the extreme.

But Amans is not alone at the end of the poem, nor is the resolution centered solely in him. What happens in the poem happens to Genius and Venus as well, and our final response to the action must be based upon an appreciation of the roles that they play in the redemption of Amans. Beyond this, we must remember a first critical principle: a poem is not comic or tragic by virtue of its ending; rather, it is the movement of the action *from the outset* that establishes the mode. The way in which

[25]Peck, Introduction, *Confessio Amantis*, p. xi.

the action creates its own complications and climaxes establishes our response, and there is a good measure of very real laughter provoked by Amans's journey to repose.

That the comic passages are intentional may be inferred from Gower's statement in the conclusion that he has undertaken "In englesch forto make a book / Which stant betwene ernest and game" (8.3108–3109). Gower's sense of "game," however, is not so far from "ernest" as the grammatical structure implies. His comedy is basically sedate, firmly grounded in his belief that civility of deportment ought to prevail at all times. Gower depends chiefly upon "civilized" provocations to laughter: verbal constructions that illuminate fallacious reasoning or exchanges of dialogue in which questions and answers do not quite correspond. In fine, Gower's comedy arises out of mental processes and manifests itself in verbal forms. The exuberant energy that propels Chaucer's characters and plots is alien to the *Confessio*; so, too, is the explosion of laughter that Chaucer exacts as his due response. Quite contrarily, Gower seems suspicious of outright laughter. What he aims for is a smile.[26]

As a comic poet Gower is remarkable neither for his inventiveness nor for his technical virtuosity. Rather surprisingly for the number of tales collected in the *Confessio*, only three may be classified unreservedly as comedies, and of these only one, "Nectanabus," is adequately sustained through its resolution.

The first comic tale in the poem, an exemplification of envy entitled "The Travellers and the Angel" (2.291–364), is hardly a tale at all but rather a synopsis that is almost forcibly subordinated to moral discourse, as if Gower did not trust the tale to illustrate morality in its own terms. The anecdote is rich in suggestions that Chaucer, for instance, would readily have amplified: strong character types, tricks that recoil upon the trickster, and surprising interpretations of key words such as *gain* and *happiness*. Gower tells the tale quite baldly. An angel who meets two men, one covetous and the other envious, promises that he will grant the first man who asks whatever he most desires, while the other shall receive "the double of that his felaw axeth." Supposing that the request

---

[26]Ernst Robert Curtius discusses early injunctions by some church fathers forbidding laughter and also unrestrained joy; Gower's attitude seems rather close to this "antique ideal of dignity" that was adopted by early monastics. Ernst Robert Curtius, *European Literature and the Latin Middle Ages*, trans. Willard R. Trask, pp. 420–22.

will be for earthly wealth, the covetous man tricks his companion into asking first. The envious man is not about to enrich his neighbor, however, though he himself will prosper. What has been presented as an opportunity for gain, he converts to a device for punishment, to provide himself happiness. He asks to be made blind in one eye. The wish is granted. On the sound of the envious man's laughter, Genius (and Gower) hastens to the admonition that man ought not rejoice in another's sorrows. The need to moralize is obvious, for the comedy is malicious, and the laughter which it provokes rejoices in man's capacity for inhumanity. But the haste with which Gower turns to morality implies an uneasiness with the tale.

The second comic tale, "Hercules and Faunus" (5.6807–6935), is also notable for its potential rather than its actual form. Told to illustrate one of the "ministers" of Avarice, stealth by night, "Hercules and Faunus" hinges on mistaken identity. Hercules and his beloved, Eolen, have taken refuge from the heat of the sun in a cave, where they indulge in idle play. When Faunus espies Eolen, he forsakes the nymphs, swearing that he will somehow win her. After night falls, he creeps into the cave, unaware that the lovers have playfully exchanged clothing. He comes to the first bed but passes it by because he feels Hercules' clothing in the dark. Now prepared to ravish Eolen, he climbs into the other bed – with Hercules. The climax ought to be a general explosion of physical activity that produces rollicking laughter, like *The Reeve's Tale,* but the farcical possibilities of the situation are almost totally blunted. The tale can only be called flat.

There remains, then, only one fully developed comic tale, "Nectanabus" (6.1790–2362). Significantly, it is the least risible of the three, and its humor derives chiefly from quickness of wit and consequent errors in judgment. Nectanabus, king of Egypt and a sorcerer, discovers that he is about to be attacked by enemies, from whom he may not defend himself, and so flees from his own land into Macedonia. Here he sees, and develops a lust for, Queen Olimpias, who is herself curious about his behavior. He comes to her, identifying himself as a clerk with a very private message: the god Amos desires to impregnate her with a son, who shall be called the god of earth. Despite Genius's recurrent comments about his wickedness, Nectanabus is a clever rogue who makes the reader suspend judgment against him at the precise moment when he is most fitting to be condemned. After her union with the "god" in the darkened temple, Olimpias expresses her sense of humility at being so honored, and Nectanabus quickly offers (6.2116–19):

> ". . . whan it liketh you to take
> His compaignie at eny throwe,
> If I a day tofore it knowe,
> He schal be with you on the nyght."

Eventually he is undone by the product of his deception, Alexander. As the two stand on a tower, Nectanabus comments that either the stars are off course or else he is to be slain by his own son. "Hierof this olde dotard lieth," thinks the "god's" son, Alexander, and he shoves the "olde bones" over the wall. In this tale, as in "Hercules and Faunus," the climax hinges on mistaken identity and on the process of acting out an error. But the emphasis here is on the mental processes rather than on the physical action. The suddenness with which Nectanabus's prophecy is fulfilled converts the physical action into a symbolic punctuation that ends an intellectual construction of guile and deception. The phrase "olde bones" removes any sense of human pain and suffering, so that the multiplication of tricks and errors redounding upon Nectanabus seems pleasingly appropriate. It is comically and morally gratifying that magic turns at last against the magician.

It is, of course, an error in judgment to suppose that these three tales sufficiently illustrate Gower's comic art. Gower is not so much a storyteller as a moralist, in the sense that all his tales exist in subordination to a moral issue. Every tale in the *Confessio* functions as the definition or illustration of a virtue or vice, and each is told for a didactic function. The three comic tales do, however, reveal a dominant characteristic of Gower's comedy as it relates to his allegory: he is more at home with the soul than he is with the body; he is closer to high comedy than to farce.[27]

The real comic achievement in the *Confessio* abides in the framework of the poem, in the conflict between Amans and Genius. Through the confession both Amans and Genius reveal themselves as rather

Laughter in the Courts of Love

ridiculous fellows, more mechanical than natural in conduct, who are engaged in a *very* polite battle to impose their wills upon each other. Genius is a garrulous instructor, a pedant, scarcely able to keep any information to himself, even when his pupil already understands the lesson thoroughly. Amans, so it turns out, is a *senex* trying desperately to retain the last vestiges of youth by engaging in a hopeless love pursuit. Genius openly chafes at being restricted to talk of love and so broadens his discourse at every opportunity. Amans, imprisoned in passion and understanding little beyond personal desire, demands that the discourse be narrowed: "Explain it to me in terms of Love." The effect, finally, is of two not-quite-human creatures—an encyclopedia and a jack-in-the-box—engaged in a highly civilized battle. Their conflicting patterns of behavior create a mental tug-of-war that can be resolved only when one contestant marshals enough energy to pull the loser across to his perspective. The winner, to Amans's eternal benefit, is Genius.

Insofar as a definable pattern of human growth and triumph can be traced in the poem, it pertains to Genius. Upon his arrival he confesses that he exists in a state of unresolved ambiguity, having one set of responsibilities to his goddess and another to the ideal of priesthood. At first he seems well suited to Venus, echoing her suspicion that all men are natural deceivers of innocent and trusting womankind. So long as he counsels according to this attitude, he urges Amans to persist in hopelessness and to expect that through some miracle he will live through winter to a new springtime. He teaches also, by implication, that the lover must regard himself as worthless. When Amans timidly ventures that his Lady is usurious, demanding his whole heart in exchange for one glance, Genius answers that quite likely her one glance is worth his heart many times over. Even his early discourses on vice are more courtly than ethical in their point: Amans must give up backbiting so that his Lady will believe him when he speaks to her of love. "She will not drink from a poisoned well," cautions Genius. Gradually, however, he gains confidence in his ability to fulfill the broader demands of his office, and he begins to leave talk of love aside.

To become a true priest, he has to go through a confession himself. First, he must come to terms with Venus, who has ordained him. This causes an awkward moment when Amans asks why he omitted her name from his list of pagan deities. Like one holding his breath before a plunge into icy waters, the confessor confesses, "Mi sone, for schame." Then he dives headlong into judgment; she is an ignorant, lustful, incestuous woman, whose only lasting gift to society has been the trade of prostitution; the man who values his soul does well to shun her lore. After this confession Genius is free to choose the lore he will follow himself, and he opts for the school of Aristotle, concluding that wisdom is preferable to sexual love because it brings profit in sundry ways to him who understands. Now he is ready to serve as priest, to wend unto the truth and let trifles be. He thus advises Amans (8.2086–89):

> "Take love where it mai noght faile;
> For as of this which thou art inne,
> Be that thou seist it is a Sinne,
> And Sinne mai no pris deserve."

The development that confession ought to foster belongs, ironically, to the confessor rather than the sinner. Genius, who at first seemed an encyclopedia, a collection of curious but useless lore, at last becomes wisdom. He is the transformed being, Reason restored from exile, for the first time frankly opposing the sinful will and ordering it to be governed. In his allegorical being, Genius is not limited merely to being the lover's reason but rather is the universal ideal of Reason, capable of functioning for all mankind. In his literal being, Genius proves to be the most truly human figure in the poem, triumphant over his past and filled with a sense of the future. It is his transformation that provides the human comedy of the poem.

Victory in the moral contest does not come easily to Genius, however, for Amans, the Old Man, is so wedded to his desire that he will not leave it of his own accord. Whereas Genius is a double figure, two priests for the price of one, Amans is his opposite, a monomaniac who is determined to love his Lady, even if it kills him. Despite his avowed love for the Lady, however, his eyes see only his own suffering. Whatever Genius says ought to be directly relevant to his narrow perspective, and so he demands, "Explain how it touches Love," or "Tell me how it affects *men* who love," or "Tell how things work in the nighttime, when I most love." When Genius says that hypocrisy is a sickness, Amans twists the words about to complain that his own heart is far sicker with love than his hypocritical face reveals. To many of the sins he must confess guilty,

though in thought rather than deed, for he is too slow and fearful to succeed as a practicing sinner. From the heights of irrationality he can say
that he is not guilty of hatred. "I hate only those men who love my Lady,"
he says, then adding, "She is so desirable that all men must love her."
When he is truly innocent of a vice, he often has to admit that virtue is
forced upon him: he has never been late for an appointment because she
has never granted him one. While Genius moves steadily toward becoming a new man, Amans clings to his old desire. "Your lesson strikes my
ear," he admits, "but it does not reach my heart."

Amans is so willfully bound to his love that he not only refuses his
counselor's advice but finally prevails upon him to take a petition to
Venus. She releases him from bondage by forcing him to see himself as
something other than an unhappy lover. After the fiery dart is removed
and an icy ointment applied, she shows the lover himself as she sees
him—and in the mirror he discovers winter. Now, he realizes, he has
been a comic fool, a *senex* chasing after youth. In admitting his age, he
sets his inner world aright. His own Reason (his personal Genius) hears
that love's rage is away and comes directly home to reign over the flesh.
Thus, concludes the lover, "I was mad sobre and hol ynowh" (8.2869).
Genius absolves him fully; Venus gives him black beads marked "por
reposer." At last he can smile and go his "softe pas" home.

If we interpret the cure of love as affecting only Amans, then the ending of the poem is melancholy. Amans gives up the whole world; in the
terms of comedy this seems a great price to pay for just one soul. But the
cure of love cannot be effected by one man alone, particularly when that
man is as diseased as the lover. Amans does not heal himself but is healed
by a divine power working through an ironic trinity of Venus, Genius,
and himself. This power, moreover, cures all love, even realigning Venus
with Nature. Redemption is a process in which all participants are
translated out of their old actions and into proper ways of being their
new selves. Ironically, Amans forces a symbolic redemption upon the
courtly pair that in turn leads to his literal rebirth. By his despair he has
forced Genius to act: the encyclopedia becomes Wisdom; the Love-
tutor, a true priest. By his persistence in an unnatural urge, he makes
Venus rise, however temporarily, from the level of cupidity to charity.
She never acts against Nature, and since Nature has made John Gower
an old man, she will cure him of love by granting him an old man's heart,

beyond desires of the flesh. In cooperating with Nature, she becomes the instrument of God's grace, which desires that the Old Man be saved. By refusing him entry into her court, she makes possible his entry into Heaven. She confers upon Amans a far greater love than she, the goddess of Love, is capable of knowing.

There is a sense of luminous tenderness encircling the final tableau as Venus, Genius, and Amans stand linked together by the desire to be kind to one another. There is, if not laughter, at least a smile as Amans turns forever from the Court of Love—the false paradise of fallen man—and goes toward the true Paradise of the new man. The smile suggests peace and comfort, the values of an old man. The divine comedy of John Gower omits joy along with hilarity, perhaps because Gower feels that these are extreme responses that attract too much attention to themselves. They are too human and too youthful to pertain to the salvation of an old man.

The vision of love in *Confessio Amantis* is designed to instruct, to teach that the Court of Love is no heaven and that Courtly Love (earthly desire) is merely a straight and narrow road to hell. Shaping the vision are Gower's often complex allegory and his didactic use of comedy to direct our proper responses to his story. In the final analysis Gower's forte is allegory. His real concern is to tell a story of one man that reveals the sin of the world and demonstrates how the world and the man can be saved from destruction. The comedy of the poem makes us laugh at sin and error and teaches us to find comfort in virtue. In this way Gower succeeds in making comedy and allegory compatible in purpose, but he does so at the expense of comedy. Instead of rejoicing in human existence, Gower's comedy rebukes and rejects many forms of existence. Gower values not laughter but a gentle smile, the smile of a man beyond the perils of the flesh.

The Dream as Nightmare

Throughout the fifteenth century the images of the court, the goddess, the Lady, and the lover continued to dominate allegorical poetry, recurring with a terrible predictability in poem after dull poem. As treated by the comic poets who succeeded Gower, however, the images become more frankly designed for didacticism and less evocative of spiritual dilemmas caused by conflicting impulses within the human heart. At the same time the comic tone grows more clangorous, and the comic devices become more patently ludicrous in their contexts. The voice of the poet nearly blends into that of the preacher, as both urge mortal man to shun vice.

In *Confessio Amantis* the Court of Love is presented as a promised land of delights, governed by an essentially just goddess, who metes out her rewards according to the laws of nature and the merits of the petitioner. The lover is cast as an outsider to both the earthly court of his mistress and the ethereal Court of Venus. Because the Lady will not accept him as a lover, he must perforce yearn after her across the distance she keeps between them. In the closing vision of the Court of Love, those lovers led by Youth are so busily engaged in acting out their traditional responses to passion that they do not notice Amans at all, while those led by Elde view him with pity and finally persuade Venus to release him from pain. This she does by excluding him firmly and irrevocably from her court. Because he is old, he is "unnatural," hence unacceptable to her. Moreover, he has been an aggressor, trying to force his way into the world of Love. There arises from his confession the impression that his Lady is the object of a hunt, the beautiful hart that the lover-hunter pursues hourly to bring to bay. Although he is himself wounded by Cupid's fiery dart, it becomes clear that Amans is the victim of his own will. Where Venus is concerned, the lover is an attacking enemy; all she does is defend herself.

There is, however, another way of viewing Venus and human lovers, which is variously demonstrated by such poems as *The Golden Targe*, *The Court of Love*, and *The Palice of Honour*. From this perspective Venus is not merely the personification of a universal impulse toward sexual love but an aggressor, actively trying to impress all men into her service. The lover does not seek admission to her court through a process of "purification." Instead he is threatened, attacked, and, if possible, bodily dragged in by what is clearly a meretricious display of power. The lover, not the Lady, is the prey; the hunter is the hunted, and, as often as not, it is not his heart but his head that Venus wants. For him the dream of love is a nightmare.

Not only does the concept of the court and the lover undergo a change, but the signification of the dream vision alters also. In *Confessio Amantis*,

Laughter in the Courts of Love

as in *The Divine Comedy*, the dream is meant clearly to have a healing function. There is, in fact, a remarkable similarity between the ways in which Dante and Gower establish the dream quality of their poems. Rather than falling asleep, the Dreamer awakens; that is, he suddenly perceives his existence on earth as a sleep and a forgetting that leads to the death of the soul. The dream into which he wakes is designed to teach him the way to righteousness, to cure him of the wounds of sin. The dream is the physician of the soul, and the suggestion that the Dreamer is awake throughout his experience implies that the cure is good for the real world too. Without saying literally that Amans goes to sleep and awakens into a dream, Gower makes the dream structure effective in his poem by his references to waking at both the beginning and the end of his confession. His dream, like Dante's, is meant to free the soul from the trap that has been made of real life.

In the later dream-vision poems, however, the dream itself becomes the trap from which the Dreamer escapes by waking into the real world. Confronted by a series of menacing opponents who want to rob him of his life, his liberty, or his happiness, the Dreamer is demoralized by fear or a sense of desolation, and he sinks into a spiritual or emotional paralysis that cannot be endured. The dream, then, is a sickness, and the real world is its cure.

This emphasis upon the dream as sickness changes the quality of the vision of life which is presented through the dream frame. While the escape from dreams to waking reality comes far closer to popular dream experience than does Gower's treatment of the dream, the correlation between poetry and reality tends paradoxically to limit the allegorical importance of the dream. The poem appeals to the reader's recognition that "this is how things really happen," but the reader's very awareness of the "realness" of sleeping and waking makes the content of the poem itself seem all the more artificial, the allegory all the more irritatingly superficial. The revelation that the nightmare is not real carries with it the suggestion that it is therefore unimportant. In a sense the dream, no matter how frightful or serious, becomes escapist poetry for the reader. A good many dream-visions of the fifteenth century suffer precisely from this inborn imputation that they are artificial and irrelevant.

In no poem, perhaps, is the sense of artificiality more palpably present than in William Dunbar's *The Golden Targe*. There has been considerable argument among critics whether Dunbar uses allegory for decoration or for revelation. "The trappings of allegory are retained," says C. S. Lewis, "but the true interest of the poet lies elsewhere, sometimes in satire, sometimes in amorous dialectic, and often in mere rhetoric and style."[28] In his explication of Dunbar's poetry Tom Scott dismisses allegory as "already dead," with its trappings pressed into service to show just how dead it is. Dunbar's so-called allegories, he says, "are not 'allegories' at all in the strict sense, but poems in which allegorical elements conflict with a sensuous impressionism, a conflict of the abstract and intellectual with the concrete and sensuous."[29] Roderick J. Lyall, on the other hand, finds in the poem a moral allegory that analyzes the deficiencies of sensuality before concluding that moderation should be a rule of conduct.[30]

Any obituary notice for allegory is, of course, premature and highly exaggerated. What seems particularly artificial and lifeless in *The Golden Targe* is not allegory itself but a misreading of one particular aspect of one particular style of allegory. The reader who approaches Dunbar's Court of Love as if it were Gower's or Chaucer's is necessarily led to the conclusion that Dunbar's is merely a company of decorative names upon a page. The personages in the court, if read by orthodox standards, are not lovers nor forces controlling man's destiny nor symbols of the vastness of love's realm.

Dunbar, however, does not create an orthodox Court of Love, nor does he intend an orthodox reading. His real interest, in fact, is not in the court but in a battle, and here the pulse of allegory is still very robust. The fact that the Dreamer is passive during the battle ought not be taken as a sign that the poet is merely working his way though a mechanical form in order to prove "his mastery of the genre."[31] Rather, it indicates that the battle is a *pyschomachia*, a conflict occurring within the Dreamer.[32] He is a double figure in the action of the poem: allegorically he is the battlefield, while literally he is the spoils of war.

[28]Lewis, *The Allegory of Love*, p. 251.

[29]Tom Scott, *Dunbar: A Critical Exposition of the Poems*, p. 332.

[30]Roderick J. Lyall, "Moral Allegory in Dunbar's 'Goldyn Targe,'" *SSL* 11 (1973):47–65.

[31]Scott, *Dunbar: A Critical Exposition of the Poems*, p. 41.

[32]Walter Scheps has entitled his study "The *Goldyn Targe*: Dunbar's Comic Psychomachia," *PLL* 11 (1975):339–56. Scheps is concerned, however, with reading the poem as an allegory of poetics, and he finds that the comedy of the poem is Dunbar's criticism of the deficiencies inherent in the dream-vision genre (p. 354).

Laughter in the Courts of Love

All this is not to deny that the poem seems artificial but to point out that allegory is neither dead nor rejected in favor of a more direct communication. The allegory seems artificial so long as it is more descriptive than active, and the sense of artificiality is heightened by the total structure of the poem. Rather than shaping the poem, the allegory is shaped to the poem; that is, it is fitted within a framework that is redolent of conscious "literariness."[33] The frame around the allegory is not the dream but the depiction of the lovely May morning, which Dunbar executes in his most aureate, hence artificial, style, ending with his expression of praise to Chaucer, Gower, and Lydgate, all of whom, he says (perhaps with tongue in cheek), could have expressed his matter far better.

In describing the setting in which the dream occurs, Dunbar stresses not the natural but the gemlike quality of time and place.[34] The fields are enameled with all colors; the pearl drops of dew shake down like silver showers; the rose is powdered with beryl drops; the purple heaven gilds the trees; the lake gleams like a lamp, reflecting the beams of the "goldyn candill matutyne." The setting thus presented is clearly no ordinary garden, but a paradise where birds sing "full angellike," and everything glows in the heavenly ambience of new creation. The apparent perfection of the scene, however, is earthly rather than heavenly, for the ear detects that the angelic choir of birds sings "upon the tender croppis / With curiouse note, as Venus chapell clerkis."[35] Beneath all appearances of peace and harmony is a subtle hint of forces that cause conflict and discord; so, when the Dreamer falls asleep and sees the ship, the vessel with a "saill als quhite as blossum upon spray" comes to the shore as lustily "as falcoune swift desyrouse of hir pray" (lines 51, 54). The Dreamer, lulled to sleep by an apparent paradise, finds that it metamorphoses into an actual hell.

The action of the poem is, in fact, metamorphosis, in which all things evolve from deceptive appearance into cruel reality. The earthly paradise of the opening stanza is first converted into a Garden of Love, when the ship lands and the ladies—that catalogue of decorative

[33]Denton Fox, "Dunbar's *The Golden Targe*," *ELH* 26 (1959):311–34. Fox argues that the poem is about poetry.

[34]Cf. Lois A. Ebin, "The Theme of Poetry in Dunbar's 'Goldyn Targe,'" *ChauR* 7 (1972):147–59, which analyzes the relationship between aureate style and moral error.

[35]William Dunbar, *Poems*, ed. James Kinsley, lines 20–21. Subsequent references are incorporated in the text.

names – enter the park "full lustily . . . all in fere." Blossoms, leaves, trees, all salute the ladies, and the birds become frankly amorous in their song, lustily warbling "ballettis in lufe." The appeal of the Love-Garden grows so strong that finally the Dreamer creeps through the leaves and is espied by Venus, a discovery, he says, that he "boucht full dere."

Now the setting metamorphoses again, into a battlefield, as Venus commands that the Dreamer be taken. The battle that follows is notably one-sided, for while the Dreamer is sought by many, he has but one defender, Resoun. This "nobil chevallere," however, is "armypotent as Mars," and the battle goes entirely in his favor until Perilouse Presence treacherously casts a powder in his eye and blinds him. With the downfall of Resoun the Dreamer is yielded up to Beautee, who quickly passes him on to Dissymulance, Fair Calling, Cherishing, New Acquyntance, and finally to Dangere, who in her turn delivers him "unto Hevynesse / For to remayne . . ." (lines 227–28).

The battlefield does not revert to Love-Garden or paradise after the fall of Resoun, however, but continues its downward evolution. The inner hell of lovesickness personified by Hevynesse is directly manifested in the outer world as the gods take to ship and leave. The fierce bugle blast from Eolus is like the trumpet that sounds the end of the world, blowing all to desolation: "thare was bot wilderness, / Thare was no more bot birdis, bank, and bruke" (lines 233–34).

The dream thus proves to be a nightmare allegory of the Fall of Man and the loss of Paradise. Dunbar's scheme of setting the dream within the frame of the real world, however, saves the poem from implying that paradise lost is mankind's finality. The Dreamer awakens into the May garden again, but now it is a natural rather than an aureate world (lines 247–49):

> Suete war the vapouris, soft the morowing,
> Halesum the vale depaynt wyth flouris ying,
> The air attemperit, sobir and amene.

Implicit in this final view of the garden is a caution against precisely that artificiality which so marked the first descriptive stanzas and appearance of Love's Court. The moral lesson is very clear, as well as trite: all that glitters is not gold, and the man who takes glitter to be gold does so at his own peril. Dunbar provides his Dreamer with a golden targe, the pure gold of Reason, as a standard for judging the false, but even Reason may be overcome by treachery. The Dreamer then can be saved only by wak- ing into reality.

Dunbar's allegory is not dead but rather is about death and so illumines death within its very structure. The Dreamer creates his own desolation out of his love of aureation: his first vision of the garden as an aggregation of jewels paves the way for his submission to sensuality: his own eyes have made a false paradise out of earth. But death is not the Dreamer's destiny, no more than the world is really aureate. When the dream becomes intolerable, the Dreamer awakens and sees now, with clear eyes, the sober wholesomeness of the natural world. Thus the total poem is, in its fullest sense, not about death at all but about rebirth, the restoration of rational vision to the Dreamer. There is, however, no im- plication of divine involvement in the Dreamer's salvation (unless some determined allegorizer would insist that the act of waking symbolizes God's saving grace). The allegory fulfills itself on chiefly rational and secular levels.

If *The Golden Targe* clearly illustrates that Dunbar has reduced the levels of allegory, it nevertheless shows that he still found allegory a useful form of communication. On the other hand, the poem is hardly a representative example of his comic powers. The same critics who find, perhaps erroneously, that Dunbar is no allegorist all agree that the most distinctive aspect of his genius is a "wild comic fantasy" of the kind that animates *The Dance of the Sevin Deidly Synnis, The Justis Betwix the Telyour and the Sowtar* and *The Tretis of the Tua Mariit Wemen and the Wedo*, the last now considered his best poem. There is within the polite limits of *The Golden Targe* little room for "wild comic fantasy" or for the scabrous exaggerations of physical grossness that mark his most characteristic works.

Yet underneath the allegorical action there pulses the spirit of laughter, as though Dunbar were emphasizing the final triviality of the nightmare that must evaporate before the clear light of waking reality. Dunbar sets his comedy in motion with a traditional disclaimer of per- sonal ability which states hyperbolically that the scene is too lovely for even Homer with his ornate style or Cicero with his sweet lips "to com- pile that paradise complete." In cataloguing the goddesses who disem- bark, he seems to chase himself in mythological circles, for he names in

Laughter in the Courts of Love

order Nature, Venus, Aurora, Flora, Juno, Apollo (hardly a goddess), Proserpina, Diana, Clio, Thetis, Pallas, Minerva (reduplicating Pallas), Fortune, Lucina (reduplicating Diana), May, April, and June. Of this remarkable list Tom Scott very cautiously suggests, "Dunbar's knowledge of classical mythology is either very shaky or he is pulling our legs."[36] Less cautiously, I would suggest that Dunbar knew his mythology well and that he is frankly mocking courtly and heroic catalogues, just as he later mocks heroic warfare in the battle between Reason and Sensuality.

In narrating the battle, Dunbar carefully deletes any real sense of danger: ". . . rycht gretly was I noucht affrayit," says the Dreamer, "The party was so plesand for to sene" (lines 143–44). While the Dreamer is defended by Resoun, "armypotent as Mars," he is attacked by improbable platoons: Beautee and her attributes wielding "mony diverse aufull instrument"; Youth and her virgins, "Grene Innocence," "schamefull Abaising," "quaking Drede," and "humble Obedience"—all who dread to do any violence—and Suete Womanhede with such warriors as Contenence, Pacience, Stedfastnes, and Sobirnes. The humor is intensified by by the great disparity between the courtly terms describing the warriors—*tender, sweet, benign*—and heroic terms appropriate to battle poetry: *scharp assayes, aufull ordynance, a cloud of arrowis as hayle schour.* The end of the battle almost equals in ignominy the great battle in the *Roman de la Rose:* Presence casts a powder in Resoun's eye that makes him go astray like a drunken man. The battle ends with Resoun playing the fool, before he is finally banished among the green boughs.

In fine, Dunbar carefully constructs his heroic battle so that it is a burlesque of the courtly romance. Underlining the burlesque is one last signal device of comedy. The dream is reported with complete objectivity so that all traces of empathy are drained away. The Dreamer has no sense of fear in the beginning; he is not frightened, indeed, until Resoun is banished and the battle is lost. His lament for Resoun, interrupting his account of how the courtly ladies beguiled him, evokes not sympathy but laughter by its very intensity (lines 214–16):

> Quhy was thou blyndit, Resoun, quhi, allace:
> And gert ane hell my paradise appere,
> And mercy seme, quhare that I fand no grace?

[36]Scott, *Dunbar: A Critical Exposition of the Poems*, p. 42.

Laughter in the Courts of Love

The intensity contrasts totally with the indolence implicit in the ladies' blandishments. By his construction and placing of the lament, Dunbar invites us not to pity but to laugh.

Unlike *Confessio Amantis*, which derives its comic vitality from the treatment of characters, *The Golden Targe* is comic in its action alone. There is virtually no attempt at characterization, not even of the Dreamer, for the poet's focus is completely upon the process by which appearances deceive the human eye and ear. The burlesque of courtly allegory is not meant as a rejection of Courtly Love (though C. S. Lewis would undoubtedly have appreciated the notion) but stands rather as a mockery of any process by which dross is made to appear gold. The poem is not suggestive or evocative like earlier love allegories;[37] that is to say, it does not appeal to an informational program lying outside the poem in the common knowledge of the reader or to earlier poems in its tradition. It is complete within itself, with the May-morning frame supplying the real action and the allegorical battle merely restating in terms of personification what is wrong with the Dreamer's waking mind. The entire allegory, then, is made a single symbol, subordinate to the descriptive frame that encloses it.

It is important to repeat that Dunbar does not eschew the traditional way in which allegory works because he no longer believes in it. His purpose is still the same as Gower's and Chaucer's: to uphold accepted values by rejecting any perversion of those values. Unlike Chaucer and Gower, Dunbar subordinates allegory to burlesque, perhaps because he lived in an age when values were less sure to be accepted without blunt statement. For Dunbar allegory still works; it still expresses the forces that work upon man to divert him from the path of truth and righteousness. Nonetheless, it is necessary to use extra measures to drive the point home, and so the entire poem, not just the allegory, is made artificial. The dream of the golden world and the dream of love are both turned to nightmare; but beyond these, the natural, wholesome world waits for the man who sees clearly.

The Nightmare as Reality

While the nightmare quality of Dunbar's love vision is confined chiefly to the dream, arising out of the gradual metamorphosis of pleasure into

[37]Fox, "Dunbar's *The Golden Targe*," p. 326.

desolation, everything about John Skelton's *The Bowge of Court* is directed toward evoking the sensation of nightmare. Dunbar's dream stands in sharp contrast to the golden May morning, a vision of folly set off against a vision of beauty. Skelton, however, prepares the way for nightmare from the very beginning when he introduces himself as a per- turbed poet, incapacitated by his own uncertainty. He wishes to write a poem in covert terms, he says, treating of vice or morality, but Ignorance discourages him with the assurance that his cunning is not nearly equal to his ambition. Of anyone who would outstrip his skill, she offers this judgment: "His hede maye be harde, but feble is his brayne!"[38] At last, worn out by the conflict in his mind, the narrator falls asleep and into a dream.

Skelton translates this waking state of perturbation into the dream, where it generates an emotional atmosphere of tension and fear. He heightens this atmosphere by making all objects and situations in the poem mutable: they flow like water from their original form into menac- ing shapes and motions that create a nagging sense of uneasiness. Even the action of the poem repeats this fluidity, changing its course and reshaping its form, until it brings the Dreamer to terror. The allegory of this poem is made up not of fixed images that have endured because they signify accepted truths and doctrines but of new images that resemble the old—but only momentarily, before they undergo change. From his use of these images it is clear that Skelton is not analyzing man's inner life as he moves between conflicting sets of values; instead, he is analyzing man's social life in a world where no values prevail.

The court that Skelton describes is not a Court of Love, nor is love the subject of the poem. Instead Skelton borrows the imagery of Courtly Love to depict the world of commerce, which, in turn, symbolizes the world of a Renaissance Court. Thus the image that has been *literalized* by Chaucer, Gower, and Dunbar is now made one of the levels of *allegorical* reference, in effect a standard of civility or gentility by which to judge the "court" of the poem. This court is a ship, steered by Fortune, and all the passengers are present because they want to profit from trade. Skelton's dreamer, Drede, boards the ship so that he too may profit, but after he has encountered seven "subtyll" passengers, he

[38]John Skelton, *Poems*, ed. Robert S. Kinsman, line 24. All subsequent references are incor- porated in the text.

becomes so fearful that he leaps overboard and ends the dream.

The dream begins calmly enough, colored by the Dreamer's initial sense of hopefulness. A fine ship anchors in the harbor, and he follows the crowds aboard, desirous of sharing in the benefits. Once on board, however, he quickly retreats into a timid carefulness not to ask for any-thing he is not certain of getting. As soon as caution hedges his ambition, the nightmare proper begins, for in the dream world all that is certain is uncertainty. He undergoes what C. S. Lewis has aptly described as "a nightmare crescendo" of responses "from guilelessness to suspicion, from suspicion to acute nervousness, and thence to panic and awakening."[39] Even the concluding stanza of the poem stresses the uncertainty of night-mare. This dream, Skelton says, may or may not contain truth as well as residue. The dream is an *insomnium*, which springs from the distress of the waking mind.[40] Unlike most other dream visions, however, *The Bowge of Court* has no resolution in which the dream is put into perspec-tive with the real world. The nightmare *is* the real world.

Adding intensity to the nightmare is the sheer energy of the poem—the swiftness and directness with which Skelton makes incident follow upon incident, the ceaseless busy-ness of the seven other passengers, nowhere better manifested than in Ryote's finding it im-possible to stand still or keep quiet, and the increasing nervousness with which Drede responds to his situation as odd-man-out. Literally nothing in the poem stands still once the ship sets sail; even Drede acts out his uneasiness, jumping, turning, and edging about to discover what perils surround him.

Before the dream turns to nightmare, however, *The Bowge of Court* seems to repeat all other dream allegories. The poem takes its initial shape from the love vision, most clearly echoing the *Roman de la Rose*. The names and characterizing behavior, if not the sex, of the figures in the Prologue to the poem are derived in the main from the *Roman*. Drede is patterned upon Peor, the unlikely warrior whose weapons of attack and defense were, appropriately, "Fear of Ostentation" and "Doubt of

---

[39]Lewis, *The Allegory of Love*, p. 252.

[40]Stanley Eugene Fish, *John Skelton's Poetry*, Yale Studies in English, vol. 157, pp. 71–72. A. R. Heiserman, however, in *Skelton and Satire*, p. 33, suggests that the dream is a *somnium animale*, a term that he believes Skelton would have found more up to date. Finally, A. C. Spearing says that the dream may be a *somnium coeleste*, though the ambiguity of the poem makes it possible to say with equal authority that it is an *insomnium*. See A. C. Spearing, *Medieval Dream-Poetry*, pp. 197–202.

Peril."[41] The lady Daunger (an uncouth man in the *Roman*) predictably taunts Drede almost as soon as he boards the ship, stressing his unworth-iness "to prese so proudly uppe." To his other side there comes up Desyre, modeled in part upon the lover's traditional friends, who urges him forward and offers to lend him her jewel, *Bone aventure*. Even the flocking of merchants to the ship evokes memories of earlier gatherings at the Court of Love. Most typical of the love allegory, however, is the magnetic and mysterious Lady, Dame Saunce-Pere, owner of the ship. She sits almost like Venus in court, behind a curtain on a brilliant throne that outshines the sun. Inscribed on the throne is a message as two-edged as that above the gate in *The Parliament of Fowls*, but instead of promising happiness or sadness, this warns, "*Garder le fortune que est mauelz et bone.*"

These similarities to traditional dream-visions suggest that the Dreamer is just another lover setting out on an amorous adventure to overcome obstacles and win the lady, but while he is still setting the scene for the action, Skelton begins to change the form of the poem from narrative to quasi-dramatic procession, and the content from the quest for love to the quest for survival. Drede learns from his acquaintance Desyre that the real Lady to pay court to is not Dame Saunce-Pere, the owner of the ship, but Fortune, who steers. When Drede asks and receives favor from Fortune, the direction and form of the poem change entirely. The illusion that this is a Court of Love vanishes, replaced by our awareness that Drede is in the court of an earthly monarch, sur-rounded by conniving courtiers. The body of the poem is written in semi-dramatic form, with Drede serving as narrator and an essentially passive participant. He introduces and listens to the "subtyll persones" but does not enter into dialogue with them. What occurs instead of formal drama is a procession in which the subtle seven accost him serially, working singly and together to do him harm.

In electing to present seven vicious folk, Skelton instantly links his poem with such moral and religious allegories as Chaucer's *The House of Fame* and Langland's *Piers Plowman*.[42] The procession of courtiers is

[41]Cf. Guillaume de Lorris and Jean de Meun, *The Romance of the Rose*, trans. Harry W. Robbins, ed. Charles W. Dunn, p. 329.

[42]The number of critics stressing Skelton's indebtedness to both Chaucer and Langland includes not only Fish and Heiserman (see no. 40 above) but also John Holloway, *The Charted Mirror:*

strongly reminiscent of Passus Five of *Piers Plowman*, which narrates the shriving of the Seven Deadly Sins, but here there is no shriving, for there is no higher authority to rebuke and reform the vicious folk. The Creator-God of this world is the pilot Fortune; the animating spirit, Favor; and the Great Commandment, "Get and hold onto good luck." This is a thoroughly secular world in which man relies neither upon his own moral knowledge nor upon God. Apart from a self-defeating trust in good luck, hope and faith are absent from the world. Even the seven personifications of vice are not the seven deadly sins but forms of vicious behavior acceptable at court or in any "racket" whose motto is "Dog Eat Dog."[43] Drede learns no positive moral values here, such as are taught in *Confessio Amantis* or even in *The House of Fame*, where Geffrey at least learns to assume responsibility for his own reputation. Stanley Fish says that the only lesson taught by the poem is "strangely nonmoral: 'When luck (Bone Aventure) fails, commit suicide.'"[44]

The absence of a "clear moral teaching" results primarily from Skelton's characterization of Drede and secondly from his rather unorthodox handling of the seven vicious persons. The personification of uncertainty, Drede has no values to hold onto; he establishes as his highest good *surety*. He follows the crowds onto the ship in order not to be left out of whatever goes on, but then he hesitates to take part in the action, not from scruples but from caution. When Desyre tells him to make friends with Fortune, he worriedly asks, "How myghte I have her sure?" Desyre's response, ". . . by *Bone aventure*," points out that Drede cannot have what he desires because the world he has entered is made up of chance and favor. In the final analysis Drede's overwhelming desire for security brings about his perils, for, rather than being content with the favors given him by Fortune, he tries to make friends of her friends, the subtle seven, and so provokes them into acting against him.

Skelton presents the action against Drede as a procession of iconographic figures who skillfully play upon his insecurity. While each

---

Literary and Critical Essays, pp. 13–17; and Norma Phillips, "Observations on the Derivative Method of Skelton's Realism," *JEGP* 65 (1966):19–35.

[43]Lewis, *The Allegory of Love*, p. 252. For a slightly longer discussion, see C. S. Lewis, *English Literature in the Sixteenth Century*, vol. 3 of *The Oxford History of English Literature*, ed. F. P. Wilson and Bonamy Dobrée, pp. 134–35.

[44]Fish, *John Skelton's Poetry*, p. 74.

menaces Drede in a mode predicted by his name – dissimulation, disdain, or deceit – the modes tend to recreate the norms established in the narrative of the Prologue, by Daunger and Desyre. Dysdayne and Disceyte repeat Daunger in attacking him forthrightly, while the others imitate Desyre's show of friendliness, only theirs is a hypocritical cloak over their real intentions. Ultimately the two modes of approaching Drede point back to the opening situation of the poem in which the poet is paralyzed by the conflict between his ambition and his confessed ignorance. Thus the waking uneasiness of mind is enacted as the literal terror of the dream.

In making manifest the true nature of the seven vicious folk, Skelton relies upon the traditional device of providing each with self-defining physical features and garments. Favell, the flatterer, wears a cloak lined with "doubtfull doublenes," and everything about Dyssymulation's body and dress is twofold and contradictory. Suspycyon shakes with palsy, and Dysdayne has an ashen, whelkish face. The outer man is an index to the inner sickness, which speech reveals even more clearly. None of them speaks straight; all quote Scripture for their own purposes, and all swear by God when they swear most in vain.[45] For them all, language is a tool for flattering, deceiving, cajoling, and threatening and for plotting murder. It, like the world they live in, has no reality apart from the perversity of personal desire.

What is most striking about Skelton's procession, however, is that he does not make it up of personification alone. Rather than presenting seven walking abstractions, Skelton introduces five vices – flattery (Favell), suspicion, disdain, dissimulation, and deceit – which are in essence merely embodied abstractions. But along with these he includes two relatively complex personages (Ryote is more human than abstract), who sum up all the negative qualities of life at court. Hervy Hafter, with his fox-furred gown and his dicing box, is the complete courtier, skilled at song, nimble afoot, and quick of tongue. He is a flatterer, a deceiver, and also a pickpocket. "Whan I loked on hym," Drede says, "my purse was half aferde" (line 238). Ryote, who clatters about blear-eyed and dressed in skimpy rags, is the ultimate version of Hervy Hafter, the portrait of what the complete courtier completely becomes. Flattering, swearing, singing snatches of song, and dancing about constantly, he tries to pick

[45]Heiserman, *Skelton and Satire*, p. 24.

Drede's pocket not directly but by urging him to wager upon anything that may be turned into a game of chance. Full of advice for getting on at court, he himself gets on by being a pimp. He is, naturally enough, but with pungent irony, the only figure to whom Drede can actually feel superior, calling him "this rybaude foule and leude" (line 414). Skelton doubles the irony when he makes clear that of all the figures on the ship only Ryote has what Drede most desires: certainty – in the reliable figure of his prostitute, Malkyn.

What is revealed by the allegory of the poem finally is the result of failing to believe in oneself. For Drede there is no certainty; to him belongs a disabling modesty that grows successively into doubt, fear, and terror. By not assuming responsibility for his own destiny, Drede lets loose the forces of darkness that lead, on the one hand, to immoral, even murderous behavior and, on the other, to suicidal despair. The five vices illustrate ways in which Drede may behave, while the two courtiers illustrate what he will become if he surrenders his destiny to the ungovernable way of the world. Skelton is undoubtedly satirizing the practices common at court, but also he is analyzing what happens to one man who lets himself become trapped between his personal Desyre and Daunger.

Because the tone of the allegory is satiric, the poem lacks the affirmation of moral or spiritual values found in *Confessio Amantis*; they are defined only by their negation. In a very real sense the allegory is "covert," as the poet intended, so that its movement is inward toward the evil that lurks in the heart of man. There is not here, as there was in the *Confessio*, a corresponding movement outward to reveal the cure for that evil. Skelton creates only half the movement and half the meaning found in other polysemous poems. He has limited allegory just as he has limited his world to its essentially negative qualities.

The Bowge of Court is traditionally classified as a satire, a genre that many critics see as distinct from comedy; so Judith Larson says that the poem is not a comedy, implying that the terms *comedy* and *satire* are mutually exclusive.[46] In terms of the poet's intentions in creating a poem, this may be true. L. J. Potts, for example, says that comedy and satire part company permanently at their point of origin; that is to say, each arises from and is

[46]"What Is *The Bowge of Courte?*" *JEGP* 61 (1962):294.

shaped by a completely different attitude toward its subject. Whereas comedy abides by the dictum that nothing in nature is alien, satire repudiates the dictum and nature too.[47] Despite their differences in attitude, however, comedy and satire are made up out of the same traditional devices, and both have as one of their goals the evocation of laughter. In her study of Renaissance aesthetics Madeleine Doran concludes that there were two modes of comedy available to the English poet, social and romantic:

> The essential difference between the two modes . . . is not so much one of realism . . . as it is one of attitude and tone. The emphasis is on a different set of human motives . . . poetic longings for love and adventure . . . [or] the grosser appetites for women, money, or power. The defining difference of tone is the difference between lyrical sentiment sympathetically expressed and critical satire.[48]

In other words, a satiric tone does not disqualify a poem from provoking laughter but rather underlines the traditional treatment of the subject. Perhaps the best way to classify *The Bowge of Court* is to say simply that it is a satirical comedy.

As a comedy the poem derives its primary impetus from the same speed that propels the nightmare to its climax. Everything occurs so quickly and abruptly, without any significant pauses for assimilation, that the reader seems to be watching a film run at double speed. The poem virtually illustrates the adage that, played fast enough, even a funeral procession or, in this case, an intended murder, is funny. The pace strips the figures of any suggestive humanity and makes them machines who merely do what they have been programmed to do. This mechanical quality is further emphasized by both their speech, which has been preordained by their names, and their physical behavior, their almost balletic circling and shuffling about. The velocity of the unfolding action is finally so great that even Drede's frightened leap overboard has little empathic value, especially since it is a leap not into water but into wakefulness and safety.

There is a strong element of farce in the poem, a stress upon the human body moving ludicrously through space. Of the seven subtle figures

[47]L. J. Potts, *Comedy*, pp. 153–54.

[48]Madeleine Doran, *Endeavors of Art: A Study of Form in Elizabethan Drama*, p. 149.

three are given to leaping: Hervy Hafter, who comes "lepynge, lyghte as lynde"; Ryote, who comes "russhynge all at ones"; and Disceyte, who jumps from behind, saying, "Boo!" At this point Drede himself jumps, punctuating the series of leaps and preparing the way for his second leap into safety. Besides jumping, the shipmates are given to creeping, stamp-ing, shuffling, and edging about, so that all bodies seem always on the verge of breaking into a hellish and ludicrous dance.

Apart from the stress upon undignified human motions, the other ma-jor source of comedy in the poem is the very apparent distortion of language. Almost all speeches are duplicities, so that there are in effect two speeches coming at the reader, as well as a palpable difference be-tween what is meant and what is said. The multiplicity of what ought to be singular undercuts any possible seriousness and exposes the hypocritical form of the speech itself. At other times the function of speech is to transfer attitudes entirely out of their proper context; thus, after Suspycyon "discloses" his mind and goes, Drede suddenly adopts his suspicious attitude—but directed against the reader: "Soo he departed; there he wolde be come, / I dare not speke; I promysed to be dome" (lines 228–29). The quintessence of distorted language and of dis-located attitudes is provided by Ryote in his discussion of his lemman, Malkyn (lines 402–403, 409–10):

> "I lete her to hyre that men maye on her ryde,
> Her harnes easy ferre and nere is soughte."

> "Who rydeth on her, he nedeth not to care,
> For she is trussed for to breke a launce."

The complete reduction of sex to bestiality is both shocking and funny because the language of the speech so carefully deletes humanity from the animal.

In constructing the procession of the vicious folk, Skelton seems to have meant Ryote to serve as a comic interlude between the open threat made by Disdayne and the murderousness implicit in Dyssymulation. He offers no physical threat, nor does he appeal to Drede's desire for secu-rity. He offers Drede a holiday from his worries, as well as a chance to feel superior to somebody. In fact, the bawdy portrait of Ryote and his Malkyn is the comic as well as the allegorical center of the poem. Ryote knows the real art of getting on with Fortune and holding onto good luck. He has found the way to live in the nightmare.

It is in the satirical tone with which the "grosser appetites for "women, money, and power" are presented that the comedy and allegory of the poem come together. The allegory functions primarily in a negative sense to reveal that self-doubt is self-corruption, while the comedy ridicules this corruption both in its extreme form and in its more acceptable appearance as Drede's desire for security. From an apparent love allegory that seemed to move upward, the poem modulates into a procession downward, with the comedy and the allegory saying alike, "This is hell." Skelton's comic allegory thus ends as far from heaven as Gower's began; and what in the earlier poem proved to be a dream of divine love in this poem resolves into a loveless nightmare.

The Triumph of Love

In his vision poems Chaucer helped establish the pattern for English poets of the succeeding century and a half to emulate: the Dreamer who comes into conjunction with the Court of Love is an outsider, either ignorant of amorous concerns or else ignobly unsuccessful in suiting himself to courtesy and to love. He is mocked by the Court of Love or by its emissaries for being unsociable, in a word, *uncourteous*. The effect of his vision, however, is not to correct him so that he may enter into love but to teach him a lesson that makes him content with being an outsider. Chaucer's Dreamer, in short, is never meant to become a lover.

While Gower makes Amans a lover, he otherwise agrees with his contemporary that the path to wisdom lies outside the Court of Love. Amans desires admission into his Lady's heart and to Cupid's company, but reason and the grace of God prevail to rescue him from sin. In Gower's poem the moral adjudication against Cupid and Venus is made more explicitly and emphatically than it is in Chaucer's poems, but there is no ethical or aesthetic disagreement between the two poets. The function of poetry is to reveal proper choices through both content and form. For this reason both poets create figures who are, from beginning to end, excluded from the Court of Love.

Both Dunbar and Skelton use this basic situation, but they have a different center of emphasis. Their Dreamer is a man in danger, a victim of a rapacious court that actively tries to seize and destroy him, either physically or emotionally. Whereas Dunbar's Dreamer is captured in battle, Skelton's yields himself up voluntarily, so that there is a sharp distinction between their fates. Dunbar's Dreamer is only handed over to Hevynesse, while Skelton's is forced to leap overboard, in effect to commit suicide.

Implicit in all these poems is the idea that entering into any court is self-destructive. The individual maintains his integrity and his happiness only in contemplative isolation. In the final poem to be considered in this chapter, however, the poet arrives at the opposite conclusion: the lover in the anonymous poem *The Court of Love* secures his happiness by leaving contemplation and entering into the Court of Love, where he finds, woos, and wins his Lady. Perhaps more than any Greek names or mischievous handling of the "Rules of Love," this elevation of the active life marks the poem as belonging to the Renaissance. Derek Pearsall dates the poem at about 1535,[49] and C. S. Lewis suggests that the poem falls after the English Reformation, saying that the anticlerical passages may "suggest a Protestant dislike of celibacy."[50] The lover in the anonymous poem prefigures the Red Cross Knight in Spenser's *Book of Holiness* in choosing to be active; but unlike Spenser and his medieval predecessors the poet creates no sense of moral dilemma that is resolved by the choice. The choice is only incidental in the lover's progress toward success.

And here is a second distinction between *The Court of Love* and its medieval predecessors. This poem is jubilantly about success. Like *The Golden Targe* it begins with the lover as an outsider summoned into the court, and much is made of his potential for falling under the wrath of Cupid; nevertheless, the lover moves unscathed to an agreement with his Lady and a joyous celebration of the power of love. He seems a golden lad who will not come to dust, or a comet in the sky, tracing a path of glory across the desolation of other lovers. Where they have failed, he succeeds; and he succeeds because, unlike them, *he* breaks the rules. He is no servile follower of the old order but one who creates the new. As creator he is the ultimate realist, taking his opportunities where they lie and letting events work for his benefit, rather than rigidly insisting that

[49]Derek Pearsall, "The English Chaucerians," in Derek S. Brewer, ed., *Chaucer and Chaucerians: Critical Studies in Middle English Literature*, p. 229.

[50]Lewis, *The Allegory of Love*, p. 257.

only one way is right. He will not wake to desolation because he is in no dream.

This marks the third distinction between *The Court of Love* and earlier love poems: the absence of the dream convention. The poet does not tie his narrative to ordinary reality by saying that the experience is a dream; rather, he lets the impossible events themselves stand for reality. Within the poem he inverts the customary dream procedure. Whereas most lovers fall into a dream because they love in their waking life, this lover comes to the court because he earlier had a dream that prompts him to seek love. The entire poem, in fact, is an inversion of what usually takes place in the procedure of dreams and in the Court of Love. It is a holiday piece in which the servant of love becomes the lord.

There is a general agreement among critics that *The Court of Love* is not a "serious" love poem but a pastiche, in both senses of the word: that is, it is a thoroughgoing parody of the courtly convention at the same time that it is made up of bits and pieces taken from earlier poems in the convention. The poet mocks the love-vision genre by omitting some of its standard features, exaggerating others, and carefully draining the usual allegorical meanings out of still others. Thus there is no sense of identification between Venus and the Virgin, nor do the saints of love call to mind Christian saints. The definition of love is thoroughly secular, an end in itself. Much of the poem is made up of slyly constructed borrowings from other poems. The convulsive lament of the clerics is modeled upon a similar, apparently sincere, lament in Lydgate's *The Temple of Glas*,[51] and the "Rules of Love" derive from the rules in the *Roman de la Rose* and, ultimately, in Andreas Capellanus's *The Art of Courtly Love*.[52] In fact, the poet has read his sources well and caught their spirit thoroughly. Accordingly, he has created a poem that is filled with contradictions, implausible situations, ludicrous resolutions, tensions that dissipate into irrelevancies, and all capped with an anthem to love that admirably re-creates the essence of Goliardic verse.

By saying this, I do not mean that the poet is ridiculing a past age or satirizing the errors of its poetry. Rather, he is in the process of recognizing and capitalizing upon such qualities as narcissism and self-negation, which are inherent in the courtly convention, the same qualities we may

[51] William Allan Neilson, *The Origins and Sources of* The Court of Love, p. 239.

[52] See the standard English translation by J. J. Parry.

Laughter in the Courts of Love

assume Chaucer acknowledged in writing his palinode to *Troilus and Criseyde* and Gower in sending his lover a "softe pas" home. Instead of making recognition lead to rejection, however, this poet is content with merely revealing – even reveling in – what he recognizes. Thus he does not reject the Court of Love outright but simply circumvents it by creating a lover whose success reveals the court's ineffectuality.

In coming to the Court of Love, the remarkably enthusiastic and energetic lover, a clerk of Cambridge called Philogenet, provides a delightfully wry criticism of Andreas's rules for lovers. He has been summoned to court by Mercury, a fact that his friend Philobone fears will go hard with him. Although he is only eighteen (the earliest age that Andreas permits for a man to come to love), Philobone charges him with having squandered years in pampered and lustful jollity. His real duty, as she explains, is

> "To Loves Court to dressen your viage
> As sone as Nature maketh you so sage,
> That ye may know a woman from a swan." [53]

Later, for one tense moment, Philogenet's advanced years do cause trouble, when an inexplicably sighted Cupid beholds him and demands, "What doth this old, / Thus fer y-stope in yeres, come so late / Unto the court?" (lines 280–82). The tension, however, relaxes when Philogenet replies that he had not come earlier because none of his friends had, an unacceptable answer that is promptly accepted. Still another tense moment arises when the court officer, Rigour, discovers Philogenet leafing through the book of rules to look at the statutes for women. Rigour denounces him to the Queen as a traitor and tells him that no man, under pain of death, is permitted to know the pleasant liberties permitted women. Again, however, nothing comes of the tension or the denunciation.

Against Philogenet's enthusiasm for love, the Court of Love stands finally for nothing but inactive rigidity, an old society that has to give way before his insouciance. The clerk triumphs over the establishment because he is so thoroughly determined to love. He exceeds even the court's requirements in his emphatic denunciation of Diana – "a fig for all

[53]*The Court of Love*, in *Chaucerian and Other Pieces*, vol. 7 of *The Complete Works of Geoffrey Chaucer*, ed. Walter W. Skeat, lines 179–81. All subsequent references are incorporated in the text.

her chastitee!" – but he is no follower of rules, particularly those that exact a futile constancy. He would like to have his first love, the girl in the
dream that inspired him to come to the court, but even more he wants
freedom to operate realistically. So he prays to Venus (lines 663–65):

> ". . . if that other be my destinee,
> So that no wyse I shall her never see,
> Then graunt me her that best may lyken me."

This, as it turns out, is precisely the Lover's destiny. While declaring
his devotion to the dream, he meets the lady Rosiall, and he is hers,
swearing eternal love and beseeching pity upon his wounded heart.[54] In
his impassioned plea for her love he goes directly to the heart of the matter, disregarding such formalities as identifying himself or proving
through service that he is worthy to make the request. Here he is
perilously close to following Andreas's suggestion that a nobleman
should attempt to win a peasant woman through flattery alone.

Rosiall, however, is no peasant to be won by flattery. She rebuts his
statement that she ought to cherish him by pointing out that she does not
even know him. She curtly demands precise facts: "Let see, com of and
say!" With no little sarcasm she questions his intentions: "But what ye
mene to servë me I noot, / Sauf that ye say ye love me wonder hoot"
(lines 909–10). She refuses to fall for a line of "sugred eloquence,"
demanding that he behave with courtly propriety, and when he swoons
from passion, she awakens him with a sharpness reminiscent of
Chaucer's Eagle: "Aryse . . . what? have ye dronken dwale? / Why
slepen ye? it is no nightertale" (lines 998–99). But for all her sharpness,
Rosiall is no "daungerous" Lady in the presence of unruly love. Although
she can refuse a man who has spent twenty years in courtly service, she
quickly promises Philogenet that she will set his heart at ease.

The lover triumphs without trial, for he has been told by his friend
Philobone that the key to success is the appeal to pity.[55] The personifica-

---

[54]Lines 922–25, in which the lover says that he has loved the lady since he began to draw toward
the Court may be taken to imply that she is the girl in his dream; however, neither the pattern of action in the poem nor several careful readings of the text support this interpretation. It seems more
likely that the lover is employing flattery in the service of desire.

[55]William Allen Neilson's evaluation of Philobone is too delightful to omit: "Now Philobone is a
perfectly proper and a very friendly young woman, and it seems almost ungentlemanly to hint that
she may have low connections. Yet this matchmaking side of her character leads us to compare her

tion Pitè lies dead from the anguish of having seen an eagle kill a fly, but Philogenet resurrects her from the tomb by his pleading. In his address to Rosiall he makes eight different appeals to her pity, before he swoons from want of it. The climax of his address is a lament for himself that is modeled upon Dido's lament in *The House of Fame*, except that here it prefaces success, not suicide (lines 974–77):

> "In wofull hour I got was, welaway!
> In wofull hour {y-} fostred and y-fed,
> In wofull hour y-born, that I ne may
> My supplicacion swetely have y-sped!"

The result of his lament and swoon is what the lover wishes: he gets the Lady. His quest and the action of the poem are resolved by a miracle, the resurrection of pity that makes love real and so defies the function of the court.

The Court of Love itself is barren of both love and miracles. As created by the poet, it is an illogical and undefinable place, resplendently glamor-ous and yet incapable of acting except in negative ways to order, to threaten, to frighten, to reduce service in love to the endurance of futil-ity. The poet constructs the court out of places, personages, and rules drawn almost at random from the literature of love and stitched together with a cheerful disregard for their earlier allegorical significance. As a physical location where action occurs, the court lacks a clearly mapped geography, partly because the poet abandons midway his early distinc-tion between the Castle of Alceste and the Temple of Venus. The Lover and his friend move from building to building and from room to room, but all places finally merge into one place, an uncharted arena filled with longing, lamenting, and shrieking.

The population that provides the noise is a curious mixture of figures: famous lovers from myth and poetry, personifications of abstract qual-ities, and representatives of the clergy. Clearly an illogical gathering, this, and the poet makes the most of it, especially in dealing with the Church. Although Andreas says that clerics are permitted to love, in-deed make commendable lovers because of their skill in maintaining secrecy, not one of the churchmen in the court has ever loved. They cry

with the obnoxious figure of the procuress who plays so important a role in love-stories from the classics onwards." William Allen Neilson, *The Origins and Sources of* The Court of Love, p. 215.

and wring their hands and curse Fortune for having taken them so soon to religion when Nature had given them "instruments in store / And appetyt to love."[56] The nuns, whom Andreas excludes from loving, suffer worse, shrieking from pangs of love. Still another group excluded by Andreas is present and complaining—the blind and physically deformed, and beside them, in non sequitur, are the suicides who curse life. A series like this defies logic, as does the court itself.

The love that is legislated by the court is an emotion entirely different from the lover's, although he does not know it. Love here is governed entirely by the rules, twenty statutes sworn to by all men entering into love. The rules are designed to lead men into abject slavery and to turn love into woeful longing.

In creating his twenty rules, the poet makes explicit what D. W. Robertson, Jr., finds implicit in *The Art of Courtly Love*.[57] They are a gathering of contradictions and impossibilities that altogether invalidates the concept of rule. They demand the heart, soul, and body of the lover, while adjuring him to remember that the Lady is one thousand times better than he. He is expected to be both secretive in love and a zealous missionary for Venus; moreover, he must look for pretexts so that he can fight for his Lady's honor. He must go without sleep and shun company and still be alert, well dressed, and companionable. He must pay constant court to the Lady and yet "be not bold." It is the sixteenth statute, however, that gives pause to all lovers (lines 453–55):

> In all the court there was not, to my sight,
> A lover trew that he ne was adred,
> When he expresse hath herd the statut red.

This statute requires that the lover "please his Lady" seven times at night, seven more times at midnight, and yet seven more at morning. Out of this rule the poet makes a comic refrain. When Rosiall accepts Philogenet, he asks at once that the sixteenth statute be either modified or repealed. Among the personages in the court Avaunter reveals his boastfulness by swearing that *he* has kept the statute. The effect of this

---

[56]Philogenet is himself a clerk, but he apparently has no meaningful connection with the Church, since only Nature, not doctrine, kept him from love.

[57]Certainly this poem is historical evidence of how the concept of Courtly Love was received by at least one person far closer in time to Chaucer and Gower than Robertson.

repetition is to reduce all the rules to "the statute," guaranteed to frighten any man not a fool. The distinction between Philogenet's and Avaunter's responses to the rule is a comic, perforce moral, distinction between truth and falsehood, success and failure in love. Success, after all, *is* morality in this comedy, where morality consists of enthusiasm, energy, and adaptability, those qualities that preserve the lover from the pitfalls of the Court.

The narrow definition of morality provided by this poem arises from the fact that the poem is a parody. While its comedy is intentional, its allegorical form is purely incidental. The poet, after all, is capitalizing upon the provocations to laughter inherent in a convention, and allegory happened to be the mode of that convention. Vestiges of allegory remain in the presence of supernatural beings and personified abstractions, but these are used as parodic details and not as revelations of other meanings. Only in one instance, when Rosiall blushes, does the poem have allegorical vitality, suggesting not only her namesake, the Rose of the *Roman*, but also Christ, the Rose of Sharon, and, more abstractly, Charity, whose symbolic color is red. The convenant of the lovers is thus blessed by a momentary aura of holiness, but at heart it remains a secular union, an active mating that results from sexual drives.

Philogenet and Rosiall exist in an entirely different world from Gower's lover. This new world rejoices in the fallen life, exults in the sexual drive. Its ideals consist of practicality and action. Allegorically the world is threadbare; comically, a rich delight. In rejecting the Court of Love, we have moved from smiles and contentment to boisterous, even bawdy laughter. Whereas Gower celebrated God's grace, this poet celebrates man, laughable, lovable, and triumphant.

4.

The Pilgrimage of Love

OR THE MEDIEVAL allegorists the Court of Love was an established image that signified the importance of choices in life, but the dominant metaphor of the period was the figure of life as a journey. This figure came directly from their Judaeo-Christian heritage and was enhanced by their knowledge of pagan myth and poetry, particularly *The Aeneid*. Taken as literal history, the Bible provided a massive compilation of journeys: the Children of Israel went out of Egypt and to the Promised Land, Joseph and Mary went unto Bethlehem, Christ went into Jerusalem, and Paul traveled throughout the Roman world. Medieval man's spiritual and poetical forefathers lived a life that was literally a journey and was to be interpreted as a figurative journey as well.

As a device for objectifying human experience, the metaphor of the pilgrimage is present, to some extent, in virtually all allegorical poems, either as the narrative action or as the implied form of the interior movement of the spirit. *Confessio Amantis* may be described figuratively, for example, as the lover's pilgrimage from darkness to illumination, or from damnation to salvation, even though the poor lover does not rise from his knees until the very end, when he goes his "softe pas" home. Whether the journey is literal or implied, we expect it, because of its scriptural and epical associations, to end on a plane of spiritual or heroical significance, even though it may have been undertaken for a thoroughly secular reason.

When the allegorical pilgrimage is related to the Court of Love, however, the significance is often more ironic and puzzling than meaningful. The metaphor of the journey suggests that the poem will lead to ethical or theological revelations that have the power to transform the pilgrim and the world through which he passes. For all its reputed capriciousness, however, the Court of Love is essentially a rigid, inflexible image, impervious to the ministrations of grace. It may be either embraced or rejected, but it truly cannot be changed. Thus when the journey leads to or through the Court of Love, the revelations tend to be either so limited and commonplace that the journey seems pointless or so cosmically vast that they seem unrelated to the rest of the poem. At times the most striking quality of the late medieval pilgrimage narratives is their power to resist our best efforts to shrink, stretch, or otherwise shape them to our interpretative expectations. They are all more stubbornly secular, more surprisingly and explicitly Christian, narrower in focus, or broader in vision—more riddling (if we confess the truth) than we feel they have a right to be.

As he provided later poets with models for a moral presentation of the Court of Love, so Chaucer also established, in *The House of Fame* and *The Parliament of Fowls,* typical patterns for the allegorical pilgrimage. The Chaucerian dream journey is, above all, a literal journey in which the Dreamer moves through space, beyond the stars, and into a heaven where he expects to see the intellectual and moral significance of his quest enacted before his very eyes. Although the Dreamer's stated objective is "to learn something," this goal has actually been chosen for him by a higher power, as is explained by the always-condescending tutelary spirit who accompanies him. The pilgrim's need for the lesson is well illustrated by his initial behavior, which reveals him as baffled by information that does not fit his questions. The lesson, however, seems equally bewildering, for it begins with a premise or vision that is virtually cosmic in scope and then closes upon a center that is best described as eccentric. Thus the presence of Africanus in a vision poem that originates and concludes in a contemplation of sexual love provides a commentary upon misconceptions of love, but the structure of the poem implies also that human sexuality should play a central role in concepts of political and national honor.

In *The Parliament of Fowls,* as in *The House of Fame,* Chaucer seems to be moving towards the Boethian vision in which past, present, and future become the omnipresence of eternity and all apparent contrarieties are resolved in the omniscient vision of God. Chaucer, however, stops short of dissolving the detail and clutter of ordinary human life into the orderliness of the ideal. Rather than denigrating the one in order to elevate the other, he encompasses both in his comic vision, making the ideal seem as extreme as the errors that necessitate the corrective vision. In Chaucer's comedy man is not merely a fool to be scorned from ideal heights. Being merely human, after all, is a necessary stage on the road to being "merely" corrected, or being "merely" saved by divine love. Chaucer's pilgrimage, then, is a comic journey toward accepting the foibles of mankind.

The poems to be discussed in this chapter reveal how variously the later poets understood Chaucer's poetical pattern and translated it into their own allegorical pilgrimages. *The Palice of Honour*, by Gavin Douglas, is explicitly Chaucerian, modeled upon *The House of Fame*, with significant borrowings from *The Parliament of Fowls*. Like Chaucer's poems it is stubbornly secular in its literal and figurative levels, despite the vision of "ane God" that climaxes the Dreamer's pilgrimage. Because Stephen Hawes follows John Lydgate, who followed Chaucer, instead of following Chaucer directly, there is little that is definably Chaucerian in the spirit or structure of *The Pastime of Pleasure*, except that the poem follows the broad outlines of the pattern that Chaucer himself traced with such exuberance. Hawes plods along his pathway with the sober good sense of a man who works eight hours, sleeps eight hours, and takes eight hours for fun. He does seem to feel, however, that comedy is a requisite part of the journey, for he includes in his poem the interlude with a clown, Godfrey Gobylyve, a scene that exists chiefly for comic relief. *King Hart*, an anonymous account of a lifelong journey through the Court of Love, is neither Chaucerian nor a pilgrimage poem on the narative level, but it is too delightful an instance of comic allegory to omit from consideration here.

Love and Honour

The Palice of Honour is a brilliant and busy poem, one that does not wear well over a series of close readings. It is a virtuoso piece, executed with all the flourishes of a man demonstrating his mastery of the devices of poetry. What the poem lacks is any sense of subtlety; every theme, every image is presented forcefully, almost violently, until the reader begins to weary of such excitement and longs for a quieter tone. But if his poem is wearing, Douglas is never dull, and he provides many surprises in his allegory of love.

He begins his poem like a completely predictable love vision. The narrator enters a May garden, expresses his wonder at the scene, prays for instruction to worship Nature, May, and Venus properly, and then falls into a vision. The vision does not come upon him in a traditional manner, however, for he is virtually knocked off his feet and into a "feminine" dizziness by a blinding flash of light. This event introduces the Christian-allegorical motif that climaxes in the apocalyptic vision (the most troublesome layer of the allegory). It is a heavily ironic parallel to the conversion of Paul on the road to Damascus, for here the blinding light leads not to life but to death.

When he awakens, he is no longer in the garden but in a wilderness, whose features are too constant and too palpable to convince the reader that they belong to the world of dreams. Rather than stylizing the scene, Douglas particularizes it, stressing the unique grotesqueness of each detail—the "fisch yelland," the gnarled and tangled branches of the barren wood, and the rumbling, stinking river. These are not merely details of local color, however, but rather elements that establish the symbolic identity of the world by arousing in the Dreamer an implacable sense of fear and desolation. The scene is a wasteland on earth reported with a good measure of objective fidelity, but it is also clearly hell.[1]

In this nightmare wilderness the Dreamer is no longer an embryonic lover but a desperately frightened man who cowers beneath tangled branches and briars as a series of courtly processions go by—the Court of Sapience, the tiny Court of Chastity, and the multitudinous Court of Venus—moving with as much pomp and ceremony as if they were traversing the original May garden rather than the wilderness.

Douglas presents these processions through a mixture of allegorical styles, which is perhaps best illustrated by his treatment of the Court of Sapience. It is the traditional company of personified figures, "Laydis fair and gudlie men arrayit / In constant weid," who show their "hie

[1] C. S. Lewis, *The Allegory of Love*, pp. 290–91.

The Pilgrimage of Love

prudence" by "ryding furth with stabilnes ygroundit."[2] But following behind, as appendages to the court, are two shambling caitiffs, Achitophel and Sinon, who are not personifications of abstractions but "real" persons, one biblical and the other pagan, who have been turned into symbols by later interpreters. The beasts on which they ride are reminders of how these false counselors brought their listeners to destruction. Achitophel's ass is the ass that carried Absalom to his death under the trees, while Sinon's "hiddeous hors" is a wooden horse that helped reduce Troy to ashes.

Between his description of the court and the Dreamer's meeting with the rogues, Douglas shifts from personification allegory to symbolism and from tableau to drama. In a confessional speech Achitophel identifies himself and his comrade and defines the nature of their membership in the Court of Sapience. Both explain that, although they are forever excluded from entering the Palice of Honour, they nonetheless intend to get within sight of it. Their anticipation of the journey ("Our horsis oft . . . will founder") and their manner of departure (". . . thay raid away as thay war skarrit") are realistic details that Douglas uses in the service of both allegory and broad, farcical comedy. These details posit their complete alienation from dignity and beauty, the proper attributes of sapience; Achitophel and Sinon are the living symbols of reason abused.

With the coming of the Court of Venus, Douglas seems to return to his original identification of the Dreamer as a lover; but he uses the scene to introduce a new allegorical motif, the trial and love judgment, which is played for broadly farcical effects. The Dreamer insults Venus by singing a true song of unhappy love, and she orders him arrested and brought to her for judgment. Fearing that he will be transformed into a beast or a fowl, he crawls into court on all fours—thereby transforming himself—and then so mismanages his defense that he must finally challenge the legality of the entire proceedings to save himself. Venus, hardly a disinterested judge, talks like a fishwife, calling him "thow subtell smy," and demands his execution until finally she is persuaded that murder is not the best testimony to love's gentle power.

[2]Gavin Douglas, *The Palice of Honour*, in *The Shorter Poems of Gavin Douglas*, ed. Priscilla Bawcutt, Scottish Text Society, 4th series, no. 3, lines 202–10. All quotations are taken from the Edinburgh edition of 1579. Subsequent references are incorporated in the text.

Laughter in the Courts of Love

Providentially the Dreamer is saved by the arrival of a fourth procession, the Court of Rhetoric, whose sovereign powers agree to provide instruction and correction. At this point begins yet another pattern of allegory, the pilgrimage. With the Muses and all worthy poets of history the Dreamer travels over the face of the earth, pausing at the Castalian Font for refreshment and entertainment provided by Ovid, Virgil, and Terence, before finally ascending a marble mountain atop which is the Palice of Honour.

Like the rest of the poem, the heaven at which the Dreamer arrives is a mixed construction, containing the Garden of Venus, the Garden of Rhetoric, and the Court of the God of Judgment. Its location atop the marble slope is derived from Chaucer's mountain of ice in *The House of Fame*, but the sulfurous pit of punishment so near the court may well be taken from the underworld in Virgil's *Aeneid*, where Tartarus is adjacent to the Elysian fields.[3] In its composition Douglas's heaven is markedly secular. Those who enjoy the pleasures of the court are there because human—especially rhetorical—opinion has put them there. The God omnipotent resembles the God of the Scriptures in his power and blinding splendor, but he functions like a king of earthly state, and his location between Venus and the Garden of Rhetoric makes him seem only a superior consort to the personification of earthly values. The heaven itself is not very heavenly in its details (the Dreamer falls head first off a makeshift bridge into a stagnant pond), and its devotion to honor defines it as less than a scriptural paradise.

In this heaven the Dreamer has three visions, which are interpreted for him by the nymph whom the Muses assigned as his guardian and tutor. Douglas uses these visions and the nymph's explanation to climax the major lines of implication that are operative in the poem; and so they do, but only in a most negative sense. First the Dreamer looks back for a view of the earth, which he sees burning, beset by tempest, with even the ship of the state of grace wrecked by the storm of sin. Next he looks into Venus's mirror, where he sees enacted the entire history of the race of man, and finally he peers through a chink in the great castle door and sees "ane God omnipotent" seated in splendor

---

[3]Douglas's major work was his translation of the *Aeneid* into Scots, and it is probable that he was familiar with the poem before 1501, the date usually assigned to *The Palice of Honour*. Cf. Gavin Douglas, *Selections from Gavin Douglas*, ed. David F. C. Coldwell, pp. xx–xxi.

on his throne. A. C. Spearing has pointed out that Douglas provides three identities for his Dreamer: as would-be lover, as priest, and as poet;[4] and these three visions seem to correspond to each identification, but in a manner that intermingles and confuses them. The vision of the world, which logically should belong to his poetical office, refers also to his religious vocation. The mirror of Venus seems appropriate to his identity as lover, and the nymph asserts that the only thing to be seen in it is the face of the Lady he serves, but what the Dreamer actually has seen is the history of mankind (the subject of poetry). The vision of "ane God" pertains to his clerical identity, but it recalls also his trial before Venus. All three visions, moreover, are marked by an emphasis upon wickedness, delusion, death, judgment, torture, and execution.

The severity of Douglas's visions differs from the usual presentation of the *contemptus mundi* theme in love visions, and the note of terror struck here is more genuine than all the fearful tremblings endured by the Dreamer elsewhere. The vision of God is the definitive statement of the spiritual pilgrimage that parallels the physical journey. Douglas prepares the way for this vision midway into the poem when, in praising God, he implies His supremacy over all other forces in the narrative (lines 775-79):

> He that quhilk is eternall veritie,
> The glorious Lord, ringand in persounis thre,
> Prouydit hes for my saluatioun,
> Be sum gude spreitis Reuelatioun,
> Quhilk Intercessioun maid (I traist) for me.

The sequence of the three visions reiterates the primacy of Christ and the urgency for man to set his spiritual course aright; the one thing man needs is not sexuality, not rhetoric, not honor, but an unsullied faith in the grace of God. The poet now speaks out of scriptural rather than rhetorical authority to provide a map of the pilgrimage man *ought* to make, set in contrast to the false paths he does take.

But because the paradise of Honour stands as the destination of the narrative action, the apocalyptic vision lies outside the general movement of the poem. It is not to be fitted into a secular world but to provide

[4]A. C. Spearing, *Medieval Dream-Poetry*, pp. 206-207.

a judgment of that world, reminding man that trust in earthly values leads to eternal death. Although honor is distinguished from earthly glory, which accrues to living man because of his wealth, power, or ancestry, it is nevertheless a terrestrial recognition of virtue, which here is defined chiefly as patriotism and valor in warfare. The great good in the paradise of Honour arises out of human rather than divine vision. The limitations of this version of heaven are made evident through the Dreamer's response upon waking. More than rejoicing in what he has learned, he regrets that he missed seeing the tortures meted out to the wretches "That Honour mankit and honestie mischeuit." What the Dreamer gains from his pilgrimage is only half a lesson, half a vision, half a truth. Despite his marvelous adventure, he is untouched by experience, still cursing his fate, lamenting his losses, and quaking with fear at whatever befalls him. Ineducable and unchangeable, he is not so much the pilgrim of an allegorical quest as the comic bumbler in a farcical misadventure.

Douglas follows Chaucer's lead in *The House of Fame* by creating his dream persona as a comic figure, but whereas Chaucer treats "Geffrey" with ironic detachment, Douglas mocks his Dreamer with heavy-handed exaggeration. Greffrey is naturally frightened by unnatural circumstances but able to relax once he has acclimated himself. Douglas's Dreamer is incapable of acclimation, and so he quakes and shivers at every occurrence until he trembles himself off the heavenly foot-log and into wakefulness. The nymph who escorts him on his journey treats him with much the same contempt that Chaucer's Eagle feels for Geffrey and once, like Africanus in *The Parliament of Fowls*, shoves him through a doorway and into the Court of God. She is, however, more shrewish than self-confident, more nagging than tutorial, until finally she provokes him to an outburst of temper. The Dreamer's one show of bravery, his challenge of the nymph, is ludicrous but is redeemed from seeming contemptible by the reader's sense that she richly deserves it.

The conflict between the Dreamer and his guardian climaxes a comic motif that is part and parcel of the allegorical theme of sexual love that generated the vision and the journey. The Dreamer falls into the vision because he wishes to serve Venus, but once in the world of love he discovers that sexual attraction also involves sexual differences. What began as a movement toward courteous love modulates into a war be-

The Pilgrimage of Love

tween the sexes. The great battle of this war, the trial scene, reaches its highest pitch when the man argues that a woman may not sit as judge. This said, he subsides into his customary trembling and tacitly admits Venus's victory. That his rescue is accomplished by another woman, the Muse Calliope, brings him relief but no honor, and his assignment to the sharp-tongued nymph is more punishment than pleasure. But while the narrative events of the poem reveal the female as triumphant, the hellish wasteland and the debased heaven suggest that her victory is the root of man's misery. The comic motif that usually implies sexual equality is thus subverted to a symbolic expression of woman's spiritual inferiority, and the cowardly man serves well in the cause of antifeminist sentiment.

The action of the comedy is essentially farcical, in the etymological sense of being stuffed with ludicrous gestures. The Dreamer is stripped of all physical dignity. We see him up a tree, then crawling on all fours, next shaking with fear, then in a dead faint, and finally falling square on his head in the pool. The nymph seems amazonian, lifting him by his hair, dragging him behind her, and carrying him in her arms when he faints. Conduct even in the heaven is rough-and-tumble, with inmates busily batting down those who would break in unbidden, through windows and over walls. In short, there is no dignity in *The Palice of Honour*.

Stylistically, too, the poem is stuffed—with the devices of comedy. Like Chaucer, Douglas is a master at modulating from formal seriousness into parody. In his hand the disability topos, in which the poet laments his inadequacy to treat a subject, becomes an enthusiastic listing of the poet's outstanding weaknesses, intoned with oratorical thunder (lines 127–35):

> Thow barrant wit ouirset with fantasyis,
> Schaw now the craft that in thy memor lyis,
> Schaw now thy schame, schaw now thy bad nystie,
> Schaw thy endite, reprufe of Rethoryis,
> Schaw now thy beggit termis mair than thryis,
> Schaw now thy rymis, and thine harlotrie,
> Schaw now thy dull exhaust Inanitie,
> Schaw furth thy cure and write thir frenesyis
> Quhilks of thy sempill cunning nakit the.

Douglas also makes considerable use of staccato lines of chiefly monosyllabic words in which the sound virtually drowns out the sense. Occasionally the line is a redundant series that resolves to a hyperbolic stutter: "I weip, I waill, I plene, I cry, I pleid." More frequently it takes the form of a compulsive catalogue, suggesting that the speaker is helpless before his urge to name every possible modification of his subject. Thus, in a lament to Fortune, the Dreamer dwindles into minute distinctions in the movement of the "quheill contrarious" (lines 174–78):

> Now thair, now heir, now hie and now deuaillis,
> Now to, now fra, now law, now Magnifyis,
> Now hait, now cald, now lauchis, now beuaillis,
> Now seik, now haill, now werie, now not aillis,
> Now gude, now euill, now weitis, and now dryis.

Yet another device of comic style is the sudden wrenching of attention from one level of reference to another. This Douglas employs when he introduces his concluding ballade, in which he commends virtue and honor (lines 2114–15):

> Till mak ane end, sittand under a tre,
> In laude of honour I wrait thir versis thre.

In place of an earnest preface he gives a description of his physical posture during the act of composition. The effect of this is to suggest that he is having one last joke at the concept of himself as a visionary pilgrim.

Through style, action, and characterization Douglas creates a vision of honor that invites laughter, as though he meant to mock the concept of honor. This certainly is not his intention, though the poem is so elaborately overwrought that it is difficult to know precisely what Douglas meant.[5] From his inclusion of the very serious apocalyptic vision it may be safely concluded that comedy is identified with the opposite of God, that it expresses man's inclination to follow the path to destruction. By no means, however, does Douglas equate honor with destruction, nor does he mock it. What the poem laughs at is man's pursuit of honor; the comedy cautions against setting it as the highest good in a world made by God. The apocalyptic vision implies the necessity of holding onto the true faith as one makes his pilgrimage toward ultimate good. The poem

[5]Priscilla Preston, Notes for *The Palice of Honour*, in Douglas, *Selections from Gavin Douglas*, p. 138.

The Pilgrimage of Love

finally resolves into a double vision: one of Good, expressed with somber urgency, and the other of Ill, ridiculed, mocked, deflated by hyperbole. For Douglas, comic technique becomes the means of revealing error, while comic vision is his recognition that error must be corrected. Beyond comedy—that is, beyond the life of man—is the final vision of man's destiny, the end of his pilgrimage.

The Perils of Pleasure

Whereas the journey toward revelation in the *Palice of Honour* evolves out of a rejection of the love governed by Venus, the pilgrimage of *The Pastime of Pleasure* is always a movement into that love. Unlike Douglas and Dunbar, who view the Court of Love as the embodiment of a predatory force, searching out man to destroy him, Stephen Hawes makes his dreamer a man who chooses freely to love and then acts upon his choice. In this sense Graunde Amoure is more akin to Amans in *Confessio Amantis* than to other dreamers of Hawes's own era, while at the same time he foreshadows Spenser's pilgrim-knights in his election of the active life with its implication that the triumph of love is in itself a desirable good.

In his final view of the doctrine of love, however, Hawes agrees with his contemporaries rather than Spenser and so rejects it, but in his method of rejection he follows the practice of Gower and "dear master Lydgate." As for Gower, so for Hawes, the flaw lies not in the Court of Love but in the pilgrim himself, and not in his being subject to instinct but in his being free to choose—more precisely, in his manner of exercising that freedom. At the end of his journey, Graunde Amoure discovers his error made in the beginning: he has put his faith in the corruptible and transitory. But unlike Douglas's pilgrim, he is given no second chance to emend the first. His pilgrimage has lasted not for just a single adventure but for an entire existence.

The pilgrimage that Graunde Amoure undertakes is remarkable for its directness and its freedom from opposition or digression. It originates in a May garden, the familiar dream locus, and comes to rest on an island paradise, which the nearly godlike hero has reached without misadven-ture. The pathway between the two is a straight line marked by occasional castles that provide the direction and encouragement needed to keep the lover moving forward.

For much of the poem Hawes seems to suggest that the pilgrimage occupies only that phase of the lover's history which the lover himself sees woven into an arras in the Tower of Doctrine. The narrative provided by the arras begins in the dream garden, where Graunde Amoure finds a fair path that brings him to a fork in the road. After some indecision he elects the path leading to Beauty and La Bell Pucell. Fame appears, urging him onward, and leaves with him two greyhounds, Grace and Governaunce. In their company he goes to the Tower of Doctrine, where, besides being instructed in the seven liberal arts, he meets and wins the provisional approval of La Bell Pucell. She, however, leaves immediately by ship to return to her island, while he follows after her on land. To reach her he passes through the Tower of Chivalry, where he is knighted; the Temple of Venus; and the Tower of Chastity. After slaying two giants, he enters the Temple of Pallas to pray for victory over his last foe, the dragon. Victory is granted and is achieved, and so he enters into the court of La Bell Pucell, there to marry her in joyous ceremony.

This is the shape of the pilgrimage that Graunde Amoure believes he has undertaken, but Hawes presents the journey as being more extensive. It goes literally beyond the grave and into eternity. Graunde Amoure lives happily until Age accosts him; then he gives himself over to avarice until Death with his dart arrests him. In a final act of contrition he gives his goods to the Church and receives final absolution. His body is laid in earth; his soul goes to Purgatory. Carved upon his tombstone is a "lytell epytaphy" that enumerates the seven deadly sins and laments the flesh's subjection to them. Fame returns, promising to spread his reputation, but Breuyacyon (Time) interrupts her, and then Eternyte arrives to declare that she is the true destination of man's pilgrimage, whether in heaven or in hell.

The modulation from love quest to spiritual pilgrimage occurs near the end of the poem, after the original quest has ended, but it has been implicit from the beginning, expressed through traditional symbols of good and evil. The fork at which Graunde Amoure makes his decision signifies the value of that choice: the right-hand (superior) road leads to Contemplation; the left, to Beauty and La Bell Pucell. The choice is between two modes of existence, and the lover elects "The actyfe waye / with all my hole entent."[6] Having chosen a lesser good, he is driven toward it by a single motivation, passion. He so burns with desire "moost hote and feruent" to see and possess the beautiful Lady that he undertakes the perilous pathway to her, never realizing that the peril dwells within his soul and so cannot be overcome by the mere slaying of giants and dragons. His discovery in death is that he fell victim to himself. Thus the pilgrimage as a literal adventure tells a story of success; as a metaphor for the life of man, it relates a narrow escape from eternal failure.

Between Douglas's and Hawes's use of the pilgrimage as structural metaphor, there are several illuminative comparisons to be drawn. To begin with, Douglas's journey occupies only the second half of his poem, and it springs from an essentially rhetorical inspiration (it is an allegorical analysis of the nature of poetry). In the company of Muses the Dreamer-poet traverses all the known world, touching especially on those places made famous through poetry, myth, and cultural tradition, and he awakens as he is trying to enter the heavenly Garden of Rhetoric. Graunde Amoure's journey is the totality of his experience, taking him beyond life and into Purgatory. The pilgrimage moves always over an interior landscape, the mind and feelings of the hero as he establishes himself as Complete Courtier and Man of the World. The terrain, the towers, the dungeons, and the persons he encounters are all personifications of the training program he follows in order to become a success. Whereas Douglas takes the actual world and makes it a symbol of the scope of poetical creativity, Hawes begins in a consciously poetical, hence unreal, world and makes it an analogy not only to the inner life of the pilgrim but also to the external pattern of progress expected by society. Following this pattern, Graunde Amoure goes to school, then trains for a profession, next proves himself on the job, and at last wins the hand of the fair young maiden who has postponed his suit until he established himself in grace with fortune and men's eyes.[7] Douglas's journey has the attraction of brilliant virtuosity; Hawes's is more plodding but also is

[6]Stephen Hawes, *The Pastime of Pleasure*, ed. William Edward Mead, Early English Text Society, o.s., vol. 173, line 112. Subsequent references are incorporated in the text.

[7]C. S. Lewis points out there is a "homely," even "Victorian," quality to Hawes's treatment of love as leading necessarily to marriage through socially sanctioned channels. Lewis, *The Allegory of Love*, p. 282.

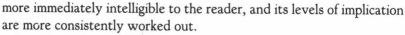

more immediately intelligible to the reader, and its levels of implication are more consistently worked out.

Second, the poets differ sharply in their use of comedy. Douglas shapes his journey to fit his comic intentions by focusing always upon the ineffectual pilgrim and ending with the anticlimactic fall into the "stank." All that is marvelous is also somehow ridiculous because of the Dreamer's inability to cope with the supernatural. Hawes attunes his pilgrimage to a note of steady sobriety, for he is dealing with probabilities of the soul and not patent impossibilities. His serious tone tells us that one may, in all goodness and sincerity, undertake, succeed, and be damned in a course of error. His purpose is to reveal this possibility through the allegorical narrative and to warn against it by direct preachment provided in the posthumous experience of the lover. In Hawes's poem comedy is not a shaping force but an interlude that provides relief from the general gravity of his analysis. Thus the comic passages in the poem are carefully separated from the mainstream of action and involve the hero only as onlooker. For this reason the comedy seems to be genuinely irrelevant. Not until the conclusion of the poem does its significance become evident; then, upon looking back, the reader sees that Hawes used it to provide an alternate perspective on the pilgrim's progress, standing in contrast to the approbation with which the lover is so generally greeted and so completely misled. The passages function as a moral guard against taking the narrative as representing truth. Hawes seems to agree with Douglas that a poem must have a passage that provides a corrective vision, but his technique is directly opposite that employed by the Scot. Where Douglas uses the seriousness of the apocalyptic vision to reveal true values in his upside-down comic world, Hawes uses comedy to call into question the values celebrated in his heroic narrative.

This interpretation of his comedy is supplied by hindsight, however, for when the comic passage occurs, it seems to underline the courtesy of Graunde Amoure and to emphasize the propriety of his conduct.

In truth, Hawes's concept of comedy seems rigidly limited to one kind of action only: a refractory mocking that is ended by drastic punishment. Ernst Robert Curtius points out that this pattern was frequently used in medieval saints' lives, where the mockery had the effect of blasphemy.[8]

[8]Ernst Robert Curtius, *European Literature and the Latin Middle Ages*, trans. Willard R. Trask, p. 428.

The Pilgrimage of Love

So too in *The Pastime of Pleasure*, where the fool's indecency makes the hero seem saintly. Hawes intends to be entertaining, but he serves up a scarcely palatable pottage of physical ugliness and spiritual doltishness in the figure of Godfrey Gobylyve. Godfrey is a professional fool, a "folysshe dwarfe" with a hood, bell, foxtail, and bag, the emblems of his occupation;[9] but Hawes turns him into a buffoon, literally one who *is* fooled. The formal entertainment that Godfrey offers is two fabliaux that center upon the undignified behavior caused by love and climax in cruel practical jokes. Love-besotted Aristotle lets a woman ride him publicly for a horse; an equally drunken Virgil is hung in a basket by his Lady but repays her by lodging a blazing coal in her nether parts and sending the citizens to light candles thereat. Godfrey is more pleasantly entertaining, though no less doltish, when he devotes himself to parody of courtly manners. In identifying himself, he mocks the traditional respect paid to noble ancestry; his noble sires are Peter Prate Fast, Sym Sadle Gander, and Davy Dronken Nole. At the Court of Venus he burlesques the love judgment by describing a witch and demanding to be told that she is uglier than he. When last he is seen, imprisoned in the dungeons of Correction and scourged for being "False Report," he is suffering the fate of all blasphemous mockers. Aesthetically, his punishment seems entirely justified, for his entertainment, like himself, has been dwarfish and ugly.

Hawes is not devoid of a modest comic talent, despite the deficiencies of Godfrey Gobylyve, but he does seem incapable of distinguishing between comedy and what his source books must have identified for him as comedy. At least twice before the Godfrey interlude he verges upon comedy, but the blunting of these passages, coupled with the clear example of Godfrey, suggests that he stumbled toward comedy without really knowing it. When he has Graunde Amoure's pandering friend Counseyle compare the lover to Troilus and Priam, Hawes strikes a vein of irony that is left unmined, possibly because he meant these comparisons to be seriously heroic.

Again, in relating an argument between Mars and Fortune, Hawes sets in motion a vigorous comic action but abandons it halfway, as soon as he has fulfilled his plan to provide information for the moral allegory. The argument takes place atop the wheel of Fortune located in the Temple of Mars, adjacent to the Tower of Chivalry. As one of the secular

[9]Enid Welsford, *The Fool: His Social and Literary History*, p. 123.

Laughter in the Courts of Love

forces propelling the lover forward, Mars promises him victory in his forthcoming battles. Fortune interrupts sharply, "Aha!" and accuses Mars of presumptuousness. She is his superior, she claims, ordained by the high God to keep the world unstable so that man will not trust in himself alone. Her motivation, however, is not to define God's working in the world but to arrogate divinity unto herself, and so, she concludes, Graunde Amoure "must pray to me." Now Mars says "Aha!" with bellicose force, accusing her of claiming divine powers when in reality she is nothing but a figure made up by poets to express how man creates his own welfare. If man were to pray to her, he would but pray to himself.

The course is clearly marked: the divine forces are on a banana-peel slide from godliness to mindless brawling; but Graunde Amoure, sorely amazed, turns away to his nobler interests. The comic pattern is visible in the fragment, but Hawes's treatment of the scene indicates that he is either unaware of or else uninterested in comedy here. His development is governed by his ideological scheme of providing a definition of the role that Fortune plays in any human pilgrimage. That done, he returns his attention to the lover's progress and so leaves the potential comedy perpetually paralyzed, forever unfulfilled.

The Pastime of Pleasure differs from all other poems in this study in that the hero is not a comic figure. Hawes presents Graunde Amoure with consistent sympathy, something like the Creator's love of man that springs from his awareness of man's fallibility. Hawes stresses that his hero is not only liked but *well liked* by the powers that it pays to have on one's side. He is, from the beginning, assured and reassured of success at frequent enough intervals to remove any suspense from his perilous trials. Upon departing from the garden of innocence and choosing the path of Beauty and La Bell Pucell, he is greeted by Fame, who tells him how to win the Lady. When he arrives at the Tower of Doctrine, he reads on the arras the prophecy of his quest, and he is thereafter prom-ised success or assistance to success by such figures as Mars, Venus, and Pallas, as well as the ladies who come from La Bell Pucell to attend him unto her. In accordance with their prophecies he proves himself an apt student, a competent knight, and a successful lover and husband. Hawes's gentle treatment of the lover arises, however, not from admira-tion at his achievements but from sorrow over his error. The poem expresses a profound pity for the man whose devotion to earthly glory teaches him to love only earthly things and thereby earns a rebuke from Eternyte (lines 5780–81):

> "Set not your mynde upon worldly welthe
> But euermore regarde your soules helthe."

By repenting before his death, the pilgrim has made sure that after purgation his soul will enter heaven, but he has irrevocably wasted his life. The seriousness of his error is reflected by Hawes's treatment of him and his journey. Out of the character of the pilgrim arise the several figurative lines of narrative that enlarge the scope of the poem from personal to universal significance. Literally, he is the hero of a romance, the knight on a quest that requires him to undergo self-examination and correction and to slay giants and dragons before he can enter into his destined paradise. His quest differs from the usual knightly adventure, however, in that it is not designed for anyone else's benefit. He is indulging his own desires by undertaking the perilous adventure, and it is he himself who is gratified by it.

On an equally important narrative plane, he is the Lover in search of the Rose, here represented by La Bell Pucell–literally, the beautiful statue.[10] When he first sees her in the chamber of Music (at the Tower of Doctrine), he is enthralled by love and despair alike, until finally he meets her at a fountain in a garden at sunrise. Their interview is as patterned and slow as a minuet, he pleading and she refusing until pity intervenes and grants him her assent. Even then their love is not consummated, for she retreats and lets Disdain and Strangeness discourage her from loving him. He follows after her, sore of heart, lamenting his estate at every feasible opportunity, and overcoming all obstacles until she admits him into her court, where they are wed by *Lex Ecclesie*.

The perils that he faces enroute to his Lady are traditional emblems of evil, giants and dragons, but each wears banners that identify it as being no universal evil but only an emotional difficulty between lovers. As a result, the knightly quest seems to function like a "clowdy figure cloking the trouthe" of the love story that motivates the quest. Of this double

---

[10]Frédéric Godefroy, ed., *Dictionnaire de L'ancienne langue français*, vol. 6. To be precise, *une pucelle is "Un grand mannequin en métal, représentant une jeune fille des mamelles de laquelle coulaient deux jets de vin."*

narrative, which so often stumbles and overlaps itself, C. S. Lewis provides a provocative explanation:

> ...Hawes, stumblingly and half-consciously is trying to write a new kind of poem. He himself believes that he is trying to revive an old kind...[But] the combination of allegory on the large scale and chivalrous romance which Hawes wants to revive, could not be revived because it had not existed.[11]

As a result, Lewis continues, Hawes moves about in the darkness of worlds not yet realized. He has neither the verbal facility nor the narrative inventiveness to let the knightly quest run freely, nor can he be at ease with the love story. His basic intention, to prove the error of the lover's choice, seems to nag at him always, making him scant art in favor of doctrine.

In the moral allegory of the poem Graunde Amoure is the student – the philosopher-king – learning all that he can about order, propriety, and harmony as they exist in ideal worlds. In the Tower of Doctrine, he is taught by the seven sciences, the trivium and quadrivium of medieval education, that all knowledge is morality. Dame Grammar welcomes him into her chambers to tell him that verb tenses exist to remind man of the brevity of existence ("all that is / shall be tourned to was," line 560), while the function of the "nowne substantyue" is to name accurately all the phenomena of existence. Out of the word, she concludes, the world was made: "The hye kynge sayde / it was made incontynent" (line 604). Dame Logic assures him that the utility of her science is learning "to deuyde the good / and the euyll a sondre" (line 632). From Rhetoric, in an extremely detailed and tedious interview, he learns that the study of rhetoric enables a poet to write fables that teach truths. In the chamber of Geometry he learns that geometry is the science of measure, or, to be more precise, of moderation and temperance, the basic rule of conduct in an ethical world. Astronomy teaches him the moral orderliness of God's world, laying particular stress upon man's intelligence, which enables

---

[11]Lewis, *The Allegory of Love*, p. 279. John N. King appears to agree with Lewis, noting that the poem gains in poetical power and quality in the final scenes when Hawes abandons the medieval pilgrimage pattern and points forward to the Renaissance allegorical pattern of the "emblematic pageant." See John N. King, "Allegorical Patterns in Stephen Hawes's *The Pastime of Pleasure*," *SLitI* 11 (1978):57–67.

him to perceive, estimate, and bring into balance his knowledge of the world.

Of this journey through the seven liberal arts it is difficult to be tolerant, let alone enthusiastic. Hawes provides some small variety by giving Arithmetic short shrift and interrupting Music with the full ac-count of the meeting and parting of the lovers, but he yields to an impulse to dilate the role of those sciences that interest him, while at the same time he is intent upon stating the precise moral utility of them all. He has, Angus Fletcher comments, entered upon a structural scheme that demands being completed, no matter how dull the product may be.[12]

Other passages devoted to didacticism and morality manage to be more dramatically educational—for example, the argument between Mars and Fortune or the hero's epitaph, which becomes a figurative pro-cession of the seven deadly sins to whom man gives hostel. Even God-frey Gobylyve serves a moral end, for he provides a direct, if ill-spirited, criticism of Graunde Amoure's pilgrimage. Despite seeming almost sacri-legious at the time, his mockery of love proves a truer vision than the hero's. His function in the poem may be aptly summed up by Northrop Frye's theory that the dwarf in romance represents "the shrunken and wizened form of practical waking reality."[13] It is against this reality, against morality at last, that the pilgrim is judged. At the end of his journey he learns that he has been ignorant, and therefore immoral, in failing to despise "The bryttle worlde so full of doublenes / With the vyle flesshe" (lines 5489–90).

As regards the specifically Christian level of allegory, Graunde Amoure is designated as the Christian knight, dressed in the whole ar-mor of God and trying to do battle against the sins of the world. After he has completed his training in the Tower of Chivalry and has been knighted by King Melyzyus, he is dressed in proper attire (lines 3375–81):

> For fyrst good hope his legge harneys sholde be
> His habergyon of perfyte ryghtwysnes

[12]Angus Fletcher, *Allegory: The Theory of a Symbolic Mode*, p. 84.

[13]Northrop Frye, *Anatomy of Criticism: Four Essays*, p. 197. O. M. Freidenberg suggests, however, that the figure of the jester is a parody of the hero, arising from the "idea of a double of the hero himself." O. M. Freidenberg, "The Origin of Parody," in *Semiotics and Structuralism: Readings from the Soviet Union*, ed. Henryk Baran, p. 278.

Laughter in the Courts of Love

> Gyrde fast with the gyrdle of chastyte
> His ryche placarde sholde be good besynes
> Braudred with almes so full of larges
> The helmet mekenes / and the shelde good fayth
> His swerde goddes wordes as saynt Poule sayth.

So outfitted, he belongs to the tradition of Sir Gawain with his Pentangle shield, while he particularly presages Spenser's Red Cross Knight. (Hawes is traditionally listed as one of the primary English influences on Spenser, and certainly he was, although essentially as suggesting things that a great poet could do better and not in the sense of a master leading his pupil). Hawes stresses also the role that Christian tradition plays in his knight's quest: he meets the Lady at Pentecost; they are wed by *Lex Ecclesie*. Graunde Amoure seems to spend his life in properly Christian pursuits, but in his death he recognizes how badly he has failed the Christian ideal. Although his soul goes to Purgatory, he laments the expense of spirit that results from not having chosen the pathway to Contemplation.

Ultimately Graunde Amoure is a redeemed man, destined to be a resident of the New Jerusalem, but there is so strong a denunciation of the misspent life that the concluding note is more hellish than joyous. Running from the report of the epitaph through the speech of Eternyte, there is so heavy an emphasis upon sin and loss that it takes a conscious effort to recall that the soul is being purified for entry into Paradise. What Hawes does in the conclusion is reject the secular life as a valid alternative to the religious, for it leads only to debasement of the spirit. Out of this conviction he ends his poem with a prayer (lines 5789–95):

> Now blyssed lady of the helthe eternall
> The quene of comforte and of heuenly glorye
> Pray to thy swete sone / which is infynall
> To gyue me grace to wynne the vyctory
> Of the deuyll / the worlde and of my body
> And that I may my selfe well apply
> Thy sone and the to laude and magnyfy.

By critical consensus Hawes's use of allegory has been termed "old-fashioned" or "thoroughly medieval." Such phrases are generally meaningless, except that they imply a value judgment of bad or dull. There is much about the poem that is dull, and occasionally some passages are downright bad, especially the inset lyrics praising measure ("Mesure / mesurynge / mesuratly taketh") and lamenting pain in love ("Wo worthe my loue"), which indicate that Hawes understood lyricism to be repetitious chanting. The weakness of the poem must be ascribed, however, not to "medievalism" nor to medieval allegory nor even to the pernicious theory that allegory was dead by the time Hawes wrote, but finally to the limitations of Hawes's poetic faculties. Hawes's allegory is not so much dead as it is weakly and mechanically realized. C. S. Lewis has advanced the theory that Hawes completely misunderstood the medieval practice of allegory: whereas the medieval poet used allegory to give voice to the speechless and body to the impalpable – to reveal – Hawes defines it as a process of cloaking truth with cloudy figures.[14] Lewis interprets Hawes's intention as being the reverse of traditional procedure, but Lewis errs by setting the two in opposition. In using the simile of the cloak, Hawes is concerned with neither revealing or concealing; what he does is justify the use of fiction by describing it as the outer covering of a moral lesson. Like the medieval poets he is providing both fruit and chaff in order to entertain and instruct his audience at the same time.

Providing the fruit of instruction is indisputably his primary interest, while the narrative exists fundamentally to exemplify what he is teaching. It is the moral lesson that links the Court of Love and the knightly quest so tightly together; it is the lesson that carries the pilgrim beyond the wedding and into Purgatory. It is the metaphor of the pilgrimage, however, that ties the units together and gives shape to the Christian argument of renunciation and purification. Among the happier choices that Hawes made in creating his poem, the best was his selection of the pilgrimage to represent the social and spiritual progress of the Dreamer.

* * *

The position of *King Hart* in this chapter is essentially that of a tailpiece that provides a commentary perhaps more decorative than useful upon preceding matters. As regards the allegorical pilgrimage, the poem can be considered only as providing an alternative understanding of how the

[14]Lewis, *The Allegory of Love*, p. 280.

metaphor works. In this poem there is no actual journey to an intended destination, nor does the hero ever consciously set a goal for himself to reach. Also, it should be noted, *King Hart* is not set in the form of a dream vision.

The relationship of *King Hart* to the allegorical pilgrimage is established by the relationship of the reader to the poem: the metaphor of the pilgrimage here is chiefly a critical term, useful for describing the progression that the poem narrates. To be sure, there is a going out upon a mission and a return, which frames the hero's adventures, but this is not the action that the word *pilgrimage* describes. The true pilgrimage of the poem is the hero's progress from youth to age and his final coming to selfknowledge, which is achieved through the slow and painful atrophy of his body. The journey moves along two levels of reality, the physical and the spiritual, to a corrected moral vision that enables the hero to see clearly what his life has been and to make a final judgment against the squandering of spirit that marked his youth and manhood.

The poem falls naturally into two parts that narrate the drama of King Hart as it is played out upon the stages of youth and age. In his youth Hart is a handsome and jolly king in a noble castle, whose only desire is to dwell forever under the wing of wantonness. He is "nocht at fredome utterlie," for he is guided and governed by such wardens as "Strenth, Rage, Grein Lust, Wantwyt, and Dyme Sicht."[15] All live together merrily, however, depending upon five noble servants to espy and warn them of danger. Within the castle they carouse, oblivious of the noise of splashing waters in the malodorous moat surrounding them.

The King's merrymaking does not go forever uninterrupted, however. Dwelling nearby is the beautiful Dame Plesance, whose behavior provokes the five servants into reporting her to Hart. Immediately he sends men out after her, who only permit themselves to be captured; then he sends out others, who are defeated in battle. Finally the King himself

---

[15]*King Hart*, in *The Shorter Poems of Gavin Douglas*, ed. Priscilla Bawcutt, lines 25-32. All subsequent references are incorporated in the text. Despite the traditional attribution of this poem to Douglas, based on an inscription in the Maitland manuscript, critics are now generally agreed that the poem is not by Douglas. Cf. Priscilla Preston, "Did Gavin Douglas Write *King Hart*?" *MÆ* 28 (1959): 31-47; and Florence H. Ridley, "Did Gawin Douglas Write *King Hart*?" *Speculum 34* (1959):402-12. The poem bears little stylistic resemblance to *The Palice of Honour;* moreover, its vocabulary cannot be checked against a glossary to the poems that are definitely known to be by Douglas.

goes and falls victim to the Lady. He is bound and locked in her dungeons, suffering from a wound that will not heal. So long as her servant Danger guards the keep, Hart has no hope of release, but eventually Fayr Calling, another of the Lady's servants, drugs Danger and brings Pietie to release the King. He rushes forth and accosts the Lady in her bedchamber, where, after an initial show of fear, she consents to accept him as her lover. The first half of the poem concludes with all going to a celebratory feast.

The second half opens with the report that the King has lived in Dame Plesance's castle for seven years when an old man knocks at the gate for admission: he is Age. Wantownness keeps him out, but Youth steals away, leaving his cloak behind as a disguise for Delyte. By ones and twos all the King's attendants depart from him as the old men—Age, Conscience, Ressoun, and Wit—come inside the gates. Hart pretends to welcome them, all the while secretly assuring Plesance that he does so hypocritically, for it is she alone that he loves. Love notwithstanding, Plesance slips away while he sleeps, and he awakes to find himself abandoned. With the old men he returns to his own castle, where he is guarded by such contumacious servants as Ire and Jalosie. Here he remains until a hideous host besiege him and break down the walls. Sorely smitten by Decrepitus, he prepares for death by making his last will and testament. Here the poem ends.

Like *The Pastime of Pleasure* and the first half of *The Palice of Honour*, this poem centers upon sensual love, analyzing it in order to reject it. The anonymous poet, who seems to have been thoroughly familiar with the *Roman de la Rose*, structures his poem according to the major stages of an amatory affair. The eyes see a desirable lady and transmit their impression to the heart. The heart, rushing impetuously into love, is held captive by the lady until she grants him permission to "capture" her. They comsummate their love and live blissfully together while the day of passion lasts. That gone, the lady abandons him, and he makes an irrevocable farewell to love.

That sexual love is treacherously alluring is indicated by the behavior of Dame Plesance. In effect she seeks out King Hart, riding by his castle so that he will discover her. She captures and then recaptures him by permitting him to "capture" her, and when he relies upon her most dearly, she steals away. Through her influence his capacity for feeling is so narrowed that the only emotions he can now admit are the base ones of jealousy and wrath. Even more serious is the damage done to his moral character. Conscience, who comes late to the King, chides noisily over his long exclusion. Ressoun, Wit, and Honour come into his life only after he grows old. Even so, King Hart is unwilling to let these moral goods replace sensuality. He may speak with them, but his heart is set upon pleasure. Clearly he suffers from a moral paralysis, seeing good and yet being unable to act upon it. This is the final reward for giving oneself over to sensuality.

While the love story provides the narrative events of the poem, the poet makes of it only the cloak that covers the *intentional* level of the poem—and at that it is a transparent cloak. As the names of the actors make clear, the world of the poem is limited to a single man. The castle is his body; the five noble servants are his senses; the guardians who lure him into riot are his own ungoverned (but not ungovernable) instincts; Dame Plesance is his sensual love of pleasure; and Conscience, Ressoun, and Wit are his intellectual and moral forces, which come to a dwarfed existence only when Age takes away his youthful indulgence. The hideous host that breach the wall are the physical infirmities of age, and the King's deathblow is delivered by his own decrepitude.

In the light of this significance, the metaphor of the pilgrimage achieves validity as a critical term describing the poem's action. King Hart travels not through space but through time, from the green leaves of youth to the barren winter of age. Although he seems at first to benefit from his journey, it proves to be a process of depletion and loss. Abandoned by all that he has valued from his youth, he himself gives the final order: "Go, send for Deid."

There is a very real affinity between this poem and the morality play *Everyman*, which is established by a similar use of personification to manifest the inward life of man as he makes his journey into death. This affinity is heightened by the narrative simplicity of the poem. Not once does the poet stop to comment upon the moral significance of an image or concept; never does he pause for the sake of suggestive description. He is as objective as a dramatist, expecting his action and actors to speak for themselves, and, like a dramatist, he commits himself to action so that his poem reveals Hart's process of *becoming* in each successive present moment.

The Pilgrimage of Love

The swift movement of the action also establishes the comic quality of the poem. In the flow of events there is no time for dignity or ennobling ceremony; there is no space for the tableaux and elaborate pageants so customary to allegorical poems, or even for characterization of the personified forces beyond what is expressed through their names and actions. Particularly in the first half of the poem, which is devoted to youth, the narrative unfolds as a lighthearted farce in which love, as a physical action, conquers all. The lover blunders through to success: he enters rashly into the battle of the sexes, assuming that it can be won as easily as a skirmish in war, and he rides squarely to defeat. The metaphor of warfare is ironically maintained even in love's triumph, when the lady "yields" herself and asks that he "do [her] nocht to smart." The feast which follows after the battle provides a traditional resolution to the comic conflict, as all are united in physical and emotional satiety.

Underlining the farcical action of Hart's youth is a consistent exaggeration of physical actions that translates them from the heroic to the ludicrous. When finally confronted, Dame Plesance lies quaking for dread, whilst the formerly ferocious Danger cowers in a nook. When the lady yields, "Dame Chastite, that selie innocent, / For wo yeid wode and flaw out our the wall" (lines 415–16). Occasionally the poet heightens the narrative exaggeration by relying upon excessive alliteration. So when the second scouting party goes out against the lady, the statement elevates valor into a flurry of fricatives (lines 193–94):

> Full-hardynes full freschlie furth he flang,
> A fure leynth fer befoir his feiris fyve.

More often, however, the poet relies upon a matter-of-fact flatness that stands in direct contrast to the extremity of the action or detail. The King's guardians number "ane milyon and weill mo," and Dame Chastite goes mad for woe.

The total effect of action, tone, and style is to make the first half of the poem a celebration of youth and its headlong rush into natural lusts, a celebration that is objectified by the feast of love. The value of this celebration, however, is called immediately into question by the second half of the poem. Here the same style prevails, the same swift alternation between hyperbole and flat, objective reporting, between inflation and deflation. There is, however, a new note introduced that corresponds to

Laughter in the Courts of Love

the King's evolution into a *senex*, the old man self-deceived into believing that he can hold onto youth. His first response to the coming of Age is surprise and irritation: "It dois me noy...Quhat haist had he!" When Conscience chides, he defends himself as having followed Nature; next he tries to blame Conscience for having been slothful all his life; and then he tries to practice hypocrisy. When he returns to his own castle – comes to himself – he discovers that he is governed by an old man's lusts. Struck down by Decrepitus, he composes a will that reflects a modicum of moral judgment and much personal ill will. To Dame Plesance he leaves his "prowde palfrey, Unsteidfastnes"; to Deliverance, his broken shin, and to Danger, his broken spear that wants the head.

The action is still farcical, with much the same stress upon speed and exaggerated physical motion as in the first half of the poem. Thus, when Dame Plesance steals away, Jelosie comes "strekand up the stair." Throughout the last part of the poem there prevails the visual image of the castle with its front door locked to keep out all comers, while from the back flows out a steady stream of defecting servants. This image not only objectifies the new perspective of the purblind man trying to stop the flow of time but also negates the earlier celebration of youthful impulse and replaces it with a deathwatch. The second half of the poem provokes little delight but much reflection and a wry laughter that criticizes a life based upon the suicide of chastity.

King Hart's pilgrimage through life is closely akin to Graunde Amoure's in its revelation of how an apparent earthly success metamorphoses irreversibly into spiritual futility; however where *The Pastime of Pleasure* brings a specifically Christian accusation against its hero, the Scottish poem judges in essentially secular terms. King Hart's error consists of drifting into sin and loving it; his correction, effected this side of the grave, calls for the death of that love.

The end of Hart's pilgrimage recalls in a deep and almost undefinable sense the end of the Canterbury pilgrimage, though the poem lacks the Christian ambience that illumines Chaucer's poem. The fires of spring, the lusts and controversies of the flesh are left behind, and in the gathering darkness the pilgrim looks to his soul's destiny. In the vast spaces of his ruined castle the broken man surveys his past and moves to complete the pilgrimage: "Send for Deid." He moves from lusty riotousness to clangorous lamentation and finally to acquiescence, while the pilgrimage

The Pilgrimage of Love

modulates from bright comedy to somber irony. Such, by the testimony of *King Hart*, is the natural shape of the pilgrimage of the unredeemed life. The fires of passion burn to the ashes of regret; the comedy of youth becomes the tragedy of loss. Only through the grace of God can the pilgrimage be redeemed and redirected; then the comedy of error becomes a song of joy.

5.

The Comedy of
The Faerie Queene

HE IMAGE OF SAGE and serious Spenser has so long dominated attitudes toward *The Faerie Queene* that most readers tacitly assume the poem to be a work of unrelenting seriousness. Much criticism of *The Faerie Queene* originates in the view of Spenser as an ambitious, intense poet who looked resolutely *through* the accidents of life to record the significance of an implied universe; then it proceeds to a similar view of his poem as soberly philosophical and thoroughly serious. *The Faerie Queene*, it is implied, must be read and reread for the philosophical theories, theological doctrines, and historical allusions that are cloaked by the fabric of the narrative. The best reader is one who recognizes each poetical construct as a disguised emblem of truth, a piece of a cosmic puzzle that must be worked out.

The critics are correct in their view that to read *The Faerie Queene* one must read allegorically, but the unfortunate fact of Spenser studies is that most critics have industriously explicated the seriousness of the poem while letting its comedy go almost unnoticed. "In volume after volume of criticism you will look in vain for any recognition of Spenser's achievements in the comic. At best, you will find some grudging comment like, 'This seems to be one of Spenser's few consciously humorous passages.'"[1] Only within the past quarter century has there been ungrudging commentary, and even this has had no remarkable success in

---

[1] Arnold Williams, *Flower on a Lowly Stalk: The Sixth Book of* The Faerie Queene, p. 113. For other studies of Spenser's comedy, see Charles B. Burke, "The 'Sage and Serious' Spenser," *N&Q* 175 (1938):457–58; Allan H. Gilbert, "Spenserian Comedy," *Tennessee Studies in Literature* 2 (1957):95–104; W. B. C. Watkins, *Shakespeare and Spenser*; and Martha Craig, "The Secret Wit of Spenser's Language," in Paul J. Alpers, ed., *Elizabethan Poetry: Modern Essays in Criticism*, pp. 447–72.

persuading other critics and general readers to recognize and enjoy Spenser's comedy. Those who do speak of his comedy, however, speak in high praise, as when Paul Alpers states, "[Book 3] is one of the great comic poems in English, and. . . to find its equal we must go to Chaucer and Shakespeare."[2] Like Chaucer, Spenser is a comic poet; like Chaucer, too, he is an allegorist; he is, in fact, the last significant maker of allegories to trace his lineage back to Chaucer, and his achievement in blending comedy with allegory thus concludes a tradition that endured in English poetry for more than two hundred years.

It is helpful to state at the outset that Spenser's comedy is quite different from Chaucer's, even when Spenser says that he is imitating his master. For Spenser, comedy is part and parcel of his allegorical intention, developed to establish and modify the "sentence" of his poem. Except for a few remarkable instances, like the Braggadocchio canto in book 2, he seldom aims for easy laughter as a primary response; rather, he develops an undercurrent of innuendos, incongruities, and surprises that culminate in a responsive chuckle or wry smile when the reader catches his drift. Through deadpan understatement, bombastic hyperbole, mocking repetition, parody, burlesque, and inappropriate, even grotesque, imagery, Spenser builds up the appearance of a character or situation and then swiftly discloses its reality for all the world to see. Yet he almost never pauses for laughter, and he seldom punctuates his humor by having a character laugh at what happens. Spenser is perhaps the most straight-faced comic poet in all of English literature.

Laughter, however, is not the only comic response man is capable of, nor is it all that Spenser tries to elicit. The range of responses to comedy is broadly outlined by Sir Philip Sidney in The Defence of Poesie, a statement of theory that coincides remarkably with Spenser's practice and probably had significant influence on Spenser's definition of his office as poet:

But our Comedients thinke there is no delight without laughter, which is verie wrong, for though laughter may come with delight, yet commeth it not of delight, as though delight should be the cause of laughter. But well may one thing breed both togither. Nay rather in themselves, they have as it were a kinde of contrarietie: For delight

---

[2]Paul J. Alpers, The Poetry of The Faerie Queene, p. 405.

wee scarcely doo, but in thinges that have a conveniencie to our selves, or to the generall nature: Laughter almost ever commeth of thinges moste disproportioned to our selves, and nature. Delight hath a joy in it either permanent or present. Laughter hath onely a scornfull tickling. For example, wee are ravished with delight to see a faire woman, and yet are farre from beeing mooved to laughter. Wee laugh at deformed creatures, wherein certainly wee cannot delight. We delight in good chaunces, wee laugh at mischaunces. We delight to heare the happinesse of our friendes and Countrey, at which hee were worthie to be laughed at, that would laugh: we shall contrarily laugh sometimes to finde a matter quite mistaken, and goe downe the hill against the byas, in the mouth of some such men as for the respect of them, one shall be hartily sorie, he cannot chuse but laugh, and so is rather pained, then delighted with laughter. Yet denie I not, but that they may goe well togither, for as in *Alexanders* picture well set out, wee delight without laughter, and in twentie madde Antiques, we laugh without delight. So in *Hercules*, painted with his great beard, and furious countenaunce, in a womans attyre, spinning, at *Omphales* com-maundement, it breedes both delight and laughter: for the represent-ing of so straunge a power in Love, procures delight, and the scornefulnesse of the action, stirreth laughter. But I speake to this pur-pose, that all the ende of the Comicall part, bee not uppon suche scornefull matters as stirre laughter onelie, but mixe with it, that delightfull teaching whiche is the ende of *Poesie*.[3]

Broadly speaking, there are two opposing responses to comedy, scorn and delight. Scorn is signified by laughter that ridicules its target, while delight is signified by the kindlier laughter or the smile of pleasure and ap-probation. Much of Spenser's comedy is aimed at breeding delight and admiration. For instance, we always admire Una and delight in Brito-mart; we rejoice also in those situations where virtue triumphs over vice. On the other hand, we laugh with a sense of superiority at figures repre-senting folly and error—Braggadocchio, Malbecco in book 3, the Egali-tarian Giant in book 5, and Sir Turpine in book 6. In *The Faerie Queene* all the great images of evil are inherently ludicrous, and they are presented

---

[3]Sir Philip Sidney, *The Defence of Poesie*, in *The Prose Works of Sir Philip Sidney*, ed. Albert Feuillerat, 3:40–41.

through comic techniques that disclose their grotesque love of corruption.

But human beings and human actions are not often so pure as to elicit a single response from the reader, and between these polar opposites of scorn and delight there is a broad range of mixed attitudes that the comedy appeals to. As Sidney says of the portrait of Hercules spinning, an image or a situation may breed both laughter and delight, because it is composed of more than one element. When Una, for instance, painstakingly teaches the Satyrs the meaning of true worship, she behaves admirably, while the Satyrs' rejection of her lesson provokes laughter:

> But when their bootlesse zeale she did restraine
> From her own worship, they her Asse would worship fayn.[4]

This is clearly a case of the matter going downhill against the bias, as Sidney says, and it elicits a rueful amusement.

It is important to point out that here, and often elsewhere in the poem, it is the situation controlled by the Satyrs and not the focal character, Una, that is primarily laughable. That is to say, although man is capable of noble conduct, he is placed in a world where nobility is an aberration, and while man tries to live up to his aspirations, the world tends to fulfill its own pattern, which honors the pragmatic and commonplace. Out of these conflicting motives arises a comedy where rueful laughter is directed at the character, the situation, and the world for making virtue seem abnormal. For instance, when Sir Guyon sails across the Idle Lake with the enchanting damsel Phaedria, he seems ludicrous in his pompous sobriety and his rejection of her gaiety, for he is out of joint with the pleasant world; but the clear fact that it is the world and not the knight that is in error redirects the reader's amusement toward the world and then toward himself as he recognizes his own erroneous tendency to accept the world as the norm and to make pragmatism his own standard for conduct.[5]

An even more complicated response is elicited by the first situation

---

[4]Edmund Spenser, *The Poetical Works of Edmund Spenser*, ed. J. C. Smith and Ernest De Selincourt, 1.6.19.8–9. All quotations are taken from this edition; subsequent references are incorporated in the text. I have modernized the printing of the letters *u* and *v*.

[5]For a discussion of the persuasive powers of the "ways of the world" in comedy, see Robert B. Heilman, *The Ways of the World: Comedy and Society*, pp. 48, 96–97.

that Britomart blunders into in Fairyland. Disguised as a knight, she is spending the night at the Lady Malecasta's Castle Joyeous. Believing her guest to be a man, Malecasta makes seductive overtures, which Britomart, being a girl, overlooks entirely. Malecasta finally succumbs to her lust and creeps at night into the "knight's" bed, but when Britomart feels someone beside her, she naturally assumes that it is a man and leaps instantly to save herself from a "loathed leachour." Malecasta screams, and six knights burst into the room to save her from supposed dishonor. For a moment all are frozen in tableau: the half-dressed, half-armed knights in the doorway, the lady in senseless swoon on the floor, and Britomart in a smock, brandishing her sword. Scenes remarkably like this, save for the detail of the sword, occur in the "golden comedies" of the silent screen—and also in *Confessio Amantis*. The situation is inherently farcical.

In this situation Malecasta is the appropriate target of scornful laughter, as are her confused defenders. Britomart behaves properly in defending herself and so should elicit admiration, and yet she too is a funny figure, appealingly feminine, yet fiercely bellicose with her sword. For the moment she is laughable too, not from scorn but from a sympathetic appreciation that she has stumbled into a comedy of errors that makes all actors foolish. Amusement is mixed with sympathy and delight in response to Britomart, not in this scene only but throughout her adventures in Fairyland. Where Britomart is concerned, the impulse toward laughter is always softened by our knowledge that she is *our* agent, acting out our quest for true love. In other words, laughter is not simply a signal of scorn, as Sidney suggests, but a complex response to our recognition of the complexities and contradictions inherent in a character or a situation.

Generally speaking, laughter is provoked more often by the situations in *The Faerie Queene* than by the characters. Most comic situations in the poem give rise to a surprised laughter that reflects the reader's sense of superiority, for these are presentations of the fallen, error-ridden way of the world. Characters who are presented comically may provoke scorn or delight; in fact, the same character may provoke scornful laughter in one situation and delighted approval in another. This is particularly true of the heroes of the different books, for most of them undergo a process of testing, failure, correction, and purification before they complete the quest they set out upon. Especially in the case of the Red Cross Knight, we laugh at him as he blunders along in error (though, to be honest, our laughter is pained, since he is our hero) but rejoice in his charity and dignity when he celebrates his betrothal to Una.

The function of comedy in *The Faerie Queene* is to highlight both the shortcomings and the triumphs of human experience so that the reader is taught to recognize and respond to both. Spenser in effect agrees with Sidney that "comedy is an imitation of the common errors of our life," even though these errors may be represented through such uncommon creatures as giants, dwarfs, beasts, and supernatural beings. The purpose of representing error is not an end in itself, however, but a means of teaching the proper sources of joy: ". . . so in the actions of our life, who seeth not the filthinesse of evill, wanteth a great foile to perceive the bewtie of vertue. This doth the Comaedie handle."[6]

Comedy, then, expresses and reinforces the morality that is communicated through the allegory of the poem. However, because each book of the poem is devoted to the presentation of a different virtue, which is in part defined by its unique set of opposing vices and errors, each book also has a different form and style of comedy. Moreover, since the triumph of each virtue elicits a type of rejoicing appropriate to itself, there are different sets of devices for creating delight also. The forms of comedy in *The Faerie Queene* are dependent upon the narrative structures of the allegory, which the comedy modifies and defines.

Each book of *The Faerie Queene* assumes its own narrative form, which in turn establishes the structure of the allegory and the style and tone of the comedy. William Nelson has suggested that for each book there is a "patron," a specific work or parental genre that helps determine the development of characters, settings, and action. The "patron" of book 1 is the Saint's Life, as taken from *The Golden Legend*; of book 2, the classical epic, particularly the *Odyssey* and the *Aeneid*; of book 3, Ariosto's *Orlando Furioso*, with special focus upon the figures of Bradamante and Angelica; of book 4, Chaucer's *The Squire's Tale*; of book 5, the myths of Hercules, Osiris, and Bacchus; of book 6, Sidney's *Arcadia* and Greek pastoral poetry in general; and of the Mutability Cantos, Ovid's *Metamorphoses*.[7] Although Nelson gives perhaps too much credit to

[6]Sidney, *The Defence of Poesie*, p. 23.

[7]William Nelson, *The Poetry of Edmund Spenser: A Study*, p. 140.

Chaucer's influence on book 4 and omits mention of it from book 3, his list of "patrons" is undeniably helpful for suggesting that the comic conventions in each book may be likewise derived from the parental work of genre. A. C. Hamilton follows essentially the same procedure as Nelson in naming a "patron" for book 1, though he selects the Book of Revelation, which he classifies as an archetypal tragedy. Hamilton interprets the first half of book 1 as tragedy (though he appears to ignore the tone of the poem in doing so), and the second half as "archetypal comedy," beginning in despair and ending with marriage.[8] Both Nelson and Hamilton agree that the ending of book 1 is designed to evoke rejoicing in the achievement of saintliness.

Holiness

The comedy in *The Legend of Holinesse* is indeed archetypal, for it celebrates the salvation of the human soul. The Red Cross Knight enacts the spiritual history of all mankind, his fall through pride and his restoration to holiness, which is effected by the grace of God. In the beginning of his career he is beset not only by human foes but also by devils who assume a garment of flesh in hopes of betraying his soul into eternal damnation. His destiny is his own responsibility, however, and no devil can betray him into hell without his cooperation. The narrative action of the poem is essentially a *psychomachia*, man in conflict with himself. Red Cross's enemies signify in dramatically concrete form his own impulses toward sin. Red Cross's greatest enemy is himself, following the way of the flesh. But once he has been cleansed of his pride, then he becomes a true "Microchristus,"[9] for as Christ humbled himself and was incarnate in the image of Red Cross and all men, so Red Cross is reshaped into the image of Christ and is renamed Saint George. Thus reborn, he slays the dragon, frees Una's parents, and then celebrates his betrothal to Una with a serenity that suggests the perfect peace and joy of heaven. The central note of the final canto is that of exultation in human triumph

---

[8]A. C. Hamilton, *The Structure of Allegory in* The Faerie Queene, pp. 60, 79. Cf., however, Georgia Ronan Crampton's rather puzzling caution that "the reader is to refrain from taking the self-congratulatory stance of comedy." Georgia Ronan Crampton, *The Condition of Creatures: Suffering and Action in Chaucer and Spenser*, p. 130.

[9]A. S. P. Woodhouse provides this term in "Nature and Grace in *The Faerie Queene*," *ELH* 16 (1949):198.

when the body and soul together transcend the errors of earth and stand, perfected but human, in the purity of first creation. The music of the spheres resounds throughout the castle, and great joy unites heaven with earth.

Set against the joyous climax of Red Cross's adventure is the more earthbound comedy of the quest, which directs laughter at his failures through pride and at the world that invites him to fail. Much of the laughter provoked by the poem is directed against the two forms that pride usually takes, vanity and hypocrisy.[10] Red Cross's comic failing is his vanity, which leads him to assume that he is much better than he is, when he is not nearly as good as he should be. Seeing himself as a remarkable slayer of dragons (overlooking the fact that he nearly fainted from nausea at Errour's vomit in his first knightly encounter), he dashes about the countryside looking for adventures that will add glory to his name.

The heroics exist in his mind, however, rather than in the adventures themselves. After all, the dragonlike monster Errour does not really want to fight and tries to turn back into her den, whereupon he attacks and provokes her to defend herself. From that point the heroic quality of the battle goes quite downhill, despite the cloak of language that sympathizes with Red Cross and directs us to be repulsed by Errour. Red Cross chokes her; she vomits; he is made faint by nausea; she disgorges herself further; in desperation he vows to destroy her or die and gathers enough force to strike her head from her body. If we observe Errour closely, however, we discover that she is as much a printing press as she is dragon, with her inky flood of books and pamphlets and her black blood. While the allegory points us in one direction toward moral philosophy, it also tends downward to burlesque. Spenser uncovers the reality of another instance of "heroic" conduct in an epic simile that describes Red Cross's battle with the proud Saracen, Sansloy (1.2.16):

> As when two rams stird with ambitious pride,
>   Fight for the rule of the rich fleeced flocke,
>   Their horned fronts so fierce on either side

---

[10]Cf. Henry Fielding, Author's Preface, *Joseph Andrews*, introduction and notes by Carlos Baker, pp. xix–xxv. Like Fielding, Spenser finds these flaws the proper targets of comedy. Spenser, however, would probably prefer to name their parent as the sin of Pride, rather than Fielding's "Affectation."

Do meete, that with the terrour of the shocke
Astonied both, stand sencelesse as a blocke,
Forgetfull of the hanging victory:
So stood these twaine, unmoved as a rocke,
Both staring fierce, and holding idely
The broken reliques of their former cruelty.

The senseless blocks, unmoved rocks, and subhuman rams are the reality of the situation, while the fierce heroism exists in the misguided mind of the warrior.

The most laughable sequence of misadventures through vanity occurs at Lucifera's palace, where Red Cross stands aloof, holding a private contempt for those proud persons who, he feels, treat him too lightly. When Lucifera rides out in state behind her grotesque counselors on their mismatched mounts, he estranges himself from their "joyaunce vaine, / Whose fellowship seemed far unfit for warlike swaine" (1.4.37.8-9). His sense of self finally becomes so great that he assumes all praise and encouragement to be directed toward himself. When, during his duel with Sansjoy, Duessa cries out to the Saracen, "'Thine the shield, and I, and all!'" Red Cross takes the vow to himself, redoubles his effort, and – to the lady's dismay – wins the shield, the lady, and all.

From this ironic triumph Red Cross continues on his career of vanity, too dull of wit to interpret properly the signs of danger that surround him. Even when Una's dwarf, Common Sense, points out the dungeon of lost souls in Lucifera's castle and persuades him to flee, he soon forgets his sense of danger and relaxes beside a spring, wishing that he had brought Duessa with him. In fact, he is so engrossed in contemplation of his own pleasures that he wishes to sit at ease, attended by both Una (if only she were pure) and Duessa, like Solomon in all his splendor. This vision of delight makes it easy for him to pour himself out in looseness once Duessa finds him and, having done so, to fall victim to the giant of pride, Orgoglio. Even long imprisonment in Orgoglio's dungeons, kept by the mumbling Ignaro, does not dissuade him from one last, almost disastrous, effort to prove that he can overcome error, in the confrontation with Despair.

So long as his love is centered on himself, Red Cross is a ludicrous figure, the proper target of laughter, though our sense of superiority is always mixed with regret and even embarrassment that he, our agent, behaves so foolishly. After he is corrected, instructed, and redirected in the House of Holinesse, then he is the source of delight in the poem. Foremost of all heroes, although Guyon, Artegall, and Calidore follow similar patterns, the Red Cross Knight evolves from a laughable to a delightful figure in his quest and so posits the complete range of comic responses available in the book.

While Red Cross represents vanity, which is one aspect of pride (or original sin), the other form that pride takes is hypocrisy, pretending to be the opposite of one's true nature. This form of pride gives rise to the duality that characterizes book 1: the two dragon fights, the two Unas, the two Red Cross Knights, the two identities for Duessa, and the two castles of pride, to name some of the more striking instances. As for the hypocritical characters—Archimago, Duessa, Corceca, Abessa, and Despair—the comic action centers upon unmasking them, for hypocrisy proceeds from a heart so hardened that it denies truth altogether. In holding up his hypocrites to scorn, Spenser relies especially upon devices of comic style: exaggeration, understatement, and metaphoric language that refocuses a subject to define it by its reality, as opposed to its appearance. For instance, when Archimago in his guise as hermit talks of saintliness, the narrative concludes (1.1.35.8–9):

> He told of Saintes and Popes, and evermore
> He strowd an *Ave-Mary* after and before.

The one word *strowd* serves a metaphorical function, turning the *Ave-Marys* from expressions of faith into tangible objects like rose petals that can be scattered about for decoration. Thus the word strips bare the attitude of the hypocrite and foreshadows what the action will make evident thereafter. In describing the apparent devotion of Corceca, Spenser uses gross exaggeration to provoke laughter. Every day she says nine hundred *Pater nosters* and twenty-seven hundred *Aves*; and, given the opportunity, she attacks with a shocking devotion to viciousness.

In the comic world of book 1, sin is laughable, for laughter is the great corrective. Spenser takes pleasure in puncturing even the most frightful of persuasions to sin by holding them up to laughter. Thus he ends Red Cross's confrontation with Despair by having Despair commit the suicide that the knight has not; yet despite having tried a thousand times, Despair cannot kill himself and so is left hanging in the halter, presumably until he gives up and cuts himself down. He cannot die any more than suicide can bring the soul into harmony with God.

But Spenser uses laughter also to heighten our sense of his hero's Christian triumph. Superstitious error and active evil still abound on earth, despite one man's salvation, and these are set off in the final canto against Red Cross's new serenity and wisdom. There is what C. S. Lewis has called a nice "Chaucerian touch" in the common folk's nervous reaction to the slain dragon, especially in the mother, "halfe dead through feare," who rebukes her foolhardy child for curiously touching one talon.[11] The breathless entrance of Archimago, interrupting the King of Eden's speech and the betrothal ceremony, belongs also to the laughing comedy of the poem, set in sharp contrast to Red Cross's dignity and Una's plain statement of truth. Scorn at error leads to admiration at the triumph of the Christian Knight.

Temperance

While *The Legend of Holinesse* evolves from a comedy of error into a comedy of joy, reflecting the transcendent Christian experience of the poem, the comedy of book 2 is essentially of one type throughout. Unlike Red Cross, Sir Guyon is not basically a comic figure, though he gets into situations that are patently ludicrous. Allegorically he resembles Christ soberly rejecting temptation in the wilderness, as well as Aeneas undertaking a preordained journey and Odysseus making the sea voyage to the enchanted island where Circe dwells.[12] He represents a classical virtue that has been subsumed into Christianity, but, as the structure of the book makes clear, it is not a virtue equal to Holiness. Guyon is distinctly unlike the Red Cross Knight: he is not a lover, not an adventurer, and not even a notably successful warrior. Neither is he clearly converted from one course of action to another during his quest. He is, instead, the "straight-man" hero of a satiric social comedy that provokes laughter against the intemperate errors of the world. As a summary of his adven-

---

[11]C. S. Lewis, *Spenser's Images of Life*, ed. Alastair Fowler, p. 89.

[12]Frank Kermode, "The Cave of Mammon," in *Elizabethan Poetry*, Stratford-Upon-Avon Studies, no. 2, pp. 151–73. For a rather different interpretation of Guyon as being closer to the "Old Adam" than to Christ, see Patrick Cullen, *Infernal Triad: The Flesh, The World, and the Devil in Spenser and Milton*, pp. 85–94.

tures will point out, he is much the same person at the end as he was in the beginning, Temperance, which the world tries to destroy.

When Guyon first appears, he is being gulled by Archimago and Duessa into bearing arms against Red Cross, but he fortunately recognizes his error and drops his spear in time to turn confrontation into a brotherly meeting. Shortly thereafter his horse is stolen, and he is forced to complete his journey as an anomaly—a *chevalier* afoot. At the house of Medina he tries to end a battle between two quarrelsome knights, Hudibras and Sansloy, but succeeds only in having both turn against him. The "straunge sort of fight" that results from his effort at peacemaking goes on until Medina herself intervenes—and here is established a pattern that will be often repeated: the temperate Guyon is drawn into an intemperate action that has to be ended by a party outside the conflict.

The next incident that befalls Guyon is even less heroic and more outrageous. He attempts to control Furor by wrestling him to the ground (2.4.8.7–9):

> Him sternely grypt, and haling to and fro,
> To overthrow him strongly did assay.
> But overthrew himselfe unwares, and lower lay.

After narrowly escaping death through this accident, Guyon discovers that he must also fight and subdue Furor's mother, Occasion, a crippled old hag. The pattern of this contest, like that of Arthur's later battle with Maleger, is taken from ancient farce: repetition of an action that becomes more nearly mechanical the more it recurs. Guyon wrestles Occasion to the ground and assumes that he has conquered her. She continues to rant and rail, however, until he has to fasten an iron lock to her tongue. Still she is not overcome, for she uses her hands to signal what she would say, and he has to tie her hands behind her back. Guyon's desire to consider the embarrassing action completed conflicts directly with her proofs that it is not, and her proofs force him to return his attention to her when he wishes to direct it elsewhere. Scarcely has this inglorious episode ended when there comes the climax to the entire situation. Fierce Pyrochles rides to attack Guyon for abusing a helpless old woman; Guyon raises his sword in self-defense and hits not his foe but the horse's neck, "and from the head the body sundred quight."

The Comedy of *The Faerie Queene*

By now Guyon has stumbled into nearly every embarrassment that can befall a knight, but his troubles still are not over. After the encounter with Pyrochles he meets Phaedria and somewhat sullenly avoids seduction. Then he concludes a three-day journey through the underworld by fainting—not faltering or advancing, not rising or falling, but merely fainting and so passing out of the action altogether. Even in completing his quest, Guyon stumbles, the Palmer having frequently to correct him and once to rebuke him severely for his fascination with the enticing exposure of "Cissie and Flossie."[13]

This summary of Guyon's career, to be sure, is abstracted from the full poetical presentation that modifies the sharp edges and establishes the precise moral values of the poem; the point is clear, however, that what happens to Guyon is comic, for book 2, in particular, is concerned with narrating the way of the world. The allegory of book 2 expresses the unending war between Temperance and those vices and errors that oppose it: excessiveness, defectiveness, and sloth. Guyon's function is to reveal and, if possible, reform immoderate conduct, or to destroy it if it is beyond reformation. But because Temperance alone cannot conquer all foes, God's grace must make intervention in the form, first, of the angel who guards the hero as he lies unconscious outside Mammon's cave and, second, of Prince Arthur, who not only defends Guyon but also overthrows original sin, an action that necessarily precedes the conquest of fruitless sensuality. The comic elements of book 2 reinforce Spenser's presentation of the world as foe to Temperance.

Throughout *The Faerie Queene*, but particularly in book 2, Spenser often turns to parody when he wishes to clarify his definition of the central virtues at the same time that he reveals vice. To create the meaning of Temperance, Spenser not only illustrates it directly but also makes two basic contrasts: first, with the vice that is its opposite, and, second, with the vice that most nearly resembles it. This second comparison constitutes what Northrop Frye has termed "symbolic parody," the inherently ludicrous spectacle of vice parading as virtue.[14] In book 2, Temperance is opposed by forms of excessiveness, Avarice and Wrath, and is parodied by Sloth. The spokesman for Sloth is Phaedria, a charming damsel who encourages man not to be excessive in his pursuits, in-

[13]C. S. Lewis has thoughtfully provided their names in *The Allegory of Love*, p. 331.
[14]Northrop Frye, "The Structure of Imagery in *The Faerie Queene*," *UTQ* 30 (1961):109–27.

deed to lay aside pursuits altogether. She detours fierce Cymochles from his pursuit of Guyon and then lulls him to sleep with a song built upon Christ's injunction, "Consider the lilies how they grow," suggesting that she speaks with scriptural authority. When she brings Guyon to the island, she makes *him* seem almost ludicrous in his rejection of her pleas-antries; and when she stops the fight between Guyon and Cymochles, she acts like Medina, who halted the three-way battle in her courtyard. The parallels suggest that she, too, is an agent of the golden mean.

The sequence of events involving Phaedria (all of canto 6) make up the central parody of Sloth imitating Temperance and the smaller parodies of Phaedria imitating Christ and Medina. As comedy the canto becomes a satiric celebration of vice in which distorted Scripture seems persuasive, true Temperance looks pompous and rigid, appearance triumphs over reality, and the righteous man is expelled from demi-Eden. What Spenser has created through parody is an incisive comedy of manners wherein behavior takes precedence over being.[15] That, after all, is the way of the world that has to be corrected or destroyed in *The Legend of Temperance*.

The world of book 2 is peopled with errant figures who instinctively oppose Temperance. When Guyon comes in contact with them, his man-ner, modest, sober, and (alas) sententious, provokes them into acting out their traditional modes of being intemperate. The foes of Temperance are drawn from the stock figures of classical comedy: the *senex*, the old woman, the soldier, the manservant, the miser, and the courtesan. The old men of the poem, Archimago and Mammon—the latter is also the miser—are appropriately impotent, capable of hating the young knight but incapable of doing him direct injury. Ironically, the most formidable warriors to oppose Guyon and Arthur are the old women, fierce and energetic hags who can run like the wind even on crutches. The sol-diers—the knights Sansloy, Hudibras, Pyrochles, and Cymochles—are mechanical figures who draw arms on all occasions, for they can act only in military fashion; however, because each has sur-

[15]Allan Rodway, like Heilman, questions the older emphasis upon the morality of comedy, saying that comedy can be "corrective without being moral." The function of comedy, he suggests, is "to in-tegrate man's nature . . . with the nature of his world, so that he can swim in his sea of troubles." Allan Rodway, *English Comedy: Its Role and Nature from Chaucer to the Present Day*, pp. 11, 22. Guyon, in other words, is out of order here, behaving like Molière's Misanthrope: moral but not correct.

rendered control of himself to his basic impulses, their actions become a parody of true chivalric behavior.

The most memorable soldier of the poem is one who does not confront Guyon but steals his horse, thereby reducing him to a pedestrian. This is the *Miles Gloriosus*, Braggadocchio. Braggadocchio is Guyon inverted, braggart, thief, bully, and would-be rapist, the embodiment of all the epithets hurled at Guyon. His encounter with the beautiful huntress, Belphoebe, is delightfully ludicrous, hinging upon a series of mistaken assumptions and misdirected actions, and climaxing with his amorous lunge that interrupts her enthusiastic oration upon the superiority of forests to courts. Both Braggadocchio and Belphoebe are single-minded, though in entirely different ways. While he assumes that everything exists for his own taking, she assumes that all men are as interested in hearing speeches on the evils of life at court as she is in making them. But while Braggadocchio is completely ludicrous, Belphoebe in her beauty and enthusiasm gives rise to a sense of true delight. She is a breeze of fresh innocence blowing across the turbid forest.

The Braggadocchio interlude is something of a surprise in book 2, so lightly connected with the rest of the action as to seem a holiday from the real business at hand; yet its function in the comic structure is vital. It is, as Harry Berger, Jr., says, a light, even brilliant variation upon the deeper comedy that arises from the basic opposition of true virtue and its parody.[16] It is one of the rare instances in the poem where the comedy advertises itself, and it is a signal that comedy occurs elsewhere as well. In illustrating the comic absurdities of intemperance, it provides a pattern for recognizing and responding to comedy in other situations. Finally, it points out that ethical gravity can be funny, depending upon the style of presentation. In a sense, canto 3 is designed to teach the reader how to respond to the comedy of book 2.

Much of the comedy of book 2 is presented through imagery that suggests the absurdity of intemperance and through mocking repetition of lines wherein focus shifts abruptly from one perspective to another. The comic image may be either "real"—that is, it states the form that the action really takes—or else figurative, a poetical construction that refers to something entirely outside the narrative. Arthur's battle with Maleger

[16]Harry Berger, Jr., *The Allegorical Temper: Vision and Reality in Book II of Spenser's* Faerie Queene, Yale Studies in English, vol. 137, p. 140.

is presented through a series of "real" images that are visually absurd: the two hags, barefoot and wrapped in rags, running as "swift on foot, as chased Stags," though one is lame and uses a crutch; Maleger riding backward on a tiger, shooting arrows as he goes; and then Maleger bouncing off the ground and into the air like a ball, returning to life as he does so. Here the presentation of original sin as a bouncing ball intensifies the comic effect of the image.

Spenser uses the figurative, or consciously poetical, image to deflate the apparent seriousness of a situation or to enhance the ludicrous impact of something that is already seen as ridiculous. In narrating the "straunge sort of fight" of Guyon, Hudibras, and Sansloy, Spenser pauses to describe a ship tossed at sea and threatened by two contrary billows—and all in Medina's courtyard. In the terms of the comparison Guyon is a tall ship, whereas Hudibras and Sansloy are merely two contrary billows, but in reality all three are merely engaged in irrational battle. The grandiloquence of the image ironically deflates the scope and significance of the combat. The use of figurative imagery to intensify the ludicrous impact of a situation occurs in its most effective form in canto 3, when Braggadocchio comes forth from the bushes to meet Belphoebe like a "fearefull fowle." Spenser reduces the man to a bird and then comes to his sharpest point of all: he is a fearful fowl that long "*her* selfe hath hid." The ethical judgment against Braggadocchio is clear, and the result is surprised, scornful laughter.

Spenser relies also on repetition as a device of comic style in book 2. In using repetition, he intends the ironic restatement of a line to signal the division between deceit and truthfulness, appearance and reality. Archimago, eager to injure the Red Cross Knight, asks Guyon, "'Vouchsafe to stay your steed for humble misers sake'"; and, in trusting courtesy, Guyon "stayd his steed for humble misers sake." The repetition mocks Archimago's duplicity while honoring Guyon's courtesy. Later when Guyon attends to the battle between Hudibras and Sansloy, they "Espye a traveiler with feet surbet" and attack. "But he, not like a wearie traveilere / Their sharpe assault right boldly did rebut." The irony that results from the repetition is the poet's direct communication to the reader of a viewpoint for evaluating the subject being viewed.

Spenser's viewpoint clearly is that the world is off course, and he not only mocks it but also scourges it with a grotesque comedy that appalls the reader, even as he laughs. This kind of comedy prevails in Guyon's encounter with Mammon in the impotent realm of greed. Spenser presents the scene through a double focus, shifting at need from Guyon to Mammon to illustrate both virtue and vice. From the focus of Guyon the trip through the underworld is heuristic, a didactic journey that instructs the reader in the corruptive and potentially damning powers of acquisitiveness. From the focus of Mammon—and it is this focus that is presented as having an emotional investment in the event—the confrontation is a grim comedy mocking covetousness. The classic miser, Mammon is first seen sitting amidst his gold, then hastily pouring it down a hole lest it be taken from him. But the instant he learns that Guyon does not want it, he offers it to him and spends three days trying to prove that gold is better than godliness. The comic point against the miser is that while he loves his gold he loves even more the envy of the man who wants it. The journey through the cave tests Mammon as much as Guyon, who is so firm in his virtue that he will not be tempted. For three days Mammon is constrained to be polite, reasonable, and courteous, though he "emmoved was with inward wrath," sore trials indeed for an old man confronted by a righteous young man who estimates all his treasures as worthless. Despite his anguish over the failure to corrupt Guyon, he must nonetheless have been relieved to be free of him.

There is much comedy in book 2 that creates a satiric portrait of the erring world and gives rise to scorn directed against the "common errors of life," but there is little comedy of delight. Guyon is not especially engaging, and the completion of his quest seems unheroic, for he systematically destroys the undefended Bower of Bliss (a Court of Love). The absence of delight, save for the brief appearance of Belphoebe, makes an important point that, I believe, Spenser directs to the reader. That is, although Temperance is the proper ideal for conduct in the world of book 2 and the real world, it is not the *summum bonum* of human existence. Compared with Red Cross's Holiness and Britomart's creative Chastity, it is truly a pedestrian virtue.

Chastity

In books 3 and 4, Spenser turns to the same theme that all the other poems dealt with in this study have expressed—the nature of love. Both

Laughter in the Courts of Love

books are essentially love stories, but love in book 3 is viewed from the perspective of private itches and passions that lead on the one hand to uncontrolled sexuality or, on the other, to the sanctified union of marriage. In book 4 love is defined primarily as friendship, the generative source of social concord. Three kinds of love are demonstrated throughout the two books (4.9.1.5–7):

> The deare affection unto kindred sweet,
> Or raging fire of love to woman kind,
> Or zeale of friends combynd with vertues meet.

But because the definition of love, and hence the allegorical point, differs between the two books, there are also marked differences between the comic structures, styles, and tones.

In *The Legend of Chastitie*, Spenser builds upon one of the oldest and surest foundations of comedy, human sexuality. While sex is the only means available to man for ensuring his fleshly immortality (and only a symbolic immortality at that), it is also the least dignified of human drives. Eating and sleeping may be accomplished with some grace, but the sexual itch turns man to his most awkward and angular postures and suggests that, no matter how angelic or courteous he may be, he is still embarrassingly like the beasts of the field. The different narrative strands of book 3 illustrate the various ways in which man responds to sexuality. If he yields to it totally, then he comes like the giants Argante and Ollyphant, rampant desire attacking any object available, for this desire sees *objects*, not ladies, knights, or squires. If he represses it completely, then he becomes like Marinell, a lover of inanimate objects, the stones and jewels of the beach. In between these poles are the agents of chastity, those who recognize sexuality and try to respond to it in socially and religiously accepted patterns; and standing outside the mating dance altogether is the embodiment of total chastity, Belphoebe, who is ironically one of the most sexually alluring creatures in Fairyland.

The titular virtue of Chastity is defined through the attitudes and experiences of the four heroines of the poem, the maiden-knight Britomart and Amoret, Belphoebe, and Florimell, who are specialized refractions of the qualities embodied in Britomart. Each guards her virginity, but for a different reason: Amoret, because she has been tutored in the Court of Love; Belphoebe, because she is unaware that either virginity or concupiscence exists; and Florimell, because she, in an exaggerated version of Britomart, is seeking one man to yield to.

The parallel between Britomart and Florimell results in two different styles of comedy in the poem. Florimell, the central figure in a sex farce played at the speed of a streaking comet, is typified by her nervous awareness of her appeal, which makes her flee the very suggestion of lust, even if it exists only in her mind. It is not Florimell, however, but the situations she gets into that cause laughter. We can sympathize with her and yet laugh when she enters the boat of the old fisherman, believing that she has found safety but discovering herself yet once more in danger of rape. As a result of her flight from supposed danger she lands in real danger, and her career through book 3 is a series of rebounds from one lecherous assault to another. Britomart, high-minded as well as single-minded in her search for her lover Artegall, seems sublimely unaware of her attractiveness as she blunders innocently into sex-centered melees. Her comedy is more complex and slower-moving than Florimell's, and it is enriched by the irony that, since she is in disguise as a knight, she is accosted sexually by women, not men.

The comic quality of book 3 is more nearly Chaucerian than anything else Spenser wrote, even book 4, which purports to be inspired by Chaucer's unfinished *Squire's Tale*. By this I do mean not that Spenser consciously imitates Chaucer but rather that, in expressing human responses to sexuality, he utilizes the same conventions as those Chaucer used in the English tradition, or Ariosto in the Italian. He sets up a basic conflict between youth and age that stresses the naturalness of love in the young and ridicules unnatural love in the old. For youth, love is a heady wine that intoxicates and inspires; filled with amorous energy, the young instinctively find ways to overcome barriers in order to gratify their desires. For the old, love becomes perversion – jealousy or avarice – that tortures them as much as lovesickness tortures the young. When the desires of youth and age come in conflict, youth triumphs, while age is overthrown.

Much of the comedy of love arises from Spenser's method of allegorical definition, in which Chastity is set off against its opposite vice, Lust, and also those modes of behavior that resemble it but arise from different motivations. The virtue that the book honors is not abstention but rather an active engagement in sex, the natural and rational direction of the love impulse toward a suitable lover. Britomart is therefore distinct from Belphoebe, who is unaware that sexuality exists, and also from Amoret, who knows all about sexuality but nothing about active chastity.

In working out his definition of Chastity, Spenser achieves a wry humor through his contrast of the twin sisters, Amoret and Belphoebe. He makes Amoret the center of sexual interest while granting true sex-appeal to Belphoebe. A child of Diana, Belphoebe inspires Braggadocchio to lunge for her and Timias to long after her. Her treatment of the wounded Timias turns into the cure that very nearly kills, for she cannot recognize and has no remedies for the lovesick heart. Her consistent diagnosis of amorous wounds as physical infirmities constitutes one of the comic motifs of the book. Amoret, on the other hand, is patterned after the courtly mistress. Brought up in the Court of Venus and well tutored in the ways of conventionalized love, she has no capacity for acting as a natural lover. Her imprisonment in the House of Busyrane is equivalent to the Rose's imprisonment in the tower in the *Roman de la Rose*, where Danger, Suspicion, Fear, and other negative emotions serve as guardians of her virginity.[17] When finally she does feel a sexual impulse, Amoret is literally seized by lust. The point of her experience is that made by C. S. Lewis throughout his book *The Allegory of Love*: "courtly love" is not love but a remarkable counterfeit that denies the active values of love and marraige. Before Amoret can be restored to Scudamore as his wife, she has to feel and be wounded in her feeling, just as he has to become manlier through his discovery that disinterested charity is a part of love also.

The spine of the comedy in book 3 is provided by Britomart, the maiden-knight, the warlike lover. Out of naiveté she blunders, but out of sincerity she sets things right. Her first deed in Fairyland is to unseat Guyon, for she represents a total giving that overgoes Temperance. At Castle Joyeous she is embroiled in the first of several comic misadventures that result from her disguise. She unwittingly inspires a wanton desire in Malecasta, who supposes her to be a man, and then has to defend herself from the midnight intruder in her bed, whom *she* supposes to be a man. The comedy of mixed designations is heightened by the detail

[17]For a discussion of Busyrane's perversion of love through fear, see Maurice Evans, *Spenser's Anatomy of Heroism: A Commentary on* The Faerie Queene, p. 164.

of the six knights in attendance, whose names form a "ladder of lechery" stating the progression of a lustful affair from first meeting (Gardante, or looking) to consummation (Noctante, or spending the night.)[18] When-ever she appears, Britomart provokes simultaneous amusement and delight in the reader: amusement because her disguise makes her seem a man to the people she meets and yet heightens the reader's awareness of her womanliness, and delight because she is the great beauty of true vir-tue in action.

Set off against the true lovers are the false lovers of the poem, who are presented with incisive irony as engaging in parodies of love. The first of these is the witch's son, who pines until his mother makes him the False Florimell to replace the true. False Florimell parodies the true; moreover, she is created *by* parody (3.8.7.1–6):

> In stead of eyes two burning lampes she set
> In silver sockets, shyning like the skyes,
> And a quicke moving Spirit did arret
> To stirre and roll them, like a womans eyes:
> In stead of yellow lockes she did devise,
> With golden wyre to weave her curled head.

The figurative lady of the Elizabethan sonnet becomes literal here, exag-gerated and impossible. False Florimell is a symbol that defines the parodic nature of false love. The second false lover is Braggadocchio, who takes away the false lady, only to give her up to the first knight who challenges him for her possession. Braggadocchio proposes that they turn their steeds and ride apart until they can meet in equal tilt; then he, "Once having turned no more returnd his face" (3.8.18.8). So the coward flies, and the false lady, pretending to chaste modesty, passes on to other hands. A third false lover is the Squire of Dames, who brings a sad report upon the moral state of womankind. He has searched for three years and found only three chaste women: a courtesan, whose fee he cannot pay; a holy Nun, who fears that he will gossip; and one truly chaste, an unso-phisticated country lass.

The other false lovers in book 3 are collected in a fabliau, a burlesque of the classical tale of the rape of Helen, which is presented with a sardonic

---

[18]Allan H. Gilbert, "The Ladder of Lechery, *The Faerie Queene*, III, i, 45," *MLN* 56 (1941):594–97.

irony reminiscent of *The Merchant's Tale*. Malbecco, old, blind in one eye, jealous, and miserly, fears that he will be robbed, and he is – of his wife Hellenore by his guest Paridell and of his gold by Braggadocchio and Trompart. When he sees Hellenore again, by creeping to her through the Satyrs' goatfold, she rejects him, and the goats attack him, in a beastly commentary upon his cuckold's horns. So beaten, he retires to a rocky cave, where he indulges himself in anguish until he is metamorphosed into the monster Gealousie. Through this satire, which provokes harsh, judgmental laughter against the counterfeits of love and chastity, Spenser heightens our appreciation of Britomart as a wonderfully comic incarnation of true love.

Friendship

The mockery and parody of the Hellenore fabliau provide a foretaste of the comic quality of book 4, *The Legend of Friendship*, wherein Spenser deals with the social aspects of love – courtesy and friendliness – virtues that are set off against discordant modes of conduct like taunting, bicker-ing, and gossiping. The personal love stories of book 3 are carried over into book 4, where they are resolved and fitted into a broader pattern of social amity. Britomart at last meets and pledges herself to Artegall; Marinell learns to love Florimell and secures her release from Proteus; and Amoret is brought into the company of Scudamour, though Spenser neglects to say that they are reunited. The awkward relationship be-tween Timias and Belphoebe seems to be resolved also, though in a baf-fling way, apparently through Timias's replacing love with friendship.

All these love stories are characterized by moments when the lovers and their actions prove laughable. When Belphoebe accuses Timias of in-fidelity as he kneels over the wounded Amoret, it is a moment of high comedy, for she leaps to a false, though logical, conclusion that is surpris-ingly jealous and out of keeping with her character. There is, moreover, a disturbing irony in her demanding constancy from Timias and a second irony in Timias's denial of his first duty to Prince Arthur in order to stay with Belphoebe.

The meeting of Britomart and Artegall is composed of multiple ironies also. He is sulking because she has unseated him at the Tournament of Beauty and thereby "stolen" his victory. Scudamour, sulking alongside

The Comedy of *The Faerie Queene*

Artegall, wishes to kill her because he believes she has stolen his lady. Britomart, after easily overthrowing Scudamour, so warms to the thrill of battle that she wishes to go on fighting even after Artegall has yielded to her sex and beauty. Not until Scudamour pronounces the savage knight's name does she realize that she is threatening to kill the man she loves, whereupon she flashes from warrior to loving lady. The delight of her success is heightened because it comes after the ironic moment in which she seems to give up her true identity and become the fierce war-rior of her disguise.

The union of Marinell and Florimell, like that of Britomart and Artegall, hinges upon an ironic reversal. The woman-hating Marinell falls into a lovesickness that only his mother can cure, by arranging his marriage to a member of the human sex that she had so carefully taught him to scorn.

The characteristic tone of the comedy in book 4 is much more sardonic, however, than these lovers' ironies suggest. The central allegorical vir-tue is concord, but it is defined largely by its absence from the world of the poem. Instead, social behavior is founded upon divisive self-interest. The poem opens with Amoret nervously and foolishly fearing that the "man" Britomart will take advantage of her, until the maiden-knight un-consciously settles matters by literally letting down her hair. Then the scene shifts to a larger social group, Blandamour and Paridell riding through the forest in the company of Duessa and Ate, "mother of debate." These four constitute a parody of the four true friends and lovers who give the book its title: Cambell, Telamond, Canacee, and Cambina. Blandamour and Paridell are quarrelsome creatures whose only activity is daring each other to prove himself at arms. In a Renaissance version of Pavlov's dogs, the sight of an approaching knight makes first one and then the other challenge his companion to tilt with the newcomer. Their pledge of friendship is a debased proverb, "The left hand rubs the right," and their highest reward for their conduct is the winning of False Florimell. When Scudamour joins the group, they resort to a cruel travesty of friendship, pretending to pity the poor man whose lady, they swear, has played him false with the strange knight, Britomart. Believing them, Scudamour turns in rage against Britomart's squire, the old nurse, Glauce; but the poor old lady cannot reveal the lie without betraying Britomart's secret. Hung on the horns of a dilemma, there she stays as long as she remains with Scudamour.

From this introductory jangle of discord it is evident that concord can exist only on a small scale, between lovers, brothers, sisters, parents and children, but not in society at large. The true nature of society is revealed by the eagerness with which the knights accept False Florimell. She passes from hand to hand, ever feigning modesty until, finally given the chance to select her own true knight, she chooses Braggadocchio. But even after she has departed with him, four knights, Paridell and Blandamour among them, fall furiously to arms for her love. Argument and pointless battle, these are the ways of this world. The Tournament of Beauty, held by Satyrane to honor Florimell's Girdle of Chastity, dwindles from an opportunity for proving prowess at arms to a display of sheer quarrelsomeness by the community of knights. The climax of the tournament comes when none of the pure ladies present, saving Amoret, can keep the Girdle of Chastity clasped about her waist. The wordly-wise Squire of Dames laughs loud and jests that they must curse the artificer for proving all the ladies "ungirt unblest."

Alongside this sharp-edged satire Spenser also sets scenes of outrageous burlesque. In the cave of Lust, Amoret and Amelia are saved from disgrace by the "charity" of the old hag, who obligingly yields herself up for the daily rape. When Timias confronts Lust, the animal-man swings the dangling Amoret before him like a shield in imitation of knightly combat. The Saracen on the dromedary, visually absurd in a world of horsemen, is another burlesque knight, a monstrous symbol of the debased values of a discordant world. True harmony does exist in nature, as demonstrated by the marriage of Medway and Thames, and in society, between lovers and true friends; however, most of mankind in book 4 seems to be staring at the hindparts of Danger (4.10.20.6–9):

> . . .hatred, murther, treason, and despight,
> With many moe lay in ambushment there,
> Awayting to entrap the wareless wight,
> Which did not them prevent with vigilant foresight.

Justice

The image of the world as threatened by the agents of danger is much like the allegorical image that defines the world of book 5. In the prefatory stanzas to *The Legend of Justice*, Spenser analyzes the world (4.1–5):

> For that which all men then did vertu call
>   Is now cald vice; and that which vice was hight,
>   Is now hight vertue, and so us'd of all:
>   Right now is wrong, and wrong that was is right,
>   As all things else in time are chaunged quight.

The world of book 5 *is* upside down, particularly in the comic scenes, which are built upon debased and violent actions, and it is Sir Artegall's task to set it right by conquering evil and establishing true justice in the land. In effect, Artegall's function is to cast out comedy.

Artegall cannot complete his quest, however, until he has undergone a process of testing and correction similar to the Red Cross Knight's. In his own way he re-creates the comic pattern of Red Cross by being a target of laughter in his errors until he learns the precise boundaries of his jurisdiction. Unlike Red Cross, however, he moves beyond the realm of comedy altogether at the end; that is, he does not arouse delight. The end of his quest is properly heroic, the serious and solemn climax to an arduous struggle against injustice and oppression. Spenser makes little of the great joy of the redeemed nation (he spends one stanza on it) but stresses instead the necessity of reestablishing justice in that "ragged commonweale."

By almost universal consensus Artegall is the least attractive of Spenser's heroes, and yet the reaction is not so much against Artegall himself as against the definition of justice that he provides. Artegall seems an unlikely hero when he first appears, covered with moss and forest leaves and bearing the legend "*Salvagesse sans Finesse.*" He seems rustic, sullen, and generally unsociable, though intelligent; yet his wits are ravished at the sight of a pretty face, especially when it is the face of a foe. The instant he shears off the ventail of Britomart's helmet and sees her, he falls to his knees in amorous subjection. In context this action seems natural enough, signifying that he recognizes his destiny and Britomart's; however, when he makes nearly the same response to the face of Radigund, the Amazon, he reveals that this is a characteristic pattern of behavior for him. As a judge of character in beautiful women Artegall is hopelessly inept. When he sees most clearly with mortal eyes, then he is blinded in his judgment, and once blind he is helpless. Not until he has gone through the ordeal of imprisonment and has learned graciousness through humiliation does he learn how to control his impulses.

As the personification of justice, Artegall seems particularly unpleasant and unsociable – and so he is, for in Fairyland, as in the real world, when people cry justice, they really mean mercy. Before absolute justice man is absolutely corrupt, deserving the penalty of death for his misdeeds; and that is why, in the world where things are not absolute and man is mortal, justice submits itself to mercy. Britomart, according to the vision at Isis's church, must set her foot upon the dragon's head and hold absolute justice in check. Allegorically it is impossible for Artegall to be both justice and mercy within himself, for then he would be God; thus, when he presumes to show mercy, he falls and languishes in prison until mercy, taking on the attributes of justice, can release him. Together Artegall and Britomart can overcome Radigund, but because judgment abdicated originally, mercy has to become the judge and the executioner, stretching itself to fill both roles.

On the level of Christian belief, the allegory of book 5 enacts the establishment of God's plan for human salvation. By God's justice man is condemned; by God's mercy he is saved, and the sentence of death is revoked. On the level of secular affairs, the poem reflects how justice ought to work in society, reasonably and impartially, not exceeding its own bounds. When passion or weakness is substituted for justice, then chaos comes. Artegall's imprisonment makes manifest the irreversible order in the working out of justice: judgment must precede mercy, or both will be meaningless.

The allegory of book 5 is more somber than that of the preceding books, and Spenser's use of comedy heightens the seriousness of his poem. For one thing, the comic passages are set to provide relief from the sober issues that precede and follow them. The capture of Guile, which comes before the trial of Duessa at Mercilla's court, is a brief interlude in which the trickster tricks himself. In short order Guile changes from self to fox to bush to bird to hedgehog, back to his own shape, and then to a snake, whereupon Talus crushes him. The speed and brevity of the scene, the repeated chase, and the trickster's momentary triumph as hedgehog are the stuff of classic comedy, constituting a little lesson in the necessity of

uncovering and eradicating deception—a lesson that is repeated ear-
nestly in the trial of Duessa.

The violent conclusion to the scene with Guile is characteristic of the
comedy in book 5. The Egalitarian Giant's frantic effort to weigh words
on his scale is climaxed with Talus's shouldering him off the cliff and into
the sea; and the wedding feast for Marinell and Florimell is highlighted
by the slashing rebellion of Sir Guyon's horse, Brigadore, who will not
suffer officious fools to peer into his mouth. Here the horse is hero, claiming as his the dignity that men do not have. In these instances a debased
action is brought to an end by a violence that rids the world of it.

In fact, all the comic scenes in the book demonstrate in their conclu-
sions the working of justice in the world. Through Braggadocchio's presence, but quite apart from his intentions, Marinell's wedding feast turns
into a court where comic quandaries are resolved. Guyon gets his horse
back, to the horse's great joy; False Florimell bursts like a bubble, and the
true one regains her estate as the only Florimell in the land. Braggadocchio, brought to justice at last, gets the punishment befitting a *Miles
Gloriosus*: his beard is shaved off, his armor dispersed, and he himself
turned out from the wedding feast.[19] By seeing him mocked, and their
past errors through him, the lords and ladies of Fairyland are at last able
to recognize truth and to laugh at their errors.

The most significant aspect of the comedy in book 5 is the pervasive influence of Sir Philip Sidney's theories upon its content and structure.
The clear moral intent of the passages reflects Sidney's principle that the
purpose of comedy is to teach man how to avoid vice by painting it in its
true features; through laughing at what is ridiculous, man becomes a better guardian of himself and takes care not to dance the same measure.
The comic center of the poem directly recreates Sidney's ideal in *The
Defence of Poesie*. The highest form of comedy, says Sidney, is that which
provokes both laughter and delight, and

> ...in *Hercules*, painted with his great beard, and furious counte-
> naunce, in a womans attyre, spinning, at *Omphales* commaundement,

[19] J. Dennis Huston raises an interesting possibility—which cannot be documented—that Braggadocchio evolves into the Blatant Beast. See J. Dennis Huston, "The Function of the Mock Hero in
Spenser's *Faerie Queene*," *MP* 66 (1969):212–17. For another analysis of the reasons for his dismissal
from Fairyland, see John M. Hall, "Braggadocchio and Spenser's Golden World Concept: The Function of Unregenerative Comedy," *ELH* 37 (1970):315–24.

it breedes both delight and laughter: for the representing of so straunge a power in Love, procures delight, and the scornefulnesse of the action, stirreth laughter.

Artegall is created in the image of Hercules as both a heroic and a comical figure, incapable of a small gesture, whether it be combating error or making a fool of himself. When Artegall falls, it is a great fall, hand-wrought by his own weaknesses. Through his strength he wins a victory over Radigund, and through his weakness, his witless admiration of a pretty face, he reverses that victory into defeat. Starting up from her swoon, Radigund snatches the victory that Artegall threw away, driving him backward across the field until he has to cry mercy, then publicly stripping him of his armor, dressing him in woman's weeds, and setting him to spin flax and tow. As a result of his emotional weakness, he who moved the world is now made the helpless object of the passions of two scheming women: Radigund, who would starve him for not loving her, and Clarinda, who tries to bribe his heart. The crowning irony of the situation is that Artegall is so ignorant of love's wiles that he does not know what the women are about. He humbly sits and spins until Britomart saves him.

In the comedy of Artegall and Radigund the world is upside down, with ordinary values inverted. The delight in the scene comes from the paradoxical way in which Artegall grows in virtue through ignorance. His ignorant love of beauty betrays him to Radigund, while his ignorance of love's schemes saves him from betraying Britomart. The scornful laughter first directed at Artegall in his awkward retreat from victory is redirected at Radigund and her handmaiden as they "chew the cud" of hopeless passion. The world inverted is a comic world, but one that must be set right if justice is to prevail. Artegall therefore passes through the corrective realm of comedy on his way to administer justice; beyond comedy, he is stern and sober, the heroic arm of a heavenly power on earth.

Courtesy

While Justice is a public virtue, establishing itself in full view of the world, Courtesy, the titular virtue of book 6, is private, the flower that blooms on a lowly stalk and then "spreds it selfe through all civilitie." The evil that Sir Calidore, the champion of courtesy, opposes, springs up everywhere also. The Blatant Beast, who has been loosed upon society by two hags, Envy and Detraction, ranges through Fairyland, with Calidore coursing him from court to city, from city to town, from the town into the country and to private farms, then to open fields and by the folds and humble cots of shepherds. The Beast preys upon man's reputation, seizing and biting victims that are vulnerable and unde-fended; and in his bite is a venom that cannot be counteracted by medicines or herbs. Rather, the victim is cured by sober attention to the scriptural injunction to shun the very appearance of evil. The evil and its cure are unspectacular, and the comedy that helps define them is simi-larly unspectacular, though it is more pervasive here than in any other book.

The comic center of *The Legend of Courtesie* is Calidore's pastoral vaca-tion from his quest, when he gives up his pursuit of the Beast to pursue Pastorella instead. The knight in shepherd's dress, fawning after Pastorella, wrestling with local lads, and descanting upon the virtues of the simple life, is an ironic figure presented half with sympathy, half with scorn. The ironies of his conduct are heightened by comparison with a second wooing, in which the captain of the brigands attempts courtesy, also to win Pastorella. Both try to efface their public identities and turn their backs to the community that depends upon them, offering to give all for love. The brigand, however, cannot quite deny his true self: "With looks, with words, with gifts he oft her wowed; / And mixed threats among, and much unto her vowed" (6.11.4.8–9). Calidore has no crim-inal traits to conceal but a courtly bearing, "queint usage, fit for Queenes and Kings," which impresses Pastorella not at all. Therefore, he becomes a shepherd, but one marked by a natural superiority that automatically rules out the rustic swains as serious contenders for Pastorella's favor. Only poor Coridon offers any competition, and he is showered with courteous kindnesses by Calidore which assure him that he has no chance. On the whole, Calidore's courtesy to Coridon strikes the reader as being exaggerated, and the kind deeds seem like sops thrown to the poor fellow after his prize has been snatched away.

The amorous evolution of Calidore from knight to shepherd is typical of pastoral romance: in Sidney's *Arcadia* two princes "evolve" into girls for the sake of love. Calidore's conduct provides an amusing inversion of the customary theme that love inspires man to elevate himself through heroic deeds. To raise himself in Pastorella's eyes, Calidore humbles himself, going daily to tend the sheep (6.9.37.7–9),

> And otherwhiles for need, he did assay
> In his strong hands their rugged teats to hold
> And out of them to presse the milke: love so much could.

The single image of the knight as milk hand gathers up all the contradic-tory elements of the pastoral interlude and shapes them into a laughable picture illustrating the power of love.

Spenser's technique here, as throughout book 6, is marked by its non-committal understatement. Our sense of the knight as a double figure is general and continuous instead of being sharply focused, and the scene goes on and on from one display of courtesy to another, but throughout Spenser speaks in two voices. With his sage and serious voice he says, "Look, this is Courtesy"; but with a lower, uninflected tone he asks, "Is it not overdone?" The two tones are apparent in the half line "love so much could," and also in the single comment upon Calidore's gracious accept-ance of Melibee's hospitality, it "being his hartes owne wish" – to stay with Pastorella, that is. Through the two tones Spenser communicates the humor of the situation: courtesy here is not the corrective to incivil-ity, not even its own reward, but the devious means to another end entirely.

The pastoral vacation constitutes one comic pattern of romance in *The Legend of Courtesie*, while a second pattern is presented through the ad-ventures of Calepine and Serena – a lamentable comedy, indeed. After their embarrassed introduction into the action when Calidore interrupts their tryst, they seem destined for disaster, with Serena bitten by the Blatant Beast and Calepine attacked by the dastardly Sir Turpine. Serena, whose behavior nowise fits her name, suffers constantly from fear of the Salvage man, from bitterness at being abandoned by Calepine, and from terror of being eaten by cannibals, as well as from the pain of her wound. She is, in many ways, another Florimell, dashing from one pitfall to another and inventing danger where none exists. The Salvage man is her savior and servant, and Calepine, whom she murmurs against, has not abandoned her but rather got himself lost while rescuing an infant from a bear. Thereafter he courses through the woods, searching vainly

The Comedy of *The Faerie Queene*

for Serena until, through wonderful accident, he comes upon the scene of the cannibals' sacrifice. He hears an anguished scream, scatters the savage band, and then returns to the altar where he finds "that Ladie... / Yet fearing death, and next to death the lacke / Of clothes" (6.8.50.1-4). In the darkness Calepine cannot see whom he has saved, and Serena, shamed to silence by her nakedness, will not speak. Thus, through ridiculous modesty, romance and heroism dwindle into embarrassed awkwardness. Ignorant of identity, the lovers sit silently by the altar through that dark night.

The two love stories are defining types of the contrapuntal patterns of action that make up the complete narrative form of book 6. One is heroic and romantic, the other pastoral; and both are comic in their ridiculous proceedings and in the foolish postures that love imposes upon lovers. Spenser makes the humbler love of Calidore and Pastorella the nobler of the two, in illustration that the naturalness of the heart's affections is purer than affection subjected to overrefined behavior. The nobility of the love relationship is predicated upon the lady's conduct, the directness and naturalness with which she responds to her lover. Therefore, Pastorella is a nobler lady than Serena, who lets her false modesty intervene between herself and Calepine.

Spenser defines both ladies as agents of Courtesy, however, and he sets them in contrast to another lady, the dolorous Mirabella, who, because she was once discourteous and ignoble in love, now is forced to make a dismal progress through ditch and briar. Mirabella is a female counterpart to the Squire of Dames in book 3, searching to undo her past and having little success. But whereas the Squire's predicament provoked laughter from Satyrane, hers calls forth sympathy and then a sober agreement from Prince Arthur that she is justly punished. In presenting Mirabella, Spenser creates two attitudes toward her—pity for her present misery and scorn for the pride brought low before Cupid—that prevents us from taking her with complete seriousness. As her scorn was once turned upon all without discrimination, so now must she be indiscriminate in her mercy, and an awareness of her consistent lack of temperance leavens pity with an impulse toward laughter.

In general the comedy of book 6 follows the ethical nature of courtesy, being everywhere possible and yet nowhere so sharply defined as to call attention to itself. Spenser's comic vision here is not a steady focus but a momentary flash coming frequently but unexpectedly. In his excellent chapter on the comedy of book 6, Arnold Williams summarizes Spenser's technique:

> ...though Book VI lacks extended comic passages of the size of the Hellenore episode in Book VI [sic], it has perhaps more short comic passages than any other, places wherein the important personages of the story become for the moment ridiculous, as Calidore is in Arcady, or Serena, who when rescued by Calepine will not speak for shame of her nakedness.[20]

The device that Spenser most consistently uses to provide the momentary flash of comedy is the visually absurd image that defines the quality of its context. Much of the action in the book either runs into or moves outward from such images. Briana sits placidly weaving a cloak of hair shorn from struggling victims; Sir Turpine and the Salvage man play tug of war over a shield; Sir Calepine rams an indigestible stone down a bear's throat and then marches off with a squalling infant; the giant Disdain with marble limbs stalks "stately like a crane . . . uppon tiptoes hie"; in the midst of the battle Timias's foot slips, and he thereby falls to defeat; the sleeping Serena is surrounded by cannibals who praise her parts and whet their knives; and Calidore lurks in the vines like a Peeping Tom to watch the naked graces dance for Colin Clout. Even the climax of the great allegorical quest is characterized by absurd images. When finally brought to bay, the Blatant Beast runs at Calidore "With open mouth, that seemed to containe / A full good pecke within the utmost brim" (6.12.26.5–6).[21] But when captured and muzzled, he "trembled underneath his mighty hand / And like a fearefull dog him followed through the lande" (6.12.36.8–9).

The effect of these incongruous and absurd images is to make their immediate contexts less dangerous or heroical, more commonplace and social. The irony brings the action down from romantic planes and sets it at home in the daily conduct of men. The evils of gossip and rudeness and slander are not so deadly as they seem, though if permitted to run unchecked, they can make society unsafe for any man. If confronted squarely, however, they will choke on their own spleen as the bear

[20]Arnold Williams, *Flower on a Lowly Stalk*, p. 120.

[21]Ibid, p. 117.

chokes over his stone, and if conquered by courtesy, they dwindle into fearful dogs.

Yet it must be acknowledged in the last analysis that comedy is a result of perspective and distance. So long as Spenser views society from outside, then he sees it as the stage whereupon the human comedy unfolds. From a distance the foes of reputation are clearly what they are, petty surrogates only pretending to be real evils like the seven deadly sins. Also from a distance man trying to be truly human can provoke laughter, for distance makes objectively clear that his greatest enemy is often himself. Once perspective is lost, however, once man is swept onto the stage and into the action himself, then the comedy is gone. Thus when Spenser abandons objectivity, the tone of his poem modulates from comic irony to sympathy or melancholy, as when he explains the appeal of pastoral retirement or the deeper pleasure of the poet's companionship with the graces. Another, more somber, note is struck when he turns at last to the real world, where the Blatant Beast ranges free, unrestrained and unrestrainable. No one, not himself, nor yet his verse, may escape the "venemous despite." With the sudden sadness of a man in the real world he closes his comedy not with laughter or delight but with regret that this poem, like his others, will be attacked by wicked tongues that wish to "bring [it] into a mighty Peres displeasure." The comedy of courtesy is over; the sadness of incivility now prevails.

Mutability

In *The Faerie Queene*, Spenser gives voice to his vision of the world and of man, the prince of that world. The allegory of the poem is Spenser's expression of what he sees, his statement of all the experiences and meanings that are available to man. The comedy of the poem is his particular focus at any given moment, when he suddenly exposes the apparent contradictions that make up the vast unity of creation. Upon occasion the contradictions seem so great or so powerful as to obliterate the unity, until laughter reduces them to proper size. Thus, in the Mutability Cantos, Spenser emphasizes the disruptive power of the Titaness, Mutabilitie, by granting her a swift succession of triumphs over earth, the moon, and Mercury; then he quickly deflates her image with a single phrase. She charges into the court of Jove, to be greeted first with shocked silence

Laughter in the Courts of Love

and then with Jove's address, "Speake thou fraile woman." The phrase refocuses the scene, reducing gods to human folk and Mutabilitie into a pretty but petulant woman.

In his history of Arlo Hill, a pastoral version of the invasion of divine privacy, wherein lustful Faunus plays Mutabilitie's role, Spenser uses the same technique of deflation, but his target this time is an angry goddess. Diana in her outrage is compared to a housewife trapping the beast that slyly drains her dairy pans. Through deflation Spenser establishes a new perspective for viewing Mutabilitie and the gods, one that is upheld by allegory. Both are properly subservient to Nature, who is herself handmaiden to the power that will change all into eternal changelessness.

In the Mutability Cantos and throughout *The Faerie Queene*, comedy is clearly in the service of allegory. By provoking laughter at inadequate or improper behavior, visions, and definitions, Spenser engages our emotional and intellectual consent to his demonstration of their deficiencies. At times the comedy merely emphasizes what we already know, like a pleasant variation upon a statement with whose terms we are thoroughly familiar. So in the Mutability Cantos, where Spenser tells us from the beginning that the Titaness is overreaching herself, the sudden reduction to "frail Woman" is a comic rephrasing of cosmic themes in terms of everyday society. At other times, however, the comedy serves a vital corrective function. In book 2 the laughter that Spenser provokes at Guyon's expense is directed against misconstructions of Temperance. Spenser's point is that while Temperance is a valid ideal for human conduct it is not the only ideal or even the best; it cannot provide delight as do Holiness and Love. Ultimately the comedy of the poem is directed through Temperance to the reader who mistakes it for the highest good in a vast universe.

Taken from this perspective, Spenser's comedy seems entirely subordinate to allegory, being meant only to enhance his ethical lessons. But Spenser is a surprising poet, and if it suits his end, he will not hesitate to make allegory serve the comedy. He casts the great battle between Arthur and Maleger (also in book 2) as comedy, perhaps surprisingly, and then invokes our understanding of the allegory to heighten the comedy. The image of Maleger hitting the earth and rebounding high into the air is ludicrous enough, but when we recognize that Spenser has just reduced original sin into a bouncing ball, then the comedy is heightened, and, as a result, the allegory is given greater validity. Likewise, when Despair tries to commit suicide for the thousandth time and cannot die, all the allegorical implications of his argument and being provoke scorn-ful laughter at his pains. His action is laughable because it grows out of the allegory and incarnates the fallacy of his position; the allegory thus encourages laughter at the wretched knave.

Despite the variances in their relationship, however, comedy and alle-gory always correspond in Spenser's art. For Spenser, allegory was a natural mode of expression. Only through it could he give voice to the complexity of his vision, and only through comedy could he evaluate that complexity. Spenser's poem covers the entire universe, but standing at its center is a figure undeniably comic: man. In Spenser's poem salvation is a comedy on the divine scale, in which man is translated out of his benighted, incomplete self and into his fully human and redeemed self, while temperance, love, justice, and courtesy are comic modes of con-duct in which man enacts his social self. *The Faerie Queene* is Spenser's image of man, incomplete but magnificent, the great comic allegory of the English Renaissance.

6.

Comedy and Allegory

T IS INSTRUCTIVE THAT many contemporary definitions of allegory sound remarkably like definitions of comedy. For instance, in his effort to map out a comprehensive view of allegory, Edwin Honig says that any allegorical work can be distinguished by its form, its genre-type, and its distinctive style. Of allegorical style he writes that it "is an admixture of tonal elements" perhaps best characterized as a "middle style," a "mixture of serious and comic (including the ironic) tones, [where] one discerns the interplay of elements of satire, pastoral, the realistic or verisimilar (formerly the epic) sense, and the tragic sentiment."[1] Among the identifying features of allegory Angus Fletcher points out particularly the obsessive nature of the allegorical character, who tends to have "an absolutely one-track mind,"[2] the "visual absurdity of much allegorical imagery,"[3] and the importance of topical allusion in making the allegory immediately meaningful to its audience.[4] In stating that allegory requires a dynamic system for enacting itself, Fletcher concurs generally with Morton Bloomfield, whose grammatical studies have led to the conclusion that particularly in personification allegory the stress is upon active verbs that present the subjects as agents, acting out their basic nature in a given context.[5] Virtually all theories of the comic agree on the primacy of agent and action in

[1]Edwin Honig, *Dark Conceit: The Making of Allegory*, pp. 15–16.

[2]Angus Fletcher, *Allegory: The Theory of a Symbolic Mode*, p. 40.

[3]Ibid., p. 105.

[4]Ibid., pp. 26, 71.

[5]Morton Bloomfield, "A Grammatical Approach to Personification Allegory," *MP* 60 (1963):161–71.

comedy. And all definitions of allegory and comedy stress the necessary presence of double focus in a poem.

In view of these dicta, the foregoing chapters may seem merely an exercise in explaining the obvious. My immediate defense, however, is the more obvious point that not all allegories are comedies, nor do all allegories contain comic passages. Occasionally an allegorical poem presents an image that is absurd or ironical enough to provoke a smile, like the figure of Fortune in *The Kingis Quair*; less frequently a poem may introduce a comic pattern of action that is abandoned before it can fulfill itself as comedy: so with the argument between Fortune and Mars in *The Pastime of Pleasure*. Only rarely, however, is a poem both allegorical and comic. Moreover, the critical definitions quoted above are generalizations abstracted from and directed toward allegory; they have only a tangential, almost accidental, relation to comedy. Finally, criticism, having a vocabulary directed toward univocal rather than equivocal expression, traditionally has tended to center upon either comedy or allegory to the subordination or exclusion of the other. Even when the critic is aware of humor in an allegorical poem, he often treats it as mere decoration or relief; thus there recurs throughout the criticism of medieval dream visions such statements as "Despite its obvious humor, this scene makes a serious point."

Comedy, however, as well as allegory, is capable of providing serious theological and philosophical statements about the nature of man and human existence, and it is natural for the two to function together. Particularly in satiric allegory the union of laughter and moral judgment is taken for granted. In *Gulliver's Travels*, for instance, or in *The Bowge of Court*, we are encouraged to laugh at those characters, attitudes, and actions that are revealed to us as morally reprehensible. The tone of the moral judgment and the sound of our laughter are equally scornful.

The relationship between comedy and allegory becomes more complex, however, when the comedy directs us to laugh at someone who is presented through the allegory as morally praiseworthy. Thus Britomart defending her chastity from the midnight advances of Malecasta, or Chaucer's Eagle lecturing through space, or Guyon cutting off the horse's head brings the reader face to face with an aesthetic and moral dilemma, for we laugh at what is clearly correct and moral – what we ought not laugh at. In these instances it seems almost monstrous to justify laughter by insisting that the character has committed a sin or fallen into error. Even the argument that poor quaking Drede in *The Bowge of Court* deserves his terror for having yielded to worldly ambition seems utterly devoid of mercy and charity. The source of laughter is the comic structure of the poem, and our laughter must be explained in comic, not allegorical, terms.

Moreover, responses to comedy are distinguished by their infinite variety. It has been said that man has only one way to cry but many ways to laugh. Whether we laugh in scorn, surprise, delight, or sympathy; whether we laugh at a character or with him; whether we laugh at the situation but not the character – these few possible choices out of many should indicate the complex nature of comedy. The poet who has a truly comic vision of life seldom relies upon one tone or one kind of laughter to express himself. It is frankly pointless to seek for a type of comedy that will characterize either Chaucer or Spenser, for both realize that the most enjoyable and meaningful laughter comes suddenly and surprisingly. At times their comedy is satiric and moralizing; at other times it is cautionary, warning against taking a doctrine, attitude, character, or action at face value; at still other times it may reflect pure delight in the imperfect humanness of mankind. At nearly all points the combination of comedy and allegory is designed to increase the complexity of their vision and expression, as though by adding the double focus of comedy to the double focus of allegory they may come closer to recreating in poetry their view of human life.

In this book I have followed a generally chronological pattern, tracing the Chaucerian tradition of comic allegory from its origins to its culmination in *The Faerie Queene*. There is, however, no significant chronological pattern of development to be found in either the comedy or the allegory. Maurice Evans points out that, as the Reformation proceeded and Calvinistic Puritanism began to take hold, critical definitions and defenses of comedy became increasingly moralistic;[6] but comedy itself does not change to fit the criticism. In fact, comedy, which is generally explained as a transitory form depending largely upon contemporary social customs and events for its meaning and appeal, is more independent of the influence of history than is tragedy: the differences between Hamlet and Willie Loman are profound and pervasive, while those between Mosca

[6]Maurice Evans, *English Poetry in the Sixteenth Century*, pp. 10–18.

and Felix Krull are largely superficial. In the poems of this book the variant comic forms come not from the times but from the poet's vision and talent. The comedy of *Confessio Amantis* is low keyed because of Gower's apparent mistrust of either ecstasy or depression; the comedy of *The Pastime of Pleasure* is weak and unpleasant because Hawes had no measurable talent for creating comedy. The difference between Chaucer's exuberance and Spenser's reticence comes from the personalities of the poets, not from the times in which they lived.

Likewise, the allegory of these poems follows no clear chronological pattern of growth and change but depends upon the poet for its development. Poets may literalize or allegorize a given construction depending upon its relation to their actual subject, but this practice does not tell us whether they "believed" in allegory, or not. Ironically, allegory has been pronounced dead by the critics at nearly all stages covered in this study: when Chaucer wrote, or Hawes, or Dunbar, or Spenser; but it was still alive when Bunyan wrote *Pilgrim's Progress* in 1678, and even in 1966, when John Barth published his *Giles Goat-Boy*. Like comedy, allegory gets its efficacy and vitality from the poet's artistry and its complexity from his vision.

The complexities of allegory and comedy, then, depend upon the art of the individual poem, and the quality of their relationship depends upon the momentary focus of the poet and his expression of that focus. They do not function in isolation from each other, nor yet may one be justified by the other's terms, unless the context makes clear that they are functioning together, in harmony with one another. For the most part they coexist in a vital tension, prompting and teasing the reader to open his eyes wider and to see through mortal clouds to the joyous complexity of truth:

> For now my sight, clear and yet clearer grown,
>   Pierced through the ray of that exalted light,
>   Wherein, as in itself, the truth is known.

> Dante, *Paradiso* (33.52–54)

Bibliography

Allen, Judson B. *The Friar as Critic: Literary Attitudes in the Later Middle Ages*. Nashville, Tenn.: Vanderbilt University Press, 1971.

Alpers, Paul J. *The Poetry of* The Faerie Queene. Princeton, N.J.: Princeton University Press, 1967.

———, ed. *Elizabethan Poetry: Modern Essays in Criticism*. New York: Oxford University Press, 1967.

Andreas, Capellanus. *The Art of Courtly Love*. Translated and edited by J. J. Parry. New York: Columbia University Press, 1941.

Atkins, J. W. H. *English Literary Criticism: The Medieval Phase*. Cambridge: Cambridge University Press, 1943.

Baker, Denise N. "The Priesthood of Genius: A Study of the Medieval Tradition." *Speculum* 51 (1976):277–91.

Barber, C. L. *Shakespeare's Festive Comedy: A Study of Dramatic Form and Its Relation to Social Custom*. Princeton, N.J.: Princeton University Press, 1959.

Baugh, A. C. "The Middle English Period" in A. C. Baugh, ed. *A Literary History of England*, pp. 109–312. New York: Appleton, 1948.

Bennett, J. A. W. *Chaucer's Book of Fame: An Exposition of* "The House of Fame." Oxford: Clarendon Press, 1968.

Berger, Harry, Jr. *The Allegorical Temper: Vision and Reality in Book II of Spenser's* Faerie Queene. Yale Studies in English, vol 137. New Haven, Conn.: Yale University Press, 1957.

Bergson, Henri. "Laughter." In Wylie Sypher, *Comedy*. Garden City, N.Y.: Doubleday, 1956.

Bethurum, Dorothy, "The Center of *The Parlement of Foules*." In Richmond C. Beatty et al., eds. *Essays in Honor of Walter Clyde Curry*, pp. 39–50. Nashville, Tenn.: Vanderbilt University Press, 1954.

———. "Chaucer's Point of View as Narrator in the Love Poems." *PMLA* 74 (1959):511–20.

———, ed. *Critical Approaches to Medieval Literature*. New York: Columbia University Press, 1960.

Laughter in the Courts of Love

Bloomfield, Morton. "Allegory as Interpretation." *NLH* 3 (1972):301–17.

———. "A Grammatical Approach to Personification Allegory." *MP* 60 (1963):161–71.

Boardman, Phillip C. "Courtly Language and the Strategy of Consolation in the *Book of the Duchess.*" *ELH* 44 (1977):567–79.

Brewer, Derek S. "Afterword: Notes Towards a Theory of Medieval Comedy." In *Medieval Comic Tales.* Translated by Peter Rickard et al., pp. 140–49. Totowa, N.J.: Rowman and Littlefield, 1972.

———. *Chaucer and His World.* London: Eyre Metheun, 1978.

———, ed. *Chaucer and Chaucerians: Critical Studies in Middle English Literature.* University, Ala.: University of Alabama Press, 1966.

Bronson, Bertrand H. *Chaucer's Hous of Fame: Another Hypothesis.* University of California Publications in English, vol. 3, no. 4. Berkeley, Calif.: University of California Press, 1934.

Burke, Charles B. "The 'Sage and Serious' Spenser." *N&Q* 175 (1938):457–58.

Burrow, John. *Ricardian Poetry: Chaucer, Gower, Langland, and the Gawain-Poet.* London: Routledge & Kegan Paul, 1971.

Caldwell, Mark L. "Allegory: The Renaissance Mode." *ELH* 44 (1977):580–600.

Chaucer, Geoffrey. *Chaucerian and Other Pieces*; including *The Court of Love.* Vol. 7 of *The Complete Works of Geoffrey Chaucer.* Edited by Walter W. Skeat. Oxford: Clarendon Press, 1897.

———. *The Works of Geoffrey Chaucer.* Edited by F. N. Robinson. 2d ed. Boston: Houghton Mifflin, 1957.

Clemen, Wolfgang. *Chaucer's Early Poetry.* Translated by C. A. M. Sym. London: Methuen, 1963.

Clifford, Gay. *The Transformations of Allegory.* London: Routledge & Kegan Paul, 1974.

Coghill, Nevill. "The Basis of Shakespearian Comedy: A Study of Medieval Affinities." *Essays and Studies*, n.s. 3 (1950):1–28.

Cooper, Lane. *An Aristotelian Theory of Comedy, with an Adaptation of the Poetics and a Translation of the Tractatus Coislinianus.* New York: Harcourt, Brace, 1922.

Cowling, Samuel T. "Gower's Ironic Self-Portrait in the *Confessio Amantis.*" *AnM* 16 (1975):63–70.

Craig, Martha. "The Secret Wit of Spenser's Language." In Paul J. Alpers, ed. *Elizabethan Poetry: Modern Essays in Criticism*, pp. 447–72. New York: Oxford University Press, 1967.

Crampton, Georgia Ronan. *The Condition of Creatures: Suffering and Action in Chaucer and Spenser.* New Haven, Conn.: Yale University Press, 1974.

Cullen, Patrick. *Infernal Triad: The Flesh, the World, and the Devil in Spenser and Milton.* Princeton, N.J.: Princeton University Press, 1974.

Culler, Jonathan. *Structuralist Poetics: Structuralism, Linguistics, and the Study of Literature.* Ithaca, N.Y.: Cornell University Press, 1975.

Cunningham, J. V. *Tradition and Poetic Structure: Essays in Literary History and Criticism.* Denver, Colo.: Alan Swallow, 1951.

Selected Bibliography

Curtius, Ernst Robert. *European Literature and the Latin Middle Ages.* Translated by Willard R. Trask. 1952. Reprint. New York: Harper and Row, 1963.

Dante Allighieri. *The Divine Comedy.* Translated by Dorothy Sayers. 3 vols. Baltimore, Md.: Penguin Books, 1949–62.

Delany, Sheila. *Chaucer's House of Fame: The Poetics of Skeptical Fideism.* Chicago: University of Chicago Press, 1972.

Donahue, Charles. "Patristic Exegesis in the Criticism of Medieval Literature: Summation." In Dorthy Bethurum, ed. *Critical Approaches to Medieval Literature.* pp. 61–82. New York: Columbia University Press, 1960.

Donaldson, E. Talbot. "Chaucer in the Twentieth Century." *Studies in the Age of Chaucer.* Publications of the New Chaucer Society, vol. 2, edited by Roy J. Pearcy, pp. 7–13. Norman, Okla.: Pilgrim Books, 1980.

Doran, Madeleine. *Endeavors of Art: A Study of Form in Elizabethan Drama.* 1954. Reprint. Madison, Wis.: University of Wisconsin Press, 1964.

Douglas, Gavin. *The Shorter Poems of Gavin Douglas.* Edited by Priscilla Bawcutt. Scottish Text Society ser. 4, no. 3. Edinburgh: William Blackwood, 1967.

_____. *The Palice of Honour.* In *The Shorter Poems of Gavin Douglas.* Edited by Priscilla Bawcutt. Scottish Text Society, ser. 4, no. 3. Edinburgh: William Blackwood, 1967.

_____. *Selections from Gavin Douglas.* Edited by David F. C. Coldwell. Oxford: Clarendon Press, 1964.

Dubs, Kathleen E., and Stoddard Malarkey. "The Frame of Chaucer's *Parlement.*" *ChauR* 13 (1978):16–24.

Duckworth, George E. *The Nature of Roman Comedy: A Study in Popular Entertainment.* Princeton, N.J.: Princeton University Press, 1952.

Dunbar, William. *Poems.* Edited by James Kinsley. Oxford: Clarendon Press, 1979.

Ebin, Lois A. "The Theme of Poetry in Dunbar's 'Goldyn Targe.'" *ChauR* 7 (1972):147–59.

Economou, George D. "The Character Genius in Alan de Lille, Jean de Meun, and John Gower." *ChauR* 4 (1970):203–10.

_____, and Joan Ferrante. Introduction. *In Pursuit of Perfection: Courtly Love in Medieval Literature,* pp. 3–15. Port Washington, N.Y.: Kennikat Press, 1975.

Evans, Maurice. *English Poetry in the Sixteenth Century.* London: Hutchinson, 1955.

_____. *Spenser's Anatomy of Heroism: A Commentary on* The Faerie Queene. Cambridge: Cambridge University Press, 1970.

Evanthius. *De Comoedia et Tragoedia.* Translated by O. B. Hardison, Jr. In *Classical and Medieval Literary Criticism: Translations and Interpretations.* Edited by Alex Preminger, O. B. Hardison, Jr., and Kevin Karrane, pp. 301–05. New York: Frederick Unger, 1974.

Fansler, Dean S. *Chaucer and the* Roman de la Rose. New York: Columbia University Press, 1914.

Fergusson, Francis. *The Idea of a Theatre: A Study of Ten Plays; The Art of Drama in Changing Perspective.* 1949. Reprint. Princeton, N.J.: Princeton University Press, 1968.

Ferster, Judith. "Intention and Interpretation in the 'Book of the Duchess.'" *Criticism* 22 (1980):1–24.

Fielding, Henry. Author's Preface. *Joseph Andrews*. Introduction and notes by Carlos Baker, pp. xix–xxv. New York: Bantam Books, 1960.

Fish, Stanley Eugene. *John Skelton's Poetry*. Yale Studies in English, vol. 157. New Haven, Conn.: Yale University Press, 1965.

Fleming, John V. *The* Roman de la Rose: *A Study in Allegory and Iconography*. Princeton, N.J.: Princeton University Press, 1969.

Fletcher, Angus. *Allegory: The Theory of a Symbolic Mode*. Ithaca, N.Y.: Cornell University Press, 1964.

Fox, Denton. "Dunbar's *The Golden Targe*." *ELH* 26 (1959):311–34.

Frank, Robert Worth, Jr. *Chaucer and* The Legend of Good Women. Cambridge, Mass.: Harvard University Press, 1972.

Freidenberg, O. M. "The Origin of Parody." In Henryk Baran, ed. *Semiotics and Structuralism: Readings from the Soviet Union*, pp. 269–83. White Plains, N.Y.: International Arts and Sciences Press, 1976.

Frye, Northrop. *Anatomy of Criticism: Four Essays*. 1957. Reprint. New York: Atheneum, 1967.

——. "The Argument of Comedy." In *English Institute Essays, 1948*, pp. 58–73. 1949. Reprint. New York: Amis Press, 1965.

——. *A Natural Perspective: The Development of Shakespearean Comedy and Romance*. New York: Columbia University Press, 1965.

——. "Old and New Comedy." *ShS* 22 (1969):1–5.

——. "The Structure of Imagery in *The Faerie Queene*," *UTQ* 30 (1961):109–27.

Fyler, John M. *Chaucer and Ovid*. New Haven, Conn.: Yale University Press, 1979.

Gallacher, Patrick J. *Love, the Word, and Mercury: A Reading of John Gower's* Confessio Amantis. Albuquerque, N.Mex.: University of New Mexico Press, 1975.

Gardner, John. *The Poetry of Chaucer*. Carbondale, Ill.: Southern Illinois University Press, 1977.

Gilbert, Allan H. "The Ladder of Lechery, *The Faerie Queene*, III, i, 45." *MLN* 56 (1941):594–97.

——. "Spenserian Comedy." *Tennessee Studies in Literature* 2 (1957):95–104.

Godefroy, Frédéric, ed. *Dictionnaire de L'Ancienne Langue Français*. Vol. 6. 1889. Reprint. New York: Kraus Reprint Corp., 1961.

Gower, John. *Confessio Amantis*. Vols. 2 and 3 of *The Complete Works of John Gower*. Edited by G. C. Macaulay. Oxford: Clarendon Press, 1901.

Gradon, Pamela. *Form and Style in Early English Poetry*. London: Methuen, 1971.

Guillaume de Lorris and Jean de Meun. *The Romance of the Rose*. Translated by Harry W. Robbins, edited by Charles W. Dunn. New York: Dutton, 1962.

Gunn, Alan M. F. *The Mirror of Love: A Reinterpretation of the* Romance of the Rose. Lubbock: Texas Tech Press, 1952.

Gurewitch, Morton. *Comedy: The Irrational Vision*. Ithaca, N.Y.: Cornell University Press, 1975.

Selected Bibliography

Hall, John M. "Braggadocchio and Spenser's Golden World Concept: The Function of Unregenerative Comedy." *ELH* 37 (1970):315–24.

Hamilton, A. C. *The Structure of Allegory in* The Faerie Queene. Oxford: Clarendon Press, 1961.

Hawes, Stephen. *The Pastime of Pleasure.* Edited by William Edward Mead. Early English Text Society, o.s., vol. 173. London: Oxford Press, 1928.

Heilman, Robert B. *The Ways of the World: Comedy and Society.* Seattle: University of Washington Press, 1978.

Heiserman, A. R. *Skelton and Satire.* Chicago: University of Chicago Press, 1961.

Henryson, Robert. *Poems.* Edited by Charles Elliott. Oxford: Clarendon Press, 1963.

Holloway, John. *The Charted Mirror: Literary and Critical Essays.* New York: Horizon, 1962.

Honig, Edwin. *Dark Conceit: The Making of Allegory.* 1959. Reprint. New York: Oxford Press, 1966.

Huppé, Bernard F., and D. W. Robertson, Jr. *Fruyt and Chaf: Studies in Chaucer's Allegories.* Princeton, N.J.: Princeton Univ. Press, 1963.

Huston, J. Dennis. "The Function of the Mock Hero in Spenser's *Faerie Queene.*" *MP* 66 (1969):212–17.

Kean, P. M. *Chaucer and the Making of English Poetry.* vol. 1, *Love Vision and Debate.* London: Routledge & Kegan Paul, 1972.

Kellogg, Robert, and Oliver Steele, eds. *Books I and II of* The Faerie Queene. New York: Odyssey Press, 1965.

Kelly, M. R. "Antithesis as the Principle of Design in the *Parlement of Foules.*" *ChauR* 14 (1979):61–73.

Kermode, Frank, "The Cave of Mammon." In *Elizabethan Poetry.* Stratford-upon-Avon Studies, no. 2, pp. 151–73. New York: St. Martin's Press, 1960.

Kernan, Alvin B. *The Cankered Muse: Satire of the English Renaissance.* Yale Studies in English, vol. 142. New Haven, Conn.: Yale University Press, 1959.

Kernodle, George R. "Excruciatingly Funny *or the 47 Keys to Comedy.*" *Theatre Arts* 30 (1946):719–22.

King, John N. "Allegorical Patterns in Stephen Hawes's *The Pastime of Pleasure.*" *SLitI* 11 (1978):57–67.

Koonce, B. G. *Chaucer and the Tradition of Fame: Symbolism in* The House of Fame. Princeton, N.J.: Princeton University Press, 1966.

Kronenberger, Louis. *The Thread of Laughter: Chapters on English Stage Comedy from Jonson to Maugham.* 1952. Reprint. New York: Hill and Wang, 1970.

Langer, Susanne K. *Feeling and Form: A Theory of Art.* New York: Scribner's, 1953.

Larson, Judith S. "What Is *The Bowge of Courte?*" *JEGP* 61 (1962):288–95.

Leonard, Frances McNeely. "The School for Transformation: A Theory of Middle English Comedy." *Genre* 9 (1976):179–91.

Lewis, C. S. *The Allegory of Love.* 1936. Reprint. New York: Oxford University Press, 1958.

_____. *English Literature in the Sixteenth Century*. Vol. 3 of *The Oxford History of English Literature*. Edited by F. P. Wilson and Bonamy Dobrée. Oxford: Clarendon Press, 1954.

_____. *Spenser's Images of Life*. Edited by Alastair Fowler. Cambridge: Cambridge University Press, 1967.

Leyerle, John. "Chaucer's Windy Eagle." *UTQ* 40 (1971):247–65.

Lyall, Roderick J. "Moral Allegory in Dunbar's 'Goldyn Targe.'" *SSL* 11 (1973):47–65.

McDonald, Charles O. "An Interpretation of Chaucer's *Parlement of Foules*." *Speculum* 30 (1955):444–57.

Mack, Maynard. "Introduction to *Joseph Andrews*." In John Jacob Enck et al., eds. *The Comic in Theory and Practice*. New York: Appleton, 1960.

Manly, John M. "What Is Chaucer's *Hous of Fame*?" In *Anniversary Papers by Colleagues and Pupils of George Lyman Kittredge*, pp. 73–81. Boston: Ginn, 1913.

Mazzeo, Joseph Anthony. *Varieties of Interpretation*. Notre Dame, Ind.: University of Notre Dame Press, 1978.

Miller, Robert P. "Chaucer's Pardoner, the Scriptural Eunuch, and the Pardoner's Tale." *Speculum* 30 (1955):180–99.

Muscatine, Charles. *Chaucer and the French Tradition*. 1957. Reprint. Berkeley: University of California Press, 1966.

Neilson, William Allen. *The Origins and Sources of* The Court of Love. 1899. Reprint. New York: Russell & Russell, 1967.

Nelson, William. *The Poetry of Edmund Spenser: A Study*. New York: Columbia University Press, 1963.

Olson, Elder, *The Theory of Comedy*. Bloomington, Ind.: Indiana University Press, 1968.

Pearsall, Derek. "The English Chaucerians." In *Chaucer and Chaucerians: Critical Studies in Middle English Literature*, edited by Derek S. Brewer, pp. 201–39. University, Ala.: University of Alabama Press, 1966.

_____. *Gower and Lydgate*. Writers and Their Work, no. 211. London: Longmans, Green, 1969.

_____. "Gower's Narrative Art." *PMLA* 81 (1966):475–84.

Peck, Russell A. Introduction. John Gower. *Confessio Amantis*. Edited by Russell A. Peck. New York: Holt, Rinehart, and Winston, 1968.

_____. *Kingship and Common Profit in Gower's* Confessio Amantis. Carbondale, Ill.: Southern Illinois University Press, 1978.

Phillips, Norma. "Observations on the Derivative Method of Skelton's Realism." *JEGP* 65 (1966):19–35.

Potts, L. J. *Comedy*. 1957. Reprint. New York: Capricorn Books, 1966.

Preston, Priscilla. "Did Gavin Douglas Write *King Hart*?" *MÆ* 28 (1959):31–47.

Ridley, Florence H. "Did Gawin Douglas Write *King Hart*?" *Speculum* 34 (1959):402–12.

Robertson, D. W., Jr. *A Preface to Chaucer: Studies in Medieval Perspectives*. 1962. Reprint. Princeton, N.J.: Princeton University Press, 1969.

Rodway, Allan. *English Comedy: Its Role and Nature from Chaucer to the Present Day*. Berkeley: University of California Press, 1975.

Selected Bibliography

Ruggiers, Paul G. "The Unity of Chaucer's *House of Fame*." *SP* 50 (1953):16–29.

———, ed. *Versions of Medieval Comedy*. Norman, Okla.: University of Oklahoma Press, 1977.

Sale, Roger. *Reading Spenser: An Introduction to* The Faerie Queene. New York: Random House, 1968.

Scheps, Walter. "The *Goldyn Targe*: Dunbar's Comic Psychomachia." *PLL* 11 (1975):339–56.

Scott, Tom. *Dunbar: A Critical Exposition of the Poems*. New York: Barnes and Noble, 1966.

Sidney, Sir Philip. *The Defence of Poesie*. In *The Prose Works of Sir Philip Sidney*, vol. 3. Edited by Albert Feuillerat. Cambridge: Cambridge University Press, 1962.

Skelton, John. *Poems*. Edited by Robert S. Kinsman. Oxford: Clarendon Press, 1969.

Spearing, A. C. *Medieval Dream-Poetry*. Cambridge: Cambridge University Press, 1976.

Spenser, Edmund. *The Poetical Works of Edmund Spenser*. Edited by J. C. Smith and Ernest De Selincourt. London: Oxford University Press, 1912.

Stevenson, Kay. "The Endings of Chaucer's *House of Fame*." *ES* 59 (1978):10–26.

Stillwell, Gardiner. "Unity and Comedy in *The Parlement of Foules*." *JEGP* 49 (1950):470–95.

Sypher, Wylie. "The Meaning of Comedy." In Wylie Sypher. *Comedy*. Garden City, N.Y.: Doubleday, 1956.

Tuve, Rosemond. *Allegorical Imagery: Some Medieval Books and Their Posterity*. Princeton, N.J.: Princeton University Press, 1966.

———. *Elizabethan and Metaphysical Imagery: Renaissance Poetic and Twentieth-Century Critics*. Chicago: University of Chicago Press, 1947.

Watkins, W. B. C. *Shakespeare and Spenser*. Princeton, N.J.: Princeton University Press, 1950.

Welsford, Enid. *The Fool: His Social and Literary History*. 1935. Reprint. Gloucester, Mass.: Peter Smith, 1966.

Williams, Arnold. *Flower on a Lowly Stalk: The Sixth Book of* The Faerie Queene. Lansing, Mich.: Michigan State University Press, 1967.

Wimsatt, James. *Chaucer and the French Love Poets: The Literary Background of* The Book of the Duchess. Chapel Hill, N.C.: University of North Carolina Press, 1968.

Winny, James. *Chaucer's Dream Poems*. London: Chatto and Windus, 1973.

Woodhouse, A. S. P. "Nature and Grace in *The Faerie Queene*." *ELH* 16 (1949):194–228.

Index

Achitophel: 109
Aeneas: 41, 143
Aeneid: 41, 105, 110, 138
Africanus: 48, 112
Alazon: 43
Alceste: 53–55, 57
Alieniloquium: 9, 35
Allegory (Defined): 7–12
  Courtly, 4–5, 11, 105–106
  Levels of, 7–10, 66–67, 71, 158
  Literalized, 29–30, 88, 172
  (See also dualism, fourfold interpretation, imagery, patristic criticism.)
Allen, Judson B.: 9–10
Alpers, Paul J.: 16n, 134
Amans: 63–79, 115
Andreas, Capellanus: 62, 98–99, 102
Anticlericalism: 31, 97
Antifeminism: 113
Apocalyptic vision: 108, 110–11, 114
Arcadia: 161–62
Ariosto: 138, 151
Artegall: 154–55, 157–60
Atkins, J. W. H.: 16n

Baker, Denise N.: 70n
Barber, C. L.: 12n
Baugh, Albert C.: 38
Bennett, J. A. W.: 40n
Berger, Harry, Jr.: 147
Bergson, Henri: 19n
Bethurum, Dorothy: 45n, 50n
Bible: 8, 105
Blanche, the Duchess: 35–38
Bloomfield, Morton: 8n, 11n, 169
Boardman, Phillip C.: 34n
Boethius: 63, 106

Book of the Duchess, The: 30, 34–38, 48, 56
Book of Revelation: 32, 139
Bower of Bliss: 3, 149
Bowge of Court, The: 57, 58, 87–96, 170
Braggadocchio: 134, 147, 148, 152, 154, 156, 159
Brewer, Derek: 22n, 29n
Britomart: 137, 150–55, 157–60, 170
Bronson, Bertrand H.: 40n
Burke, Charles B.: 133n
Burlesque: 86, 140, 147, 156
Burrow, John: 8

Caldwell, Mark L: 10n
Calidore: 160–64
"Canace and Machair": 68
Canterbury Tales: 4, 27, 29, 30, 57, 130
Charity: 70
Chastitie, The Legend of: 149–54
Chaucer, Geoffrey: 4, 20, 21, 27–56, 87, 96, 99, 106–107, 134, 138–39, 143, 151, 171–72
Chaucer persona: 50, 112
Chaucerians: 10, 27, 58
Christ: 8, 39, 71, 103, 139, 143
Clemen, Wolfgang: 28, 56
Clifford, Gay: 8n
Coghill, Nevill: 12n
Comedy (Defined): 12–22
  Aristophanic, 17
  Archetypal, 139
  High Comedy (Comedy of Manners), 73, 75, 146
  New Commedy, 17, 32, 47, 48
  Old Comedy (Processional form), 17–18, 41, 43–44, 90–95
  Transformational Comedy, 18
Comic relief: 118, 158

Common profit: 47, 49–50, 65
Confessio Amantis: 58, 62–79, 91, 105, 115, 137, 172
Confession: 23, 31, 76–77
Consolation: 36, 71–72
Consolation of Philosophy, The: 63
Cooper, Lane: 12n
Court of Love: 52, 57, 59–61, 96, 105, 150
Court of Love, The: 57, 80, 96–103
Courtesie, The Legend of: 160–65
Courtly Love: 4, 61–62, 66, 152
Cowling, Samuel T.: 64n
Craig, Martha: 133n
Crampton, Georgia R.: 139n
Cullen, Patrick: 143n
Culler, Jonathan: 7n
Cunningham, J. V.: 6n
Cupid: 52, 54–55, 59, 62, 67, 97, 99
Curtius, Ernest R: 34n, 73n, 118

Dante: 3, 12n, 13–14n, 15, 63–64, 172
Defence of Poesie, The: 15, 134–36, 138, 159
Delany, Sheila: 29n, 40n
Delight: 15, 130
Diana: 49, 99, 152
Dido: 41, 42, 53, 101
Divine Comedy, The: 63–65, 172
Doctrine of Love: 60–62
Donahue: Charles: 11
Donaldson, E. Talbot: 27n
Doran, Madeleine: 94
Douglas, Gavin: 27, 107–15, 117–18
Dream vision: 32, 81
Drede: 88–96, 171
Dualism:
  in Allegory, 5, 9, 11, 21, 142, 149, 162
  in Comedy, 13–14, 21, 45, 50, 94, 162
Dubs, Kathleen E.: 47n
Duckworth, George E.: 12n
Dunbar, William: 27, 57, 81–87, 96–97, 115, 172

Eagle: 41–45, 69, 112, 170
Ebin, Lois A.: 83n
Economou, George D.: 60–61, 70n
Eiron: 43
Energy: 46, 89
Errour: 140
Evans, Maurice: 152n, 171
Evanthius: 6n
Everyman: 128
Exaggeration: 129

Exegetical critics: 28
Exemplification: 8
Exemplum: 67–68
Experience v. Authority: 45

F and G Prologues: 52–55
Fabliau: 119, 153–54
Faerie Queene, The: 3, 11, 133–67, 171
Fansler, Dean S.: 30n
Farce: 94–95, 109, 113, 129, 144
Fergusson, Francis: 12n
Ferrante, Joan: 60–61
Ferster, Judith: 34n
Fielding, Henry: 140n
Fish, Stanley E.: 89n, 91
Fleming, John V.: 32
Fletcher, Angus: 9, 10n, 123, 169
Fortune: 14, 88, 114, 119–20, 170
Fourfold interpretation: 7–8, 66–67
Fox, Denton: 83n, 87n
Frank, Robert W.: 52n
Freidenberg, O. M.: 123n
Friendship, The Legend of: 154–56
Frye, Northrop: 17n, 18, 19, 61, 123, 145
Fyler, John: 40n

Gallacher, Patrick J.: 64n
Gardner, John: 29n, 52n
Geffrey: 13, 40–47
Genius: 32, 62–79
Gilbert, Allan H.: 133n, 153n
Godfrey Gobylyve: 107, 119, 123
Golden Targe, The: 57, 58, 80, 81–87, 97
Gower, John: 5, 62–79, 87, 96, 99, 103, 115
Gradon, Pamela: 8n
Graunde Amoure: 115–24
Guillaume de Lorris: 32, 63, 90n
Gunn, Alan M. F.: 32n
Gurewitch, Morton: 22n
Guyon: 3, 136, 146–49, 152, 170

Hall, John M.: 159n
Hamilton, A. C.: 139
Hawes, Stephen: 27, 107, 115–25, 172
Heilman, Robert B.: 22n, 136n
Heiserman, A. R.: 89n, 92n
Henryson, Robert: 22–25, 27, 57
Hercules: 138, 159–60
"Hercules and Faunus": 74
Holinesse, The Legend of: 139–43
Holloway, John: 90–91n

Index

Honig, Edwin: 10n, 169
House of Fame, The: 9, 13, 20, 39–47, 48, 56, 90–91, 106–107, 110
Huppé, Bernard F.: 7, 30n
Huston, J. Dennis: 159n
Hypocrisy: 142

Imagery:
  Allegorical, 58, 135–36
  Comic, 147–48, 157, 164
Inversion: 17, 19, 52–53, 98, 157–60, 161–62
Irony: 28, 177
Isidore of Seville: 9, 35

Jealousy: 154
Jean de Meun: 32, 33, 63, 90n
John of Gaunt: 37
Justice, The Legend of: 156–60

Kean, P. M.: 35, 40
Kellogg, Robert: 4n
Kelly, M. R.: 47n
Kermode, Frank: 143n
Kernan, Alvin: 21n
Kernodle, George: 19n
King Hart: 107, 125–31
King, John N.: 122n
Koonce, B. G.: 7, 40n
Kronenberger, Louis: 21n

Lady Philosophy: 69n
Langer, Susanne: 13n, 14n, 24
Language: 5, 20, 28, 29, 95
Larson, Judith: 93
Laughter: 3, 4, 14–15, 32, 58, 85, 130, 134–35, 170–71
La Vieille: 31
Leonard, Frances M.: 18n
Lewis, C. S.: 8–9, 61, 64–65, 66, 67, 69–70, 71, 82, 87, 89, 91n, 97, 108n, 117n, 122, 125, 143, 145n, 152
Literalized images: 29, 36, 47, 88, 172
Literary criticism: 53
Litotes: 20
Lyall, Roderick J.: 82
Lydgate, John: 27, 57, 83, 98, 107, 115

Macaulay, G. C.: 62n, 65
Mack, Maynard: 17
Malarkey, Stoddard: 47n
Maleger: 166–67

Manly, John M.: 40n
Mazzeo, Joseph A.: 8n
McDonald, Charles O.: 47n
Merchant's Tale, The: 154
Mercy: 158
Metamorphoses: 37, 138
Metamorphosis: 83–84
  (See also Comedy, Transformational.)
Miles Gloriosus: 147, 159
Miller, Robert P.: 71n
Miller's Tale, The: 20
Morall Fabillis: 22
"Mundus and Paulina": 71
Muscatine, Charles: 13
Mutability: 165–66

Nature: 47–48, 50–51, 52, 62, 78
"Nectanabus": 71, 74–75
Neilson, William A.: 98n, 100–101n
Nelson, William: 138–39
New Jerusalem: 124
New Man: 78

Odysseus: 143
Old Man: 63, 77
Olson, Elder: 15n
Ovid: 110, 138
Oxymoron: 20, 39

Palice of Honour, The: 80, 107–15, 127
Parabolic plot: 17
Paradise: 49, 67, 79
Paradox: 71
Parliament of Fowls, The: 20, 47–52, 56, 90, 106–107
Parody: 24, 32–33, 55, 98, 113, 119, 145, 153
Pastime of Pleasure, The: 107, 115–25, 127, 130, 170, 172
Pastoral: 138, 161
Patristic criticism: 7, 13, 21, 28–29
Pearsall, Derek: 5n, 65, 68, 97
Peck, Russell A.: 63, 65, 68n, 69, 70, 71–72, 75n
Persona: 38–39, 54, 112
Personification: 9, 11, 41, 42, 49, 87, 92, 109, 117, 128
Phillips, Norma: 91n
Pilgrimage, metaphor of: 105–107, 116–18, 125–26
Potts, L. J.: 12n, 18n, 19n, 21n, 93–94
Preston, Priscilla: 114n, 126n
Pride: 140–42

Laughter in the Courts of Love

Prologue to *Confessio Amantis*: 65–66, 69
Prologue to *The Legend of Good Women*: 52–55
Purgatory: 116, 124
Psychomachia: 70, 139

Raison: 32, 69
Reason: 77, 84–85
Red Cross Knight: 29, 97, 124, 138, 139–43
Redemption: 13, 13–14n, 71–72, 130–31, 139–40
Repetition: 147, 148
Rhythm: 14, 20
Ridley, Florence: 126n
Robertson, D. W., Jr.: 7, 16n, 30n, 60, 61n, 62, 71n, 102
Robinson, F. N.: 28
Rodway, Allan: 22n, 146n
Roman de la Rose: 10, 30–33, 53, 62, 63, 65, 89–90, 98 103, 127, 152
Ruggiers, Paul G.: 12n, 40n, 63n

St. Paul: 105, 108
Saints of Love: 98
Sale, Roger: 16n
Satire: 21, 38, 43, 46, 93–94, 170
Scheps, Walter: 82n
Scott, Tom: 82, 86
Senex: 76, 129–30, 146
Sex: 13–14, 149–52
Shakespeare: 15, 17, 134
Sidney, Sir Philip: 14n, 15, 134–35, 138, 159–60, 161
Skelton, John: 27, 57, 58, 88–96
Slapstick: 32
Somnium Scipionis: 32, 48–49, 52
Spearing, A. C.: 35n, 89n, 111

Speed in comedy: 129, 194
Spenser, Edmund: 3, 4, 21, 27, 97, 115, 133–67, 171, 172
Squire's Tale, The: 151
Steele, Oliver: 4n
Stevenson, Kay: 40n
Stillwell, Gardiner: 51
Structuralist critics: 28
Symbolism: 9, 11, 40, 109, 117
Sypher, Wylie: 13

"Tale of the Fox and the Wolf, The": 22–25
Temperance, The Legend of: 143–49, 166–67
"Travellers and the Angel, The": 73–74
Travesty: 155
Troilus and Criseyde: 4, 7, 29, 54, 99
Tropological interpretation: 8, 67
Tuve, Rosamund: 10–11

Una: 136, 139–43
Unity: 25, 40

Vanity: 140–42
Venus: 49, 52, 59, 62, 67, 80, 86, 90, 96, 98, 100, 108, 109, 110, 111
Virgil: 69, 119

Watkins, W. B. C.: 133n
Way of the World: 145
Welsford, Enid: 119n
Williams, Arnold: 133n, 164
Wimsatt, James: 30n
Winny, James: 28
Woodhouse: A. S. P.: 139n